The Sociolo D1089280
Spatial Inequ....ty

THE SOCIOLOGY

OF SPATIAL

INEQUALITY

Edited by

LINDA M. LOBAO
GREGORY HOOKS
ANN R. TICKAMYER

STATE UNIVERSITY OF NEW YORK PRESS

11385793

Published by
STATE UNIVERSITY OF NEW YORK PRESS
ALBANY

For information, address
For information, contact State University of New York Press, Albany, NY
www.sunypress.edu

Production, Laurie Searl
Marketing, Fran Keneston

Library of Congress Cataloging-in-Publication Data

The sociology of spatial inequality / edited by Linda M. Lobao, Gregory Hooks,
Ann R. Tickamyer.
     p. cm.
   Includes bibliographical references and index.
   ISBN 978-0-7914-7107-4 (alk. paper) — ISBN 978-0-7914-7108-1 (pbk. : alk. paper)
 1. Equality. 2. Social stratification. 3. Human geography. 4. Spatial behavior.
 5. Demography. 6. Political sociology. I. Lobao, Linda M., 1952– II. Hooks, Gregory Michael.
 III. Tickamyer, Ann R.
   HM821S655 2007
   306.201—dc22

2006021968

10   9   8   7   6   5   4   3   2   1

Contents

PART II
STUDIES OF SPATIAL INEQUALITY

PART III
THE SOCIOLOGY OF SPATIAL INEQUALITY:
TOWARD A COMMON VISION

Acknowledgments

This volume grew out of collective efforts to bring a spatial lens to the study of power and privilege in sociology. To address spatially oriented inequality questions, sociologists increasingly have been branching out beyond traditional subfields, linking previously disparate literatures and focusing on social action across a wide range of territorial settings. To help carve out the conceptual, empirical, and methodological contours of the sociology of spatial inequality, Linda M. Lobao, one of the editors of this volume, was awarded a Fund for the Advancement of the Discipline Grant, a program sponsored by the American Sociological Association and National Science Foundation. The purpose of the project was to convene a workshop to develop scholarly publications that would advance the sociology of spatial inequality. This volume is the outcome.

A number of individuals and organizations aided in the development of the volume and the editors would like to acknowledge their efforts. Foremost we thank the American Sociological Association and National Science Foundation for their interest and investment in the entire project. Their support made possible the initial workshop held at The Ohio State University, Columbus, Ohio, in fall 2002. Its purpose was to sort out approaches to the study of spatial inequality in order to advance a more coherent and distinct sociological view. Approximately twenty-five scholars attended, a mix of sociologists whose work represents different approaches to spatial inequality and geographers committed to joining a dialogue with sociologists on the topic. The editors specifically would like to thank geographers Lawrence A. Brown, Kevin Cox, Meipo Kwan, Edward Malecki, and Alan Murray for sharing their time and ideas regarding the project. At The Ohio State University, funding and in-kind support for activities connected to the workshop were provided by the Center for Urban and Regional Analysis, the Department of Geography, the Department of Human and Community Resource Development, the Department of Sociology, and the Initiative in Population Research.

In the year following the workshop, the editors began planning the present volume, and in 2004, we solicited manuscripts from workshop participants. We selected a mix of manuscripts that illustrate different approaches to the topic and reflect thoughtful consideration of spaces, places, and inequality. Developing an edited volume is often said to be as challenging as writing a monograph itself. While this probably was true in terms of time the editors devoted to the project, the contributors made the task much easier. They provided careful, thoughtful response to our comments and those of the external reviewers. It was a pleasure working with them all and we hope that feeling was mutual.

The State University of New York Press sent the completed manuscript to two reviewers, Leslie McCall and Charles M. Tolbert III, who provided careful reading and excellent suggestions. We are especially grateful to them for sharing their time, ideas, and comments that served to improve this manuscript.

At the State University of New York Press, our editor, Nancy Ellegate, shepherded the manuscript from its initial conception to its completion. We much appreciate her encouragement, advice, and assistance. We also thank editorial assistant Allison Lee for her help in preparing the manuscript and Laurie Searl for her work in finalizing production.

A number of other individuals provided assistance with the manuscript as a whole or individual chapters and we thank them for their efforts. Greta Wryick at The Ohio State University provided the initial copyediting of the manuscript. Ann Bennett at Ohio University provided assistance with manuscript figures, and Erin Fink helped create the index for the volume. We extend a special thanks to Megan Comstock at Washington State University. She made time in a very busy schedule to take the individual chapters and turn them into a book while cleaning up a myriad of formatting problems along the way. Many students assisted in this research, but we particularly thank Stacey Watson for her innumerable contributions to the manuscript. Wenquin Chen and Gunhak Lee of the Center for Urban and Regional Analysis at The Ohio State University and Erick Lobao developed the maps used in chapter 2. Cecil Williams shared his excellent skills in helping with graphics. We also thank Larry Brown for his comments on various chapters.

The editors also would like to acknowledge external sources of support on their individual chapters. The research reported by Lobao was supported by the USDA National Research Initiative Competitive Grants Program (grant number 00–35401–9254). Hooks's research into spatial inequality has been supported by the Open Society Institute and the National Science Foundation (grant number 0518722). The research reported by Tickamyer and her colleagues was supported by grants from the Joyce Foundation, USDA National Research Initiative Competitive Grants Program (grant number 97–35401–4561), Ohio State Legal Aid and Legal Aid Society of Greater Cincinnati, and Ohio University.

As with all book projects, efforts expand to those who share our daily lives and we particularly would like to thank our families. For Linda this includes Larry, Erick, and Traci; for Greg it is Jane, Allie, and Josh; and for Ann, Cecil, and YukiAkari are the mainstays of daily life.

This book is dedicated to Linda's mother, Helen Lobao, and Greg's mother, Faithe Hooks, both of whom passed away as this book was conceived, and to Ann's father, Irving Friedman, whose death predates the book but who always believed that something like it was in the works.

ONE

Introduction

Advancing the Sociology of Spatial Inequality

LINDA M. LOBAO
GREGORY HOOKS
ANN R. TICKAMYER

GEAUGA COUNTY, OHIO, reflects a portrait of national affluence, with a median household income of over $52,000 per year and a poverty rate of an even 5 percent. Several hours due south, residents of Meigs County realize a median household income half that of Geauga's population and confront a poverty rate four times as high. These statistics are evidence of the vast differences in material resources and life chances for residents of the two areas, ranging from the likelihood of obtaining a college education to differences in wages for the same degree and from availability of health care to quality of general public services. Geauga County is comprised of wealthy bedroom communities for the Cleveland metropolitan area; Meigs is in the heart of Appalachian Ohio, a region of legendary persistent deprivation. Yet the two counties are part of the same state, subject to the same legal and administrative system. Differences between these two counties and the regions in which they are embedded are discussed in one of the chapters in this volume. These differences reflect the very real significance of geography in shaping opportunity structures and the complex ways that social and spatial organization interact to construct enduring inequalities.

Inequality—the study of who gets what and why—has been at the heart of sociology since its inception. However, this simple formula fails to acknowledge that *where* is also a fundamental component of resource distribution. Barring a handful of traditions, sociologists too often discount the role of space in inequality. In this volume, we revise sociology's core question to ask *who gets what where?*

The studies in this book stand apart from most research on social inequality due to their sustained attention to space. *Where* becomes the focus of articles addressing theory, research, and policy. Spatial inequality is increasingly used by sociologists to describe this body of work (Lobao 2004; Tickamyer 2000). The study of spatial inequality attends to stratification across a range of territories and their populations. This book is among the first to address spatial inequality as a thematically distinct body of work that spans sociological research traditions.

The first set of chapters takes stock of sociology's conceptual treatment of space and inequality, denoting its missing links. The second set provides examples, at different geographic scales, of spatial approaches to topics including welfare reform, health and mortality, poverty, community service provision, and migration. Each of these chapters provides a theoretical rationale for taking a spatial approach, methodological tools to accomplish this task, and empirical analyses demonstrating the importance of spatial research on inequality. The final set of chapters reflects on sociologists' efforts to build a more coherent field of spatial inequality and outlines an agenda for future action.

SPATIALIZING THE STUDY OF SOCIAL INEQUALITY

Sociology has long been concerned with inequality and with the spatial settings in which social life occurs. But these two concerns evolved rather separately through independent subfields, bridged today in limited ways. Even when analysts attend to the intersection of inequality and space, differences in scale fragment our understanding. Literatures on spatial inequality are most developed at the scale of the city and nation-state or global system. In emphasizing their respective territories of focus, these literatures tend to reinforce differences among others. They sometimes leave the impression that different territories are distinct species of social settings, whose principles of understanding are unconnected. Further, certain geographic scales, such as those involving regional, rural, or other subnational territory, remain neglected or relegated to the backwaters of the discipline, while others are privileged through extensive exploration.

The contributors to this volume believe that fragmentation in research on spatial inequality is detrimental, but we do *not* believe this fragmentation is inevitable. In an era of globalization and regional reconfiguration, it is important to self-consciously situate social processes in spatial context. This volume is directed to understanding how social inequality is influenced by space, especially at and across spatial scales and in places bypassed by much conventional literature.

Sociology's interest in inequality, the differential allocation of valued resources across social groups, traditionally focuses on class, race, gender, and other forms of social stratification. The discipline's core grounding in stratification sets it apart from other social sciences, such as economics, political science, and geography. However, until the 1980s, sociologists studying inequality in advanced nations neglected and, to some degree, resisted consideration of geographic territory as a base of stratification (Soja 1989). More recently, interest in space and place has blossomed, along with a new generation of theory, methods, and substantive work addressing territorial sources and outcomes of inequality.

Thus, a broad movement to spatialize sociology is underway, witnessed by recent reviews assessing progress toward this goal (Gans 2002; Gieryn 2000; Lobao 1993, 2004; Tickamyer 2000). This book showcases work that contributes to this effort.

The study of spatial inequality bridges sociology's pervasive interest in social inequality with a concern for uneven development. It examines how and why markers of stratification, such as economic well-being and access to resources as well as other inequalities related to race/ethnicity, class, gender, age, and other statuses, vary and intersect across territories. The territories of interest are wide ranging and beyond sociology's familiar focus on nations and urban areas: they include regions within a nation, states, counties, labor markets, and other locales. The study of spatial inequality thus entails the investigation of stratification across places at a variety of spatial scales. By spatial scales, we mean the geographic levels at which social processes work themselves out, are conceptualized, and are studied. Beyond recognizing variation in a descriptive sense, the goal is to identify how and why spatial context contributes to inequality. This literature recognizes both the importance of where actors are located in geographic space and how geographic entities themselves are molded by and mold stratification.

By breaking from sociology's past limited treatment of space, this recent generation of research opens up new topics for theory, empirical investigation, and public policy. Increasingly, sociologists view geographic space alongside race, class, gender, age, and sexuality as an important source of differential access to resources and opportunities in the United States. The wide disparities in power and privilege across the nation indicate that the spatial components of inequality must be scrutinized along with sociology's more familiar social statuses.

This collection of articles is aimed at advancing sociology's ongoing spatialization project. It addresses gray areas in this project—topical and conceptual issues that remain less developed or have ambiguous meaning and history in the discipline. In doing so, the volume seeks to make visible a new generation of work on inequality across a variety of scales and places.

(Re)Searching Gray Areas, Seeking the Missing Middle,
and Studying Inequality at Various Scales

Despite sociology's spatial turn, well-established literatures on inequality are found mainly at two opposite scales, the global system of nation-states and the city or local area. Large literatures theorize the development of nation-states and cities, denote their salient conceptual attributes, and systematically attend to questions about power and privilege. While numerous unresolved methodological and conceptual issues remain, these too are typically discussed in large literatures.

Insofar as the sociological imagination has been drawn largely to cities and nation-states, we are left with disciplinary gaps: a large swathe of places, people, and substantive topics are left out of systematic investigation because they do not fall into the usual categories by which sociologists carve up space. One objective of this collection is to fill in gray areas that have received limited scrutiny, particularly those not centrally captured in established traditions. The theoretical importance of this effort is examined by Lobao and Hooks in chapter 2, which focuses on sociology's missing middle: the subnational scale, the territory beyond the reach of the city but below the level of the nation-state. Other pieces, including those by McLaughlin et al., Saenz et al., and Tickamyer et al., follow suit to bring in new literatures and conceptual frameworks to understand subnational inequalities. This focus on an intermediate scale is useful for exploring recent forms of inequality and for extending previously aspatial or underspatialized theories to ground-level, territorial settings.

In moving beyond established traditions and particularly to the subnational scale, researchers often use place-units less familiar to sociologists, for they fall outside the customary limits of the city. This raises questions about how such places are to be conceptualized and treated empirically. Contributors to this volume also reflect upon these issues, as they present comparative analyses of states, regions, counties, labor markets, and other areas. Chapters by McLaughlin et al., Saenz et al., and Tickamyer et al. each use counties as places of study, but in very different ways, as reflected in their methods of analysis and the meanings they assign to these units. The chapter by Irwin centers on methodological and conceptual issues involved in studying spatial processes across a range of places at different spatial scales.

Other gray areas arise as researchers work outside established spatial inequality traditions. One involves how to bring space into underspatialized literatures and subfields. The chapter by Leicht and Jenkins, for example, outlines the importance of extending political sociology spatially in order to address theoretical and substantive gaps. Another gray area involves less visible bodies of work. The chapter by Lobao and Hooks, for example, discusses rural and environmental sociology that generate a great deal of empirical work on subnational inequality but without wide incorporation into stratification literatures outside these fields.

Even where the more familiar urban scale is site of attention, as in chapters by Cotter et al. and by Oakley and Logan, the authors demonstrate gray areas in studying spatial inequality. Conceptual and measurement issues in multilevel and intra-urban processes are tackled, respectively, in these chapters.

Taken together, the articles in this collection introduce a way of looking at inequality across space different from sociology's conventional traditions. Studies of sociological subfields demonstrate that spatial traditions are largely segmented from inequality traditions and that spatial traditions are segmented by their geographic territory of interest (Daipha 2001; Ennis 1992). By contrast, contributors to this volume share a view, outlined below as well as in the two concluding chapters, of the similarities among approaches that study inequality at different scales. These similarities include the recognition that analysts are addressing essentially common questions about stratification across scales, building from critically oriented theory, and using comparative methodological approaches. At the same time, within sociology the topic of spatial inequality itself remains unevenly developed. Included in this volume are both articles falling outside the realm of established literatures as well as others providing novel extensions of sociological traditions. In exposing the gray areas in theory and research and in calling for recognition of commonalities among approaches, the articles aim to collectively advance sociology's spatialization project.

A New Generation of Research on Spatial Inequality: Commonalities across Literatures

The new generation of spatial inequality research is characterized by a blooming of work beyond the established urban and national/cross-national traditions. Sociologists seeking to bring space into the study of inequality outside these traditions tend to follow two different paths. One starts from a spatially oriented subfield, such as demography, human ecology, or rural sociology, then brings in questions about inequality. The other starts from underspatialized literatures concerned with power and inequality (such as stratification, political sociology, and economic sociology), then brings in questions about space. Since the scale of focus is not fixed a priori, both approaches have generated much empirical work at a variety of scales. They have contributed to a new generation of work that is critical and theoretically informed as well as spatially comparative. Much of this work is directed to the subnational scale. Studies that examine both space and inequality have increased rapidly over the past decade, producing a wealth of different insights into theory, methods, and the topic of inequality, but they remain fragmented by subfield and by approach. Nevertheless, as we argue, these seemingly disparate studies can be seen as giving rise to a new research tradition on stratification across space. By bringing in more fluid ways of addressing spatial inequality, this new generation of work advances sociology's spatialization project in general, beyond the city and nation-state. This advancement has numerous advantages for the discipline. For sociological theory, aspatially framed or national generalizations about development and socioeconomic well-being may be challenged, rejected, or revised to take into account the inherent diversity within a variety of spatial settings. For methodology, spatial analysis brings innovative ways of conceptualizing research questions and analyzing data. Addressing the causes and consequences of inequalities at and across a range of scales also opens up new opportunities for public sociological intervention and policy engagement.

In brief, this new generation of research shares the following characteristics, elaborated more fully below in this and later chapters.

- Its foremost concern involves research questions about how and why socially valued resources are differentially allocated across space.
- This literature stresses flows and processes over analytic strategies that emphasize the sui generis nature of cities, communities, or any other geographic unit.
- Its method of argumentation is critical and theoretically informed. Theory is enlisted for a number of purposes, such as interrogating and extending underspatialized frameworks to demonstrate the manner in which they work out on the ground across actual territorial units. Theoretical efforts are also directed toward examining the spatial dimensions of social constructs, such as the state, civic society, and industrial structure, and how these relate to inequality. In turn, actors such as capital, labor, the state, and civic society—the staples of critical theories of stratification—figure prominently in the literatures introduced to analyze spatial inequality.
- The empirical approach is comparative across places. Research may be qualitative or quantitative, but interest in charting differences among many territorial units necessarily lends itself more to quantitative work or to systematic selection and analysis of qualitative comparative case studies.

This volume grew out of discussions among the editors and contributors, who have longstanding interest in how geographic territory is related to different forms of inequality. Since a spatial perspective is not explicitly a part of a number of stratification-related literatures, we found ourselves working at the margins of different research traditions, wholly captured by none. Innovations are said to come into disciplines from the margins, where outside approaches are introduced into established perspectives (Dogan and Pahre 1990). Because our research was not captured by sociology's established subfields, we found ourselves in a continual quandary. We had to rehash the same issues in publishing our work, such as justifying why the research questions we address are worthwhile. Why is it important to bridge the study of inequality with the study of space? Why should sociologists care about inequality and power relationships at the subnational scale across regions and localities? Another set of issues involved methodology. Reviewers were often unfamiliar with or even suspicious of the use of counties, states, regions, or other nonurban units of analysis. Those who were familiar often were inconsistent about how these units should be handled in research designs and statistical models. Finally, most contributors to this volume are motivated by social justice issues, recognizing the need for progressive policy and public sociological outreach. Making a wider arena of sociologists, policymakers, and the public aware of these issues is hampered, however, when research is not visible in a coherent body of work.

Recognizing the need to move research on spatial inequality forward, the American Sociological Association and National Science Foundation provided a Fund for Advancement of the Discipline Award to convene a workshop with the goals of promoting dialogue, critical reflection, and development of an edited book. This volume is the result of that effort. Each contributor has been charged with self-consciously reflecting on theory and method to show how taking a spatial approach makes a difference to a specific substantive question about inequality.

Our focus is inequality across geographic areas within the United States. Contributors approach this topic largely by examining material resources and life chances, their structural determinants, and the ways in which inequality relationships are mediated by spatial processes. Of course, sociologists examine inequality at other scales, ranging from the more micro-levels of the body and household to the macro-, cross-national level. They address spatial inequality from other approaches, such as by focusing on individuals' daily lived experiences and by analyzing discourses about social power and exclusion (Lobao 1994; Tickamyer 2000). And they examine forms of inequality beyond those related to economic well-being, health status, service allocation, government devolution, public welfare provision, and others addressed here. A single volume cannot cover all the previous topics; we make no effort to do so. Rather, this volume takes steps toward systematically articulating conceptual issues, research approaches, and methodologies to address general territorial inequalities within nations. Individually and collectively, the contributions to this volume show the difference a spatial approach makes in conceptualizing research questions across distinct substantive areas, address comparative geographic methods, and discuss how spatial approaches illuminate key public policy issues.

Sociology, of course, is not the only social science to grapple with the issues discussed here. Geography, political science, and economics devote independent attention to the uneven distribution of resources across space and have literatures concerned with regions or subnational territory. This volume emphasizes sociology's distinct approach. That is, it starts from sociology as a discipline, takes its longstanding questions of inequality as primary, and questions the difference a spatial approach makes. Various chapters are informed by geography and other social sciences (and several authors have formal affiliations or training in these disciplines). We also take stock of sociology's approach from outside the discipline, providing a view of our project from the lens of geographers. Nevertheless, our interest is to look within sociology at how a spatial approach enriches the discipline and to make visible existing efforts that connect the study of inequality with spatial concerns.

SPACES AND PLACES

To explain the contemporary terrain of spatial inequality, it is useful to bring in the fundamental concepts of space and place. Space is the more abstract concept insofar as it is "everywhere," while place, as a particular spatial setting, is located "somewhere" (Taylor 1999:10). Geography has voluminous literatures centering on conceptualization of space (for reviews, see Gregory 1994; Harvey 1989; Lefebvre 1991; Massey 1994) and place (for reviews, see Agnew 1987; Entrikin 1991; Hudson 2001). By contrast, sociologists have rather recently begun explicitly exploring the ontology of both concepts. Reviews of sociologists' treatment of space are found in Friedland and Boden (1994), Lobao (1996), and Tickamyer (2000); and for reviews of place, see Falk (2004), Gieryn (2000), Lobao (1994), and Orum and Chen (2003). Studying space and place remains fraught with complexity and debate. As we take up this task, sociologists have much to learn from geographers' well-worn ground.

In sociology, discourse about space and place sometimes considers them as fixed, binary concepts, in opposition to one another. This is particularly seen where place is narrowed to symbolic meaning and emotional attachment that a social actor has for a specific location, as in place authenticity or "sense of place." By contrast, if space is defined to mean an abstract and dehumanized environment, it becomes of less interest than place (Gieryn 2000). The view from geography varies. Rather than clear differences between the two concepts, geographers see tension and overlap (Domosh and Seager 2001; Massey 1994; Rose 1993; Taylor 1999). Places may be conceptualized as sites of materially based social relationships as opposed to sites of community identity and culture (Agnew 1989; Massey 1994). Space may be brought in to theorize social relationships at a variety of spatial scales (Massey 1994; Taylor 1999) or simply introduced to account for externalities associated with distance. Thus, rather than treating space or place as singular concepts, it is more appropriate to talk about the kinds of spaces and places conceptualized by social scientists.

Neither space nor place is a stand-alone concept. Their meaning and significance depends on the research question at hand and the theoretical perspectives informing it. In the discussion below, we consider space a concept that can be introduced to illuminate research questions about inequality in new and different ways. Bringing in space requires attention to the scale or geographic levels at which social processes occur. How space is used to inform theory and research and at which spatial scales, in turn, is linked to conceptualizations of place.

BRINGING SPACE INTO RESEARCH ON INEQUALITY

Space, like its counterpart time, is a concept that can be explicitly used to explore research questions. It tends to be treated in three ways in inequality research. Most frequently, space is not explicitly addressed or is a taken-for-granted empirical backdrop of where a study was conducted. Deductive modes of theorizing and interest in generalizing across populations tend to lead researchers to downplay the role of space in inequality processes.

A second way of treating space is as a concept producing "noise" in social relationships, an interference to be bracketed out or incorporated in some controlled way. Distance is a concept introduced to tap space in this way. For example, poverty, educational attainments, demographic characteristics, and economic structure tend to cluster at similar levels around neighboring units. Since this clustering can interfere with primary relationships of interest, analysts often use measures or methodologies that incorporate distance between spatial units.

Space is also studied as an object of interest in its own right and is brought in to address questions about inequality in different ways. As we noted, a few subfields, notably urban sociology and cross-national/development sociology, have established traditions in framing inequality questions in terms of geographic space. But most others require reframing and going beyond conventional literatures to bridge the study of space and the study of inequality. In general, sociology's major subfields such as general stratification, economic sociology, and political sociology give central attention to power and inequality but comparatively little to space. Alternatively, subfields such as demography and rural sociology, while having strong spatial roots, historically have given less central attention to power and inequality.

In contrast to sociology's limited, fragmented approach, geographers use space to understand discipline-wide research questions and extend these questions across spatial scales (Lefebvre 1991; Massey 1994; Tuan 1977). Some geographers argue for theorizing social relationships in space as a "power-geometry," "a complex web of relations of domination and subordination, of solidarity, and co-operation" (Massey 1994:265). Power-geometries may be studied at any scale, from the household to the global system, as well as across scales (Allen 2003; Hudson 2001; Massey 1994). For sociology, this highlights the importance of studying stratification processes beyond conventional settings. It suggests that the topic of spatial inequality itself can be understood as a power-geometry across spatial scales.

Once space is brought in, how does it become part of the explanation for inequality? The answer, of course, varies by the research question analysts ask, but some overall strategies can be noted. One is to recognize that space intersects with primary social statuses in complex ways (McCall 2001). Class, gender, and race/ethnic differences exist not only in how populations are distributed across space, but also in how space is used and experienced by different social groups. For example, gender differences in the use of space are illustrated by home-to-work movement patterns of women, which vary from those of men (Domosh and Seager 2001). Second, space is seen as channeling inequality processes, sometimes constraining, sometimes amplifying their effects (Clegg 1989; Swanstrom et al. 2002). For example, much work establishes that the likelihood of an education in improving an individual's earnings is spatially variant: in rural areas, returns to investment in a college degree tend to be lower than in urban areas. Third, there is recognition that space itself is created through inequality processes. Social relationships are space forming (Soja 1989). Rounds of struggle and negotiation between actors, such as capitalists, labor, the state, and citizens, create spatially varied social structures, built environments, and uneven regional development (Hooks 1994; Hooks and Smith 2004). Pockets of poverty, such as in Appalachia and the rural south, are outcomes of these territorial stratification processes. Finally, spatial and inequality processes can be treated as causally intertwined. Forces such as industrial restructuring and state-society shifts such as recent welfare reform have a spatial dynamic inherent to them: to understand how they operate and how they affect inequality requires considering their embeddedness in spatial settings.

No matter how space is incorporated into the study of inequality, the task is inherently complex and messy. Because space is "one of the axes along which we experience and conceptualize the world," it has a taken-for-granted quality that makes it difficult to define and study with precision (Massey 1994:251).

Place in Society, Society in Place

To understand spatial inequality, it is useful to distinguish two ideal types of conceptual traditions on place. A longstanding tradition is to start with a place (or places) of intrinsic interest, such as a nation-state, city, region, or local community. The purpose is to illuminate the distinct character of this place and potentially generalize outward to other settings. In sociology, the sine qua non concept of place itself is often equated with the discernible "places" studied in this manner (Gieryn 2000). Examples of this tradition are found across sociological subfields and theoretical perspectives. Older variants of this tradition often drew from human ecology. They were concerned with cataloging characteristics that highlighted place distinctiveness and less so with studying structural inequalities. Sociology's human ecology school addressed the development of the city, cities in the central place system, and the south as a distinct region (Odum and Moore 1938). In a similar fashion, long-standing community perspectives emphasize the study of particular places, especially attending to the processes by which local identification with places is created and maintained. More recently, Marxian political economy, other critical theories, and postmodern approaches employ specific cities and regions as touchstones for illuminating capitalism. Social constructionist approaches (Gieryn 2000) that stress place identity and hearken back to earlier community frameworks also are applied to study particular places. Other analysts blend frameworks incorporating political-economic forces, culture, and key historical events to explain how places become differentiated from one another (Molotch et al. 2000).

Pursuing research questions through the lens of specific places can be described as the *place-in-society* tradition. That is, research centers on the distinct character of a place (in comparison to other places) in a society and in light of social theory. Theoretical perspectives aimed at understanding the distinct qualities of places are varied, as shown above. Some emphasize local identification with a place, while others, such as political economy perspectives, see any local identification as problematic and contested. Although starting out with place specificity, analysts are typically interested in generalizing upward, to say something about how a given place illuminates broader theory or societal processes. In this volume, the chapter by Tickamyer et al., which focuses on Appalachia, exemplifies aspects of this approach.

A second tradition, the *society-in-place* approach (Agnew 1989:11), tackles place from the opposite angle: it starts at the societal level and then moves to the level of specific places. Analysts are less interested in the intrinsic quality of a given place and more interested in how social processes work out across them. For example, analysts may theorize how causal forces generating inequality, such as economic restructuring and dismantling of the welfare state, are manifest across places. This tradition of analyzing place has roots in Marxian geography (Hudson 2001; Harvey 1996; Massey 1994; Peck 1996), critical regional science and planning (Glasmeier 2002; Markusen 2001; Harrison 1994), and the British locality studies of the 1980s to early 1990s (see Massey 1994). According to Massey (1994:5), this tradition challenges "some influential conceptualizations of place . . . [that attempt] to fix the meaning of particular places, to enclose them, endow them with fixed identities, and to claim them for one's own."

From the society-in-place tradition, places are "particular moments" of intersecting social relations (Massey 1994:120). Thinking about place in this way "reveals a complex and unbounded lattice of articulations . . . of power and inequality" (Hudson 2001:257). This view of places corresponds with conceptualizing social relationships across space as a power-geometry (Massey 1994). As the focus on a particular place is diluted, it follows that territorial boundaries are more mutable. "Boundaries may be needed for the purposes of certain types of studies but are not needed for the conceptualization of place itself" (Massey 1994:155). At the same time, analysts recognize places are different from one another—indeed, that is a reason for studying how general social processes work out across them. Places have their own unique structured coherence (Harvey 1989) or social relationships that "come together contingently in specific space-time combinations" (Hudson 2001:261–62). From the society-in-place tradition, the social relationships of primary interest center on production and reproduction, or relationships between actors, such as capital and labor or state and citizens. Nonmaterial forces, such as culture, circumscribe these relationships. The unique combination of these social forces "together in one place may produce effects which would not happen otherwise" (Massey 1994:156).

In sum, from the society-in-place tradition, broader social processes are first emphasized, with places grounding their study. Places have meaning. They require conceptualization. But this conceptualization should be based on the social processes of interest, not taken for granted or based on a priori criteria and narrow definitions like shared social identity. This tradition also assigns no particular priority to studying cities, the nation-state, community, or other territorial unit. Rather, a variety of bounded or unbounded territories relevant to the research question at hand may be studied. In short, this approach sees place in an array of conceptualized territories. The quantitative studies by Cotter et al., McLaughlin et al., and Saenz et al. featured in this volume adopt the society-in-place tradition.

How places are conceptualized affects research design. Those working from the place-in-society tradition tend to focus on a limited number of territorial units and collect richly detailed data about them. Case studies and comparative qualitative designs are often used. The society-in-place approach, by contrast, is more place extensive, lending itself to a larger number of cases and quantitative analysis. In either case, qualitative or quantitative analyses are not precluded. Further, insofar as both traditions represent ideal types, researchers may blend the two. For example, Oakley and Logan largely adopt the society-in-place tradition, as their primary interest is examining community service distribution across places, in this case, neighborhoods. Because their study is situated in New York City, they are able to draw from its distinct history of service provision to shed light on these distributional patterns.

Both the place-in-society and society-in-place traditions are valuable. In sociology, however, discourse about the concept of place largely focuses on the former, making it the more recognized approach to studying—as well as defining—places (see Gieryn 2000). Explicit, detailed articulation of processes creating inequality is also largely confined to the first, as in the large literatures on the development of cities and nation-states. The second tradition, which starts with some question about inequality, then explores it across places variously conceptualized, particularly characterizes the research on subnational inequality.

These two traditions provide overlapping insights that inform each other. To understand inequality across places, recognition of place distinctiveness and a range of place attributes must be a touchstone. At the same time, limiting the study of inequality to a set of special places can be problematic. It not only circumscribes the study of spatial inequality itself but also the ability to compare the experiences of different places, including those at other spatial scales.

SOMETHING OLD, SOMETHING NEW: THE EMERGENCE OF CURRENT WORK ON SPATIAL INEQUALITY

The study of stratification developed with indifferent if not hostile reaction to consideration of space. The classical theorists themselves placed greater emphasis on time and history over space and geography (Soja 1989). Marx's and Weber's central concern, the subsumption of precapitalist societies to capitalist market relations, directed attention toward temporal dimensions of social change and anticipated leveling of geographic differences. Later Marxist-oriented, radical frameworks saw spatial forces like regionalism and nationalism as barriers to a united proletariat (Soja 1989). Place-based inequalities and potentially progressive influences of spatial identities and forces were discounted. Similarly, a spatial research agenda conflicted with sociology's more pervasive, liberal social reformist tradition that included functionalist sociology (Soja 1989). From this view, spatial differences were becoming part of a bygone era because modernization and its benefits were expected to advance across entire populations. Finally, throughout the last century, intellectual priority was given to grand theory (Storper and Walker 1989). The intrinsic specificity of spatial settings muddled grand theory and deductive research agendas that assumed generalizations applied everywhere (Lobao 1993).

Sociology has undergone a remarkable shift over the past few decades. A number of changes have resulted in a blooming of interest in space beyond traditional spatial subfields and at the same time transformed these subfields by making them more sensitive to structural inequalities. Here we denote changes giving rise to the new generation of work on spatial inequality, particularly at the subnational scale.

First, in the 1980s, the top-down, structural orientation of stratification theories was revised to acknowledge a greater role of human agency in creating social structure (Giddens 1981; Bourdieu 1989). This approach necessitated the examination of ordinary social interaction occurring in spatial settings such as the community and household. The concept of human agency also implied that political struggle against inequality was not to be found only in the factory (or at other points of production) but also at the point of consumption or in the community, as evidenced in new social movements. For example, the environmental movement and political actions revolving around NIMBY ("not in my back yard") issues represent attempts to protect places that matter to people.

Second, sociologists moved from a restricted focus on class stratification to the study of social inequality more generally. In the 1980s, they began to devote increased attention to the extra-economic bases of inequality, with a focus on race/ethnicity, gender, and the role of the state. In the 1990s, sexuality and the intersection of race/class/gender and other statuses became important topics. Interest in inequality across space, including subnational territory, is in part a function of expanding the substantive scope of stratification research.

Third, sociology as a whole has witnessed a long-term movement away from deductive theory or covering laws applicable regardless of time and place, and a movement toward historical as well as spatial contextualization. Relationships are increasingly seen as contingent upon time and place. The importance of a spatial approach for informing, challenging, and transforming existing theory is explicitly being recognized. For example, a number of studies now center on questioning whether abstract, macro-level theories are supported on the ground, across subnational territories (Baller and Richardson 2002; Grant and Wallace 1994; Lobao and Hooks 2003; Lobao et al. 1999; Tolbert et al. 1998).

Fourth, theoretical and methodological literatures from human geography and regional science have diffused into sociology. From the 1980s onward, sociologists increasingly drew from them to explore how space structures class relationships and, in turn, variations in socioeconomic well-being (Lobao 1990; Soja 1989). A number of conceptual points from these literatures guided subsequent work on spatial inequality. First, by the 1980s, economic and political geographers had demonstrated the compatibility of critical, neo-Marxian theory with spatial issues (Agnew 1987; Harvey 1989; Storper and Walker 1989). In doing so, geographers explained the role of space in shaping class relations. Observing the movement of capital, firms, and jobs on a global scale, they saw space as less constraining for economic activity than in the past and as a key factor in the search for profits (Massey 1984; Storper and Walker 1989). Business relocation or threats of relocation were central for capital to remain competitive and for management to suppress class struggle. Second, geographers (Massey 1984; Smith 1984) and regional scientists (Markusen 1987) outlined broader principles of uneven development. They argued that capitalists respond to the configuration of social forces at various spatial scales, continually seeking out new opportunities for profit that generate unbalanced growth across geographic areas. These insights opened up the topic of uneven development at the subnational scale to sociological scrutiny. Finally, geographers became intensely interested in the transition from Fordism to a post-Fordist economy. While most attention was to production shifts, some work also considered how poverty and other social inequalities varied regionally in different epochs of capitalism (Dunford and Perrons 1994; Peck 1996, 2001). This literature has served as a theoretical guide for sociologists interested in why the economic conditions of states and localities vary in different historical periods (Grant and Wallace 1994; Lobao and Hooks 2003; Lobao et al. 1999).

Methodological contributions of geography and regional science also spread to sociology. Sociologists periodically addressed analytical approaches to areal data (Duncan et al. 1961), but linkages with other disciplines brought in a newer wave of methodologies. As they tested hypotheses about spatial relationships (Land and Deane 1992; Tolnay et al. 1996), they increasingly drew on spatial analytical methods, such as spatial regression (Anselin 1988). More recently, Geographic Information Systems (GIS) has come into greater use, particularly for descriptive purposes. Still at present, these methodologies are not a staple of most sociologists' research toolkit.

Besides cross-fertilization with other disciplines, interest in spatial inequality also came from sociologists' independent observations that space figured into a series of profound changes in U.S. society from the 1980s onward. Observing the restructuring of regions, communities, and livelihoods, sociologists sought to understand the growing inequalities created. Long-term regional changes were noted such as the decline of the northern manufacturing belt and rise of the sunbelt (Falk and Lyson 1988) and the ongoing restructuring of rural America (Falk et al. 2003). New pockets of prosperity such as California's Silicon Valley were observed (Saxenian 1994). To understand how people and communities coped with economic restructuring, sociologists also turned to the household (Nelson and Smith 1999; Falk 2004; Falk et al. 2003). Research on plant closings (Perrucci et al. 1988) and its rural counterpart, the farm crisis of 1980s (Lasley et al. 1995), addressed the intersection of community and household well-being. Sociologists also observed massive restructuring at the global level (McMichael 2000). They recognized that global changes in industries and trading patterns filter downward (and sometime back upward) to communities producing specific goods for global markets (Gereffi 1994; Anderson 2000). Fortunes of communities ebb and flow with these global changes. Sociologists also recognized that collective desires to protect communities could create progressive responses to change. In response to restructuring, new social movements often sprang from local or regionally based identities, organizations, and networks (Buechler 1995; Castells 1983).

As a result of all of these changes, sociologists working in traditional, spatially oriented subfields of urban sociology, rural sociology, and demography became more critical in their approach, while those working in critically oriented subfields such as stratification and economic sociology became more spatial in theirs. Demography, urban sociology, and rural sociology largely developed from human ecology, a theoretical orientation that devoted little attention to the issues of power and inequality (Walton 1993). By the 1980s, critical traditions from political economy and feminist theory infused urban sociology (Walton 1993) and, to some degree, rural sociology (Lobao 1996; Tickamyer 1996). More recently, a critical demography has emerged (Horton 1999). While this critical theoretical affinity links all three subfields to a much greater degree than previously, limited dialogue remains between them. Separate professional organizations—the ASA section on Urban and Community Sociology, the Rural Sociological Society, and the Population Association of America—reflect the broader segmentation of literatures. Of these three subfields, urban sociology has produced the largest, most coherent body of work on spatial inequality, an advancement discussed in more detail in the following chapter. Meanwhile, by the 1980s, sociologists taking a critical approach to the role of work in inequality allocation became concerned with how relationships varied across labor markets. A large literature on labor markets that contextualized relationships between work and inequality developed, engaging those concerned with general social inequalities as well as economic sociologists (Singelmann and Deseran 1993). For other subfields concerned with power and inequality, such as political sociology, interest in spatial processes is growing, as discussed in the chapter by Leicht and Jenkins.

Shifts in sociological subfields have fostered research on spatial inequality by creating a community of scholars from diverse backgrounds who share a critical theoretical orientation and common methodological approaches. While they may situate their research question within a traditional specialty area, studying spatial inequality, especially at subnational levels invariably ushers in research issues beyond their respective specialties. Thus, the topic itself is creating greater cross-fertilization of literatures and subfields. This volume provides an example of how authors reflect and build upon literatures in stratification, economic sociology, and political sociology, as well as draw from spatial traditions of urban sociology, rural sociology, and demography.

In sum, a new flourishing of research addressing spatial inequality beyond traditional subfields and outside the confines of the urban and national scales has occurred. This is resulting in a real paradigmatic shift in how sociologists conceptualize inequality. The growing body of work on inequalities at the subnational scale, not fully routinized or captured by classification systems within sociology, is part of this broader shift. As sociologists increasingly integrate spatial thinking into their research, new lines of inquiry will emerge. To advance sociology's spatialization project, this volume brings together recent work that articulates the development of a more broad-based spatial agenda within sociology.

CONTENTS AND SCOPE OF THIS VOLUME

As we noted, this volume grew out of research and discussions exchanged at a workshop on spatial inequality sponsored by the American Sociological Association and National Science Foundation's Fund for Advancement of the Discipline. Participants were invited to craft papers that illustrated their distinct approaches to the topic. Authors were asked to consider three basic sets of issues:

1. Why is taking a spatial approach to your research topic important? How does it differ from approaches traditionally used to study your topic?
2. From a theoretical standpoint, how does drawing upon space illuminate your research question and inform your broader area of specialization within sociology?
3. And for empirical chapters (Part II), how do you use space in terms of research design? Why is the place unit you have chosen significant to your research question? What types of spatial methodology are useful to answer your research question?

We selected papers that illuminate different aspects of the spatialization of sociology. The collection showcases the current generation of work applying spatial perspectives to the study of inequality, work that extends spatiality into the heart of the discipline. Taken together, the articles address processes creating inequalities in society and space and, reciprocally, the outcomes of these inequalities. They treat gray areas in sociology's spatialization project, including giving particular scrutiny to the subnational scale. Collectively, they reveal the gaps left when space is ignored and the enhanced ability to theorize, analyze, and address policy and social justice issues when it is not.

The volume is divided into three sections. Part I centers on conceptual and methodological issues applicable to the general study of spatial inequality. Part II brings together empirical pieces that use different methodological and conceptual approaches to bridge the study of space with the study of inequality. Part III completes the project with an assessment of the overall effort and an inventory of future research needs and initiatives.

Part I begins with a chapter on subnational perspectives. Two editors of this volume, Linda Lobao and Greg Hooks, argue for the importance of studying sociology's "missing middle"—the spatial scale between nation and city. Privileging the national and urban scales has led to a gap in our understanding of structures and processes across people and places situated in substantial territory. Yet the subnational scale provides opportunities for spatializing theory and a window onto some of the nation's worst inequalities. This scale is also important for studying new forms of inequality arising from devolution and other changes in state and society. Research on subnational inequality is fragmented but coalescing into a more coherent body of work. Lobao and Hooks supply a systematic examination of subnational research, focusing on the different conceptual approaches studies can take and their overall contributions as well as shortcomings.

The broad overview of subnational perspectives is followed by a critical discussion by Kevin Leicht and Craig Jenkins of similar issues applied to political sociology. They argue for the need to explicitly integrate space into a peculiarly underspatialized subfield, an ironic omission since political sociology assumes territorial bases for political action and institutions. Additionally, they address varieties of political action that are subnationally based, illustrating with a discussion of their own research on state-level economic development programs. They contribute to the book's conceptual attention to spatial scales, considering how political processes are territorially embedded and how they diffuse across places at different scales. Their chapter provides a framework for filling the gap created by past failures to adequately theorize and research political action below the levels of the national state.

The final chapter in this section links conceptual and methodological aspects of spatial analyses. Mike Irwin outlines the conceptual and empirical origins of commonly used territorial units and how these units can be applied to study inequality across spatial scales. He illustrates his discussion with census units, such as tracts, blocks, zip code areas, and counties. He demonstrates the impact of decisions about using different place units on data reflecting three dimensions of inequality—race, wealth, and occupational status—then shows how resulting relationships vary at different scales. His article addresses two thorny issues in spatial inequality research. One is how differences in place-unit choice may influence the degree of inequality observed. The other is the issue of spatial autocorrelation, the potential for spatial clustering among units that affects inferences drawn from statistical models. This chapter clarifies why spatial analysis matters and provides examples of how to interpret this type of analysis.

Part II showcases the recent generation of work on spatial inequality with a series of empirical studies. These chapters illustrate different treatments of place, comparative methodologies, and conceptual approaches blending the study of space with the study of inequality. The first chapter in this section begins the scrutiny of different spatial perspectives by illustrating the "place-in-society" approach, with a comparative case study using qualitative data and methods. The next four studies all use quantitative methods and move closer to a "society-in-place" approach to spatial inequality. That is where their similarities end, however. They differ in the specific units, spatial scales, methods, types of analyses, and dimensions of inequality, providing a broad sample of the different varieties of quantitative spatial analyses that may be employed. Each chapter illustrates a different methodological approach. Showcased are: qualitative comparative research; quantitative models using places as units of analysis; multilevel models featuring individual and place effects; and analysis using places whose boundaries are constructed through GIS.

The studies featured in Part II also illustrate different ways of bridging the study of inequality and the study of space to address substantive topics. Some authors are interested in bringing in space to address topics germane to general inequality research, economic sociology, and political sociology. Others extend traditional spatially-oriented literatures, such as those in demography and rural sociology, through more detailed scrutiny of income and ethnic inequalities. For other authors, the more developed urban inequality literature becomes the starting point.

This section is headed by Ann Tickamyer, one of the editors, and her colleagues. They use a spatial lens to study welfare reform, a topic of considerable interest to inequality researchers, political sociologists, policymakers, and advocates for the poor. Their article moves in the direction of a place-in-society approach with qualitative methods. Tickamyer et al. use intensive research on selected Ohio counties to study the impacts of welfare reform and broader governmental devolution. In many ways their analysis represents a version of a multilevel approach as well as analysis of regional differences with local communities embedded in two different definitions of region—rural/urban and Appalachian/non-Appalachian. The results show that welfare reform has different implications for localities in Appalachia than those outside this region. The results also reveal urban-rural differences. The outcomes are both shaped by preexisting inequalities organized spatially and, in turn, are complicit in maintaining and reconstructing spatial difference. The authors argue that there are profound public policy implications due to the reorganization of the spatial scale of welfare.

Diane McLaughlin and her colleagues continue this section by bringing demographic and inequality literatures together to address determinants of mortality across the United States. The authors explore mechanisms by which income inequality is linked to mortality by introducing sets of local conditions expected to mediate the effects of income inequality. These conditions include unique local attributes such as social cohesion and environmental risks as well as more commonly employed social structural and health variables. Although previous studies rooted in ecological models demonstrate a relationship between income inequality and mortality at different levels of analysis, this research moves beyond past work to explicitly incorporate and test spatial models. Their county-level analysis, spanning urban and rural areas, is a prime example of a subnational approach to spatial inequality.

David Cotter, Joan Hermsen, and Reeve Vanneman are interested in extending the study of poverty spatially. They select metropolitan areas as places of study which they employ in a multilevel research design. Substantively, the authors use metro-area characteristics to show how variation in economic prosperity and inequality is associated with the risk of poverty for families, with particular attention given to the mediating effects of labor supply and family structure. Methodologically, this study provides a classic example of multilevel quantitative modeling that delineates how geographic context affects individuals' life chances. Conceptually, the study exemplifies a structural approach, as it focuses on economic conditions of places and their relationship to family poverty, while simultaneously maintaining a sensitivity to race and gender inequalities.

The three previous chapters use existing place units to explore spatial dimensions of inequality. The next two papers provide intriguing examples of more flexible approaches to studying space, including emphasis on movement and flows and the ways these empirically yield different categories of places. Saenz and his colleagues bridge literatures on migration and ethnic inequality, extending both topics in the process. They examine Mexican-American migration from its core or "homeland" location in the American Southwest into peripheral and frontier regions, places of more incipient Mexican American growth throughout the United States. These flows are conditioned by push and pull factors operating differently in regions. Inequality and discrimination drive Mexican-Americans to seek new opportunities and resources, while human capital and social capital, including kin and community ties, direct this traffic to either peripheral or frontier regions. The authors provide novel contributions through their construction of places based on flow patterns and also by addressing territorial bases of social capital that underpin ethnic migration.

Oakley and Logan build from the spatial inequality tradition in urban sociology to assess the allocation and patterning of community services in New York City. Like Saenz et al., they put forth a flexible definition of place units, in this case using spatial analytic tools. They begin with census tracts to empirically construct neighborhood clusters based on income, then use them to investigate patterns of inequitable service delivery. This study, with its quantitative spatial analysis across neighborhoods, typifies a society-in-place approach. However, the authors' intrinsic interest in the case of New York City adds elements of a place-in-society approach. The study presents a unique analysis of inequality in urban service delivery and a model for using existing units to construct new spatial boundaries based on geographic patterns of inequality. It also yields findings that challenge prevailing views of service provision found in urban research: community services tend to be similarly allocated across neighborhoods despite socioeconomic and racial composition. To explain these findings, the authors draw from New York City's unique history with regard to zoning policies.

Part III concludes with an assessment of the spatialization project outlined in this volume, first from the lens of geography. We invited Vincent Del Casino and John Paul Jones, the latter a recent editor of the discipline's flagship journal, *The Annals of the Association of American Geographers*, to comment on the overall effort to integrate the social and the spatial. They see the studies straddling two metatheoretical camps in human geography, "socially-relevant spatial science" and "critical realism." From the spatial science approach, research questions are explored largely through variable-based models, drawing from determinants reflecting local, regional, national and other characteristics. The spatial science approach is a dominant tradition in geography, from which GIS and other spatial analytical methods emerged. Some of this work casts a critical theoretical eye and raises prospects for social transformation. Critical realism argues for viewing social and spatial processes as intertwined: social relations, actors, and institutions operate in tandem with space. Outcomes of social processes are contingent on place settings. For example, macro-level processes such as industrial restructuring work out differently across places due to their unique contextual attributes. Both geographical approaches are applied across spatial scales, but each takes a different view of scale itself. While research from these two camps is used to explore many topics in geography, the authors note the usefulness of blending both traditions to study inequality and for drawing from sociology, which has a deeper inequality tradition. In turn, sociologists stand much to gain from engagement with these traditions that study relationships and processes across scales.

In the final chapter, the editors conclude with a broad-based call for advancing the study of spatial inequality. This chapter summarizes lessons drawn from the volume and other ongoing work, and outlines an extensive agenda for future research. It is our hope that this collection will provide some of the foundational building blocks for moving the project of spatializing sociology forward.

REFERENCES

Aglietta, Michael A. 1979. *Theory of Capitalist Regulation: The U.S. Experience*. London: Verso.

Agnew, John. 1987. *Place and Politics: The Geographical Mediation of State and Society*. Boston: Allen and Unwin.

———. 1989. "The Devaluation of Place in Social Science." Pp. 9–29 in *The Power of Place: Bringing Together Geographical and Sociological Imaginations*, edited by John A. Agnew and James S. Duncan. Winchester, MA: Unwin Hyman.

Allen, John. 2003. *Lost Geographies of Power*. Malden, MA: Blackwell Publishing.

Anderson, Cynthia D. 2000. *The Social Consequences of Economic Restructuring in the Textile Industry*. New York: Garland.

Anselin, Luc. 1988. *Spatial Econometrics: Methods and Models*. Dordrecht, The Netherlands: Kluwer

Baller, Robert and Kelly Richardson. 2002. "Social Integration, Imitation, and the Geographic Patterning of Suicide." *American Sociological Review* 67: 873–888.

Bourdieu, Pierre. 1989. "Social Space and Symbolic Power." *Sociological Theory* 7:14–25.

Buechler, Steven. M. 1995. "New Social Movement Theories." *Sociological Quarterly* 36:441–464.

Castells, Manuel. 1983. *The City and the Grassroots: A Cross-Cultural Theory of Urban Social Movements*. Berkeley: University of California Press.

Clegg, Stewart R. 1989. *Frameworks of Power*. Thousand Oaks, CA: Sage Publications.

Daipha, Phaedra. 2001. "The Intellectual and Social Organization of ASA 1990–1997: Exploring the Interface between the Discipline of Sociology and its Practitioners." *American Sociologist* 32:73–90.

Dogan, Mattei and Robert Pahre. 1990. *Creative Marginality: Innovation at the Intersections of Social Sciences*. Boulder: Westview Press.

Domash, Mona and Joni Seager. 2001. *Putting Women in Place*. New York: Guildford Press.

Duncan, Otis Dudley, Ray P. Cuzzort, and Beverly Duncan. 1961. *Statistical Geography: Problems in Analyzing Areal Data*. Glencoe, IL: The Free Press.

Dunford, Michael and David Perrons. 1994. "Regional Inequality, Regimes of Accumulation, and Economic Development in Contemporary Europe." *Transactions, Institute of British Geographers*. 19:163–182.

Ennis, James G. 1992. "The Social Organization of Sociological Knowledge: Modeling the Intersection of Specialities." *American Sociological Review* 57:266–273.

Entrikin, J. Nicholas. 1991. *The Betweenness of Place*. Baltimore: Johns Hopkins University Press.

Falk, William W. 2004. *Rooted in Place: Family and Belonging in a Southern Black Community*. New Brunswick, NJ: Rutgers University Press.

Falk, William W. and Thomas A. Lyson. 1988. *High Tech, Low Tech, No Tech: Recent Industrial and Occupational Change in the South*. Albany: State University of New York Press.

Falk, William W., Michael D. Schulman, and Ann R. Tickamyer, eds. 2003. *Communities of Work: Rural Restructuring in Local and Global Contexts*. Athens, OH: Ohio University Press.

Friedland, Roger and Deirdre Boden. 1994. *Now Here: Space, Time, and Modernity*. Berkeley: University of California Press.

Gans, Herbert J. 2002. "The Sociology of Space: A Use-Centered View." *City and Community* 1:329–339.

Gereffi, Gary. 1994. "Capitalism, Development, and Global Commodity Chains." Pp. 211–231 in *Capitalism and Development*, edited by Leslie Sklair. London: Routledge.

Gereffi, Gary and Miguel Korzeniewicz, eds. 1994. *Commodity Chains and Global Capitalism*. Westport, CT: Praeger.

Giddens, Anthony. 1981. *A Contemporary Critique of Historical Materialism*. London: Macmillan.

Gieryn, Thomas F. 2000. "A Space for Place in Sociology." *Annual Review of Sociology* 26:463–496.

Glasmeier, Amy K. 2002. "One Nation Pulling Apart: The Basis of Persistent Poverty in the USA." *Progress in Human Geography* 26:155–173.

Grant, Don S. and Wallace, Michael. 1994. "The Political Economy of Manufacturing Growth and Decline Across the American States, 1970–1985." *Social Forces* 73:33–63.

Gregory, Derek. 1994. *Geographical Imaginations*. Cambridge, MA: Basil Blackwell.

Harrison, Bennett. 1994. *Lean and Mean: The Changing Landscape of Corporate Power in the Age of Flexibility*. New York: Basic Books.

Harvey, David. 1989. *The Urban Experience*. Oxford: Blackwell.

———. 1996. *Justice, Nature, and the Geography of Difference*. Cambridge, MA: Basil Blackwell.

Hooks, Gregory. 1994. "Regional Processes in the Hegemonic Nation: Political, Economic, and Military Influences in the Use of Geographic Space." *American Sociological Review* 59:746–772.

Hooks, Gregory and Chad L. Smith. 2004. "The Treadmill of Destruction: National Sacrifice Areas and Native Americans." *American Sociological Review* 69:558–575.

Horton, Haywood. 1999. "Critical Demography: The Paradigm of the Future?" *Sociological Forum* 14: 363–367.

Hudson, Ray. 2001. *Producing Places*. New York: Guilford Press.

Land, Kenneth C. and Glenn Deane. 1992. "On the Large-Sample Estimation of Regression Models with Spatial or Network Effects Terms." *Sociological Methodology* 22:221–248.

Lasley, Paul, F. Larry Leistritz, Linda M. Lobao, and Katherine Meyer. *Beyond the Amber Waves of Grain: An Examination of Economic and Social Restructuring in the Heartland*. Boulder: Westview Press.

Lefebvre, Henri. 1991. *The Production of Space*. Cambridge, MA: Basil Blackwell.

Lobao, Linda M. 1990. *Locality and Inequality*. Albany: State University of New York Press.

———. 1993. "Renewed Significance of Space in Social Research: Implications for Labor Market Studies." Pp. 11–31 in *Inequalities in Labor Market Areas*, edited by Joachim Singelmann and Forrest A. Deseran. Boulder: Westview Press.

————. 1994. "The Place of 'Place' in Current Sociological Research." *Environment and Planning A* 26:665–668.

————. 1996. "A Sociology of the Periphery Versus a Peripheral Sociology: Rural Sociology and the Dimension of Space." *Rural Sociology* 61:77–102.

————. 2004. "Continuity and Change in Place Stratification: Spatial Inequality and Middle-Range Territorial Units." *Rural Sociology* 69:1–30.

Lobao, Linda M. and Gregory Hooks. 2003. "Public Employment, Welfare Transfers, and Economic Well-Being Across Local Populations: Does Lean and Mean Government Benefit the Masses?" *Social Forces* 82:519–556.

Lobao, Linda M., Jamie Rulli, and Lawrence A. Brown. 1999. "Macro-Level Theory and Local-Level Inequality: Industrial Structure, Institutional Arrangements, and the Political Economy of Redistribution, 1970 and 1990." *Annals of the Association of American Geographers* 89:571–601.

Markusen, Ann. 1987. *Regions: The Economics and Politics of Territory.* Totowa, NJ: Rowman and Littlefield.

————. 2001. "Regions as Loci of Conflict and Change: The Contributions of Ben Harrison to Regional Economic Development." *Economic Development Quarterly* 15:291–298.

Massey, Doreen. 1994. *Space, Place, and Gender.* Minneapolis: University of Minnesota Press.

McCall, Leslie. 2001. *Complex Inequality: Gender, Class, and Race in the New Economy.* New York: Routledge.

McMichael, Philip. 2000. *Development and Social Change.* Thousand Oaks, CA: Pine Forge Press.

Molotch, Harvey, William Freudenburg, and Krista E. Paulsen. 2000. "History Repeats Itself, but How? City Character, Urban Tradition, and the Accomplishment of Place." *American Sociological Review* 65: 791–823.

Nelson, Margaret K., and Joan Smith. 1999. *Working Hard and Making Do: Surviving in Small Town America.* Berkeley: University of California Press.

Odum, Howard E. and H. E. Moore. 1938. *American Regionalism; A Cultural-Historical Approach to National Integration.* New York: Henry Holt.

Orum, Anthony M. and Xiangming Chen. 2003. *The World of Cities: Places in Comparative and Historical Perspective.* Malden, MA: Basil Blackwell.

Peck, Jamie. 1996. *Work-Place: The Social Regulation of Labor Markets.* New York: Guilford Press.

————. 2001. *WorkFare States.* New York: Guilford Press.

Perrucci, Carolyn, Robert Perrucci, Dena Targ, and Harry Targ. 1988. *Plant Closings: International Context and Social Costs.* New York: Aldine De Gruyter.

Rose, Gillian. 1993. *Feminism and Geography: The Limits of Geographical Knowledge.* Minneapolis: University of Minnesota Press.

Saxenian, Anna Lee. 1994. *Regional Advantage: Culture and Competition in Silicon Valley and Route 128.* Cambridge, MA: Harvard University Press.

Singelmann, Joachim and Forrest A. Deseran, eds. 1993. *Inequalities in Labor Market Areas.* Boulder: Westview.

Smith, Neil. 1984. *Uneven Development: Nature, Capital, and the Production of Space.* Oxford: Basil Blackwell.

Soja, Edward. 1989. *Post-Modern Geographies: The Reassertion of Space in Critical Social Theory.* London: Verso.

Storper, Michael and Richard Walker. 1989. *The Capitalist Imperative: Territory, Technology, and Industrial Growth.* Oxford: Basil Blackwell.

Swanstrom, Todd, Peter Dreier, and John Mollenkopf. 2002. "Economic Inequality and Public Policy: The Power of Power." *City and Community* 4:349–372.

Taylor, Peter J. 1999. "Places, Spaces, and Macy's: Place-Space Tensions in the Political Geography of Modernities." *Progress in Human Geography* 23:7–26.

Tickamyer, Ann R. 1996. "Sex, Lies, and Statistics: Can Rural Sociology Survive Restructuring?" *Rural Sociology* 61:5–24.

———. 2000. "Space Matters! Spatial Inequality in Future Sociology." *Contemporary Sociology* 29:805–813.

Tolbert, Charles, Thomas T. Lyson, and Michael Irwin. 1998. "Local Capitalism, Civic Engagement, and Socioeconomic Well-Being." *Social Forces* 77:401–28.

Tolnay, Stewart E., Glenn Deane, and E. M. Beck. 1996. "Vicarious Violence: Spatial Effects on Southern Lynchings, 1890–1919." *American Journal of Sociology* 102:788–815.

Tuan, Yi-Fu. 1977. *Space and Place: The Perspective of Experience.* Minneapolis: University of Minnesota Press.

Walton, John. 1993. "Urban Sociology: The Contribution and Limits of Political Economy." *Annual Review of Sociology* 19:301–320.

PART I

Extending the Sociological Imagination Across Space: Conceptual and Methodological Issues

TWO

Advancing the Sociology of Spatial Inequality

Spaces, Places, and the Subnational Scale

LINDA M. LOBAO
GREGORY HOOKS

DESPITE WIDESPREAD INTEREST in spatializing sociology, consideration of space in research on stratification remains limited. Well-recognized, coherent literatures on stratification are found mainly at two opposite spatial scales, the city and the cross-national level. A large urban literature explores inequalities of poverty, racial segregation, crime, and other conditions within and across cities. Much of it focuses on large, world cities such as New York, Chicago, Los Angeles, and Atlanta. At the other extreme, cross-national literature charts the socioeconomic position of entire nations in the global system. But there is a missing middle: large swathes of places, people, and substantive topics are not systematically investigated because they fail to fall into the relatively binary pattern by which sociologists carve up space. Illustrating this lack of attention is that sociology has no customary term for the middle geographic scale between city and nation-state.

This restricted focus is problematic for much broader disciplinary issues. Take the two most recent presidential elections, for example. If sociologists' customary populations of interest were in the position to dictate electoral outcome, George W. Bush would have been defeated by such wide margins in 2000 and 2004 that disputes over small fractions of votes in Florida and Ohio, respectively, would have little historical significance. However, because the study of spatial inequality has stayed so close to its urban tradition, sociologists have difficulty answering Thomas Frank's (2004) query: *What's the Matter with Kansas?* Sociology has a poor understanding of people of modest means who reside outside major metropolitan areas, including their perceived interests and their reasons for voting against the interests sociologists assign to them.

A growing body of research makes headway against this impasse. Its interest is regional inequality beyond the metropolis but below the level of the nation-state. It addresses this scale through the comparative analysis of states, counties, labor markets, and other place units. The places studied are less familiar to sociologists because they typically fall outside traditional city limits. This research has its own mode of analysis: it centers on delineating shared attributes of groups of places with the purpose of examining how social processes and attendant inequalities unfold differently within a nation.[1] We refer to this body of research as the *subnational* approach to spatial inequality. Certainly sociology has older traditions, such as human ecology and social indicators research, that understand subnational areas largely through a non-critical sociological lens. Rural sociology and demography also address subnational areas. How these older traditions feed into current work is discussed in more detail elsewhere (Lobao 1996, 2004). Here we give attention to a new generation of work that bridges the study of social stratification and uneven development. Sociological work on subnational inequality is still in an emergent phase. It has evolved from discrete studies responding to different research traditions, giving the body of work a fragmented character. This fragmentation limits development of an accumulated knowledge base and integrative theory. However, in recent years, research is consolidating as analysts recognize they share overarching interests and approaches.

This chapter explains how research on subnational inequality advances the study of stratification. First, to situate the subnational approach, we bring in the concept of spatial scales and how it relates to spatializing inequality and conceptualizing places. Second, we take stock of sociology's ongoing spatialization project. We contrast literatures on the nation-state and urban scales with subnational research, bringing together bodies of work often kept separate in scholarly debates. Third, we critically assess the status of subnational research. We then turn to our own work to highlight issues current studies tend to overlook, such as recent state-society shifts. Finally, we outline areas where further research is needed. Interest in subnational inequality exists across the social sciences. While we bring in other disciplines, our focus is how the sociological imagination is deployed at the subnational scale. Sociologists have produced numerous studies on subnational inequality that merit visibility as a distinct approach. Geography and other disciplines have internal debates on the topic separately articulated by scholars elsewhere.[2]

Rather than providing a dogmatic definition of the subnational scale, we see it as occupying the gray areas of regional territory between the nation and city that sociology has not coherently addressed, a scale encompassing states as well as other regions of the nation as a whole. A general example of inequality at the subnational scale is illustrated by mapping median family income, a commonly used indicator of well-being. Maps in figure 2.1 show relative rankings of counties into high (top third of distribution), moderate (middle third), and low family income (bottom third) based on data from the last four U.S. censuses for 1969 to 1999. Most counties retain relative rankings over time, reflecting deeply rooted trends. There are also some shifts, particularly where northern and western counties lost advantaged positions over time. Sociologists have barely scratched the surface of understanding many of the reasons behind these spatial-temporal trends.

SPATIAL SCALES, SPACES, AND PLACES

Spatial scales, along with spaces and places, illuminate key issues in subnational inequality as well as gaps in sociology's spatialization project. As noted in the introduction, rather than viewing any of these as fixed concepts, it is useful to consider the spaces, spatial scales, and places conceptualized by analysts. Space can be brought into the study of inequality in different ways. Subfields such as cross-national, rural, and urban sociology have an inherent spatial focus. But others remain underspatialized. For example, chapters in this volume explain how taking a spatial approach to political and economic sociology enriches these fields. Bringing in space requires attention to the scale at which social processes occur. Addressed widely in geography (Gough 2004; Smith 2003), the concept of spatial scales has received little direct attention in sociology. It refers to the territorial resolution at which social processes work out, are conceptualized and studied (Smith 2003:228).

Social scientists privilege certain scales in understanding social processes. The urban and national scales have generated distinct explanatory discourses which Swyngedouw (1997) calls "scalar narratives." Scalar narratives tend to assert the primacy of their scales of focus while crowding out others. For example, discourse about large, world cities may be directed upward to explain global paths of development, or it may be directed downward, so that subnational development is reduced to a network of large cities. Generalizations about the nation-state may be uncritically assumed to apply at lower scales, leaving regional level processes and explanations unquestioned. Privileging certain geographic scales creates an unbalanced view of inequality (Lobao 2004). For the most part, ordinary, unexceptional places, such as slow-growing or marginal regions and the subnational scale at large, are left out of discussion. Neglecting these areas and focusing on propulsive urban centers contributes to over-emphasis of globalization as opposed to localization processes (Cox 1997) and change over stasis in inequality and development.

1969

1979

1989

1999

Low
Moderate
High

FIGURE 2.1. Median Family Income

Social processes are also fluid and cut across spatial scales. Any one scale provides but a snapshot of a causal moment in studying inequality (Swyngedouw 1997:140). In different historical periods, different geographic scales emerge as significant to social processes. The subnational scale, for example, is increasingly important for understanding the allocation of inequality in part due to decentralization. States and counties have greater responsibility for economic growth and social welfare today relative to the past and the federal government (Lobao and Kraybill 2005).

Finally, the scale at which one chooses to direct theory and research affects conceptualization of places. In our introduction, we discussed two traditions, the place-in-society approach, more conventional to sociology, and the society-in-place approach, more articulated in geography, which sees *place* in an array of conceptualized territories. Much work on subnational inequality takes the second approach. Here the intrinsic character of places is of less interest, but places still require conceptualization based on the social processes earmarked for attention. Since social processes cut across scales, one way to view *place* is as a "particular articulation" of those processes (Massey 1994:5). That is, a place represents a particular mix of social relationships originating from sources at different scales, both internal and external to that place.

The literature on spatial scales challenges confining inequality research to cities and nation-states. It opens up the subnational scale as worthy of investigation and increasingly important under neoliberal governance. It cautions against fixing the study of place itself at any particular scale. Finally, it provides an alternative way of thinking about places, as nodes of intersecting relationships involving power and inequality from different scales (Massey 1994).

Spatial scales, space, and places expose gray areas in sociology, evident in the language describing the subnational scale and the units comprising it. As noted earlier, sociology has no customary term for the subnational scale. In geography, *region* is often used, but in sociology, this word is usually understood as region of the country, such as North or South. Relatedly, the place units of study are a territorial mosaic and no widely-used term describes them. The term *localities*, while potentially useful, does not convey that states are also studied. Geography too has no consistent term for place units in subnational research (Taylor 1999). To simplify discussion, we use *places* for the various subnational units that analysts conceptualize and operationalize.

SCALAR TRADITIONS OF SPATIAL INEQUALITY: SIMILARITIES AND DIFFERENCES

Space, spatial scales, and place help to describe current sociological research traditions on spatial inequality. In brief, these traditions range from those where spatially framed research questions are aligned with established scales and concrete places of study to those where this tripartite alignment is diffuse and/or lacking. At the latter extreme are less charted areas of spatial inequality, where the subnational research resides. Spatial inequality traditions are large and varied and we cannot provide a detailed inventory. Rather, our goal is to explain how subnational research compares with other traditions. It should be stressed, however, that research traditions are porous and not mutually exclusive, so that literatures and researchers themselves span traditions.

Sociological traditions of spatial inequality share similarities irrespective of their scale of interest, although subnational research is less developed on some dimensions. These traditions recognize both the importance of where actors are located in geographic space and the fact that geographic entities themselves are subject to processes of stratification. They pose similar research questions: How and why are varying forms of poverty and prosperity distributed across populations in different territories? How do territories themselves become stratified from one another? The first question addresses unequal distribution, while the second is more concerned with uneven development. Places are conceptualized through the place-in-society and the society-in-place approaches. Research designs and statistical methods are similar. Multilevel and aggregate-level quantitative modeling and comparative, qualitative analyses characterize spatial inequality research. Social actors and groups, as well as structural forces reflecting the market, state, and civic society that are important to the study of stratification, likewise figure prominently in spatial inequality research.

In table 2.1, we present a brief synopsis of sociology's spatial inequality traditions, with the purpose of contrasting subnational research with the established cross-national and urban traditions.

ESTABLISHED TRADITIONS OF SPATIAL INEQUALITY:
THE CROSS-NATIONAL AND URBAN SCALES

Well-recognized inequality literatures are situated at the cross-national and urban scales. The scale of interest of the former is the nation-state or beyond, while for the latter, it is the city or local area Research at both scales has produced theoretical perspectives, applicable concepts, methods, and research topics routinized by decades of systematic inquiry. As a consequence, cities and nation-states are widely accepted as *places* from which to study inequality. Urban and cross-national sociology have strong place-in-society traditions. Intrinsic interest in a particular city or nation-state, respectively, often forms the basis of systematic study. We by no means suggest that gray areas do not exist within these subfields. However, although unresolved methodological and theoretical debates remain, these too are typically discussed in large literatures.

TABLE 2.1
Spatial Inequality: The Subnational Approach Compared to Established Traditions

	National/Cross-National	Urban	Subnational
		Overview	
Contributing subfields	Cross-national, development sociology	Urban sociology	Mixed: spatially-oriented traditions and inequality-oriented traditions
Spatial scale of interest	Nation-state, global system	City or local area	Between nation-state and city: all subnational territory, regions, states
Common research designs	Comparative, cross-national; multilevel (individual-nation state); studies of specific countries. Both qualitative and quantitative research.	Comparative, cross-urban; multilevel (individual-city-neighborhood); studies of specific cities, including inequality within. Both qualitative and quantitative research.	Comparative, cross-territorial units; multilevel (individual-subnational unit); studies of specific regions, including inequality within. Both qualitative and quantitative research.
Typical concrete place units of analysis	Nation-states	Large cities, intracity units such as neighborhoods	Territorial mosaic: states, labor markets, counties, both rural and urban communities

(continued on next page)

TABLE 2.1 (continued)

	National/Cross-National	Urban	Subnational
	Coherence of Theory and Research		
Research tradition	Established: relatively well-recognized coherent literature	Established: relatively well-recognized coherent literature	Emergent: literature in consolidation phase
Theoretical development	Commonly-used well-known theories about development of nation-states and inequality between nation-states	Commonly-used, well-known theories about development of the city and inequality within and between cities	No commonly-used current sociological theories directed to uneven development or to inequality at the subnational scale
Research questions, spatial scale of resolution, and place units of analysis	Well defined and aligned	Well defined and aligned	Not routinized

(continued on next page)

TABLE 2.1 (continued)

	National/Cross-National	Urban	Subnational
	Contributions to the Study of Spatial Inequality		
Spaces: The ways in which space is brought in to answer questions about inequality	Inherent focus on inequality questions with reference to geographic space	Inherent focus on inequality questions with reference to geographic space	Varied: some work, such as that on labor markets, has an inherent focus on inequality questions with reference to geographic space; other work seeks to extend underspatialized inequality literatures
Conceptualizing places	Includes strong place-in-society tradition	Includes strong place-in-society tradition	Weak place-in-society tradition; places seen mainly from society-in-place approach
Consideration of subnational territory	Limited. Some work on regional underdevelopment within developing societies.	Limited. Some work on city-regions, suburbanization processes. Subnational territory sometimes treated as a network of large cities.	Central but under-theorized
Contribution to the study of spatial inequality	Nation-state and globally centered view of spatial inequality	City-centered view of spatial inequality	View of spatial inequality as a power-geometry across subnational space

Sociological interest in cross-national inequality has resulted in a general cross-national tradition (Firebaugh 2003; Lenski 1966) as well as specific attention to developing nations (McMichael 2000). Researchers theorize the development of nation-states and their articulation in the global system (Chase-Dunn and Grimes 1995; Frank 1967; Wallerstein 1979). Cross-national research provides a direct understanding of social forces creating inequalities. Forces internal to nations, such as class actors, state and market conditions, and external forces such as trading patterns, financial markets, and first-world hegemony, affect national paths of development and attendant inequalities. Customary types of inequalities are examined, most frequently conceptualized by economic well-being, but also by demographic, health, gender-related, environmental and other indicators of inequality (Esping-Anderson 1990; Firebaugh 2003; Jorgenson 2003; Moller et al. 2003; van der Lippe and van Dijk 2002). There are established methodological protocols. Researchers share common substantive topics that have recognized importance for advancing the field. The end result is that research questions are framed with a global and/or national spatial resolution in mind, with nation-states serving as concrete testing grounds and places of study.

Similar parallels can be drawn with inequality research at the urban scale. Two sets of work, each focusing on how the urban context molds stratification, can be delineated. One is more concerned with inequality processes internal to cities, reflected in research on intracity segregation, poverty, and other social exclusion (Brooks-Gunn et al. 2000; Wilson 1987), and also in research on local development such as through urban growth machines (Logan and Molotch 1987; Molotch et al. 2000). The second body of work is concerned with inequality processes across cities, reflected in research on comparative urban development (Sassen 2000; Zukin 1991). From the Chicago school onward, sociologists have theorized urban development (Feagin 1998; Soja 1989; Walton 1993). They also have long identified specific social forces creating inequalities across and within cities. For example, forces internal to the city, such as class actors and labor market, racial/ethnic, political, and cultural attributes as well as external forces such the global economy and state policy, are often implicated (Molotch et al. 2000; Walton 1993; Zukin 1991). The urban literature has a set of inequalities commonly addressed, typically poverty, unemployment, housing, education, segregation, and crime (Charles 2003; Gottdiener 1994; Jargowsky 1997; Logan et al. 2004; Massey and Denton 1993; O'Connor et al. 2003; Small and Newman 2001; Wilson 1987). There are established methodological protocols (Brooks-Gunn et al. 2000; Sampson et al. 2002; Small and Newman 2001). Research questions are framed with a city or locally centered resolution in mind, with cities and neighborhoods as concrete testing grounds. In sociology, the city is virtually synonymous with *place* as seen in recent books (Frazier et al. 2003; Jargowsky 1997; Orum and Chen 2003).

The subnational scale tends to be defined by omission in both the cross-national and urban inequality traditions, but some interest has always been evident. Some development sociologists turn downward to examine regional inequalities (Bunker 1985; Bunker and Ciccantell 2005; Cardoso and Falleto 1979). Contemporary urban researchers have reached beyond city limits. Some argue for a view of the city as a "metropolitan region" whose political economy influences hinterland development (Feagin 1998; Gottdiener 1994). Researchers studying poverty in the urban core link it to suburbanization processes and labor market mismatches (Fernandez and Su 2004) and to regional political economic forces denoted in the "metropolitics" literature (Dreier et al. 2001; Orfield 1997). For both the cross-national and urban traditions, however, attention to inequality broadly across subnational space remains outside their customary domains of concern. The former provides a nation-state and globally centered view of inequality where subnational variation is typically taken into little account; the latter provides a city-centered view that while illuminative in its own right, runs the danger of reducing subnational territory to a network of large cities and obscuring inequality processes outside these areas.

BETWEEN SOCIOLOGY'S DOMINANT SCALE TRADITIONS:
CURRENT WORK ON SUBNATIONAL INEQUALITY

Sociologists turning a spatial lens toward inequality outside the urban and cross-national traditions confront gray areas. Here, theory, research questions, their appropriate spatial scale of resolution, and their concrete places of focus are less defined and aligned. There tends to be no a priori view of the primacy of a particular place unit or scale of social action. Research questions are examined across scales from micro-settings, such as the household, and on upwards.

Two alternative ways sociologists address spatial inequality outside the urban and cross-national traditions can be delineated. Both are the foundation for current research on subnational inequality. One is to start from traditional spatially oriented subfields, such as demography and rural sociology, then bring in questions about inequality. The other is to start from underspatialized inequality-oriented subfields, then bring in questions about space. Since the scale of focus is not fixed (i.e., primacy is not given to any one scale), both approaches yield research at the subnational as well as other scales. However, less conceptual and methodological routinization, coupled with segmentation of literatures, add contention and ambiguity to research efforts. At the same time, by bringing in more fluid ways of addressing spatial inequality, both approaches advance sociology's spatialization project beyond the city and nation-state.

Research from the two approaches shows that a range of significant questions about inequality can be usefully explored at the subnational scale and that a body of empirical work has now been amassed. Most studies examine how and/or why well-recognized stratification indicators, such as poverty, income inequality, employment opportunities, as well as inequalities by race/ethnicity and gender, vary across subnational territories. Other forms of inequality, such as environmental degradation (Hooks and Smith 2004), collective violence (Tolnay et al. 1996), and state resource capacities (Lobao and Kraybill 2005), are sometimes addressed.

Researchers have overlapping motivations for invoking the subnational scale. They may have conceptual interest in processes at this scale, as in studies on regional uneven development (Duncan 1999; Hooks 1994; Falk et al. 2003; Lyson and Falk 1993; McGranahan 1980; Mencken 2000), devolution of federal responsibilities to subnational governments (Lobao and Kraybill 2005), state-level economic development (Leicht and Jenkins 1994), and social welfare policy (Soule and Zylan 1997). A second motivation is theory-testing and extension of underspatialized literatures. For example, labor market research has long extended our knowledge of how general stratification theories work spatially. More recently, sociologists have been interested in whether aspatial political economic theories hold within nations (Grant and Wallace 1994; Lobao et al. 1999; Nielsen and Alderson 1997). Third, analysts may study the subnational scale as part of extant disciplinary traditions. Finally, they may have policy interests and social justice purposes or what Markusen (2001) calls the "politicization of space." Here, subnational territory is used to analyze multiple interlocking oppressions requiring documentation to create change.

Although subnational research is less routinized than urban and cross-national research, it employs comparable research designs and statistical methods. It also raises distinct issues such as spatial autocorrelation (Voss et al. 2006), which is given central attention in Irwin's chapter in this volume.

Our discussion below casts the net broadly in considering the subnational scale as territory composed of multiple communities extending regionally beyond the city, thereby potentially encompassing both urban and rural areas. In practice, studies addressing the subnational scale range from those completely covering national territory to those covering portions such as certain regions. Studies using metropolitan areas as labor markets also provide a partial window on the subnational scale, insofar as they reach to be inclusive across national territory (Cotter et al. 1997; Huffman and Cohen 2004; McCall 2001). Finally, while research often uses local units of observation, scholars' interests lie beyond the local, to processes systemic to broader subnational territory. They are concerned with a higher order of explanation about territory formed as a combination of local, state, or other units of analysis.

The research discussed below lays the groundwork for a more comprehensive approach to subnational inequality. It also points to incomplete tasks that must be addressed. In contrast to urban and cross-national/development sociology, sociologists working at the subnational scale have no commonly used theories directed to this scale. Linkages across different traditions below tend to be weak. These studies represent the status of sociology's subnational spatialization project—not fully formed and wrestling with a number of issues.

Spatially-oriented traditions: bringing in inequality. In demography and rural sociology, it is often customary to frame research questions with explicit consideration of subnational space. Both traditions emerged from strong human ecology roots, which saw spatial variations as resulting from humans' adaptations to different ecological settings. Critical perspectives that view spatial variations in terms of power and inequality, produced by capitalist development, are more recent (Horton 1999; Lobao 2004). Both traditions span the urban and rural divide and a fair number of rural sociologists are also demographers (Champion and Hugo 2004; Kandel and Brown 2006).

Demographers have long used geographic units in entirely aggregate-level analyses and more recently in multilevel studies linking individual outcomes with place context. Voss (2007) notes that quantitative demographers once depended almost entirely on data based on geographic units, but turned more to individual-level data as it became publicly available. Interest in spatial demography reemerged in the 1980s onward (Voss 2007). Demographers' research moves beyond questions about economic inequalities to how a variety of well-being indicators, such as migration, fertility, mortality, family formation, health status, and crime, are spread across populations (Brown 2002; Lichter et al. 1997; McLaughlin and Stokes 2002; South and Messner 2000) and to variations in inequality by ethnic group (Fosset and Seibert 1997; Saenz 1997) and gender (Lobao and Brown 1998). Intrinsic, detailed place characteristics are usually not of foremost concern; rather the purpose is to generalize across many ecological units. As a consequence, places tend to be represented by a few variables or may be simply taken-for-granted population containers. Some studies explicitly address the link between place conceptualization and concrete units, such as the choice of counties as marriage markets (Lichter et al. 1997) and villages (Entwisle et al. 1989) as contexts for demographic decision making. Place attributes that matter to demographic outcomes continue to be sorted out. One debate concerns the relative importance of income levels versus income inequality in determining mortality, addressed in this volume by McLaughlin et al.

In rural sociology, much empirical work on subnational inequality exists, but it is segmented by substantive topic (Lobao 2004). Research questions center on the disparities in well-being indicators and their causal determinants. Counties, labor market areas, cities, and towns are typically used as either units of analysis directly or as contexts surrounding households and individuals. One set of work reflects a general rural inequality tradition: it builds from literature on rural poverty (Duncan 1999; Rural Sociological Task Force on Persistent Rural Poverty 1993; Weber et al. 2005), labor markets (Singelmann et al. 1993), demography (Brown and Lee 1999; Brown and Hirschl 1995; McLaughlin et al. 1999), and racial/ethnic segregation processes (Saenz and Thomas 1991). Most attention is on how poverty and other well-being indicators vary within rural areas and between urban and rural areas. Explanations for these variations tend to focus on economic structure, such as manufacturing employment, and sociodemographic and ecological factors. A second set of work centers on determinants of subnational inequality from agricultural and environmental/natural resources sociology. Agricultural sociologists have long studied how industrialized farming relative to family farming impacts regions and communities (Lobao 1990). Environmental sociologists similarly study the impacts of natural resource-based and other industries on socioeconomic and environmental conditions across regions (Freudenburg and Gramling 1994; Rudel 2002).

Finally, though not addressing the subnational scale in a broad sense, community research should be noted. Typically focusing on a single or few communities, it epitomizes the place-in-society approach. It has traditionally emphasized questions of social solidarity over power and inequality but some research reflects an evolution toward a more critical and comparative approach. For example, a comparative communities literature exists that examines how plant closings, other downturns, and new industrial and residential development affect the well-being of small and rural communities (Falk et al. 2003; Salamon 2003; Winson 1997).

Inequality-oriented traditions: bringing in space. Another approach to subnational inequality is to begin from a body of work whose foremost concern is inequality, then bring in space to this underspatialized literature. Specific subfields in sociology illuminate different aspects of inequality allocation. Literature on stratification addresses how valued resources are allocated according to class, gender, race/ethnicity, and other statuses. While much of the stratification literature centers on allocation of economic resources, there is attention to other forms of inequality, such as health, schooling, crime, and environmental indicators (see Neckerman 2004). Sociologists also study inequality from the opposite end, by focusing on the social actors and institutions responsible for allocating inequalities. For example, economic sociology examines how economic actors and institutions make earnings and employment opportunities available to different social groups. Political sociology examines state mechanisms central to allocation processes. Focus is on the role of government and capitalist elites, labor, and civic society, as well as state policy in creating economic inequalities. Bringing in space to the study of stratification, economic sociology, and political sociology has expanded since the 1970s. However, theoretical extension of these subfields is carved out largely at the city or nation-state level.[3] For example, the chapter by Leicht and Jenkins in this volume discusses how political sociology overly relies on the nation-state for theorizing.

Perhaps the literature on labor markets is the most recognized contribution of subnational research to the study of general stratification. The chapter by Cotter et al. in this volume provides an example. Labor market literature sheds light on why earnings, income, and poverty rates are not constant across populations. Researchers examine how differences between labor market areas, particularly in the quantity and quality of jobs, affect individual as well as aggregate economic outcomes (Beggs 1995; Browne and Misra 2003; Cotter 2002; McCall 2001; Singelmann et al. 1993). This literature also shows that returns to earnings from human capital attributes and from the race, ethnic and gender statuses of workers vary by labor market. As McCall (2001) demonstrates, the effects of labor markets on different social groups are complex and often cannot be anticipated by aspatial stratification theories.

Turning to social forces involved in inequality allocation, researchers have shown how a subnational approach matters. Economic sociologists have extended questions about industrial structure to subnational areas (Bloomquist et al. 1982; Grant and Wallace 1994; Lobao 1990; Lobao et al. 1999; Lorence and Nelson 1993; Tomaskovic-Devey 1987). This literature tends to find that industries such as durable manufacturing and producer services known to produce higher earnings for workers also have beneficial effects across places. Some political sociologists look to the subnational scale to examine state policy and institutions. Federal policy involving the defense industry (Bloomquist and Hooks 1992; Hooks 1994) and state-level economic development programs (Leicht and Jenkins 1994) create uneven playing fields for generating economic growth. Social welfare policy adoption varies across states, with more punitive requirements enacted in states with less institutional protections for citizens (Soule and Zylan 1997). Public employment and social welfare expenditures vary subnationally, affecting the economic well-being of populations (Lobao and Hooks 2003). Other researchers extend the civic society literature subnationally, showing that places higher on civic society measures, have lower out-migration and economic inequality (Tolbert et al. 1998).

The previous studies situate their arguments within an underspatialized literature, then discuss why a spatial approach is needed. Comparative analyses are drawn across places such as states, counties, labor markets, and metropolitan areas. The fact that sociology is balkanized into different subfields on inequality allocation has important implications. It highlights the complexity of how inequalities are created and distributed, and points to the need for linked approaches. Extant research on the subnational scale also shows how the economic, political, and stratification literatures in sociology can be extended by bringing in space. There are costs of introducing space into underspatialized literatures, however. A spatial approach may be unappreciated insofar as it challenges customary ways of addressing theory and research. It opens up potential criticism that a study no longer belongs within its "home" subfield but has entered the realm of others, such as the spatially-oriented traditions noted above. Thus, spatial research may be banished from the subfield it wishes to influence.

ADVANCING RESEARCH ON
SUBNATIONAL INEQUALITY

Addressing the knowledge gap at the subnational scale has broad importance for sociology. Serious inequalities exist at the subnational scale. One example is recent development patterns where economic growth is combined with income polarization, as seen in the bicoastal West and Northeast (Lenz 2004). Another is long-standing patterns of inequality involving economic well-being, health status, public services, and racial/ethnic segregation that have persisted across regions for decades (Glasmeier 2005). Numerous questions about business and government can only be rigorously assessed through comparative, subnational research, such as the effects of low-wage businesses such as Wal-Mart on poverty rates and social welfare expenditures, the impacts of environmentally polluting industries, and the impacts of government policy. The subnational scale is central to a major political economic shift, the neoliberal rollout of social policy (Peck 2001). Here, devolution is creating a new round of spatial instability more specific to state and county than in the past, with the consequence that poorer places may fall further behind in well-being.

Most importantly, the subnational scale is significant for building theory. As noted earlier, neglecting subnational space creates an unbalanced view in how we theorize development. Macro- or national-level theories also often depend on subnational relationships seldom directly analyzed. This may lead to ignoring part of the overall theoretical story or to more serious problems. For example, cross-national studies often implicate industrial restructuring as a cause of the United States' high growth of inequality relative to other nations in the post-1970 period; however, the distinct U.S. pattern can only be understood through the movement of industries, firms, and jobs from snowbelt to sunbelt, which helped reduce the earnings of the aggregate working class. More seriously, Massey (1994:128) argues that in failing to trace out the subnational implications of macro-level theories, analysts may assume causal relationships not empirically warranted. Since general, national relationships are in some sense a summary of relationships occurring subnationally, it is essential to address this scale directly. Causal forces considered in macro-level theories also operate subnationally (Massey 1994). For example, political economy theories see institutional arrangements between capital, labor, and the state as regulating national growth and redistribution. These insights have been extended to posit the existence of subnational modes of regulation (Peck 1996) and "structured coherences" (Harvey 1989) where industrial structure and institutional arrangements coincide in distinct patterns. In turn, the subnational scale is important for theorizing urban inequality. Researchers increasingly recognize that to adequately theorize poverty in the urban core, broader regional processes must be incorporated (Drier et al. 2001). The subnational scale is also a site for theorizing connections between local-level processes and national/global ones (Brenner 2004; Chen 2005; Orum and Chen 2003). As Del Casino and Jones point out in their chapter in this volume, attention to the subnational scale in some sense allows researchers to "split the difference" between explanations for inequality that are locally centered on the one hand and globally centered on the other.

Finally, subnational research indicates different social problems and inequities in different areas, so political responses need to vary accordingly. Conclusions drawn at the national level about policy or political action cannot be assumed universally applicable within nations. Conversely, cities and communities are embedded in regional contexts that can constrain or enhance local efforts to improve socioeconomic conditions.

Moving Beyond the Limits of Current Work

To advance subnational inequality research, a number of issues must be tackled. With the eclipse of the human ecology framework, sociologists have no widely used theories to study this scale. This contrasts with research at the urban scale, where the eclipse of human ecology was met with extensive theory building from Marxist and other approaches. Conceptualization of subnational inequality is limited to a handful of disparate determinants. As each study tends to focus on one or two main determinants, the body of research appears as if it were a series of different stories as opposed to a concerted effort to address inequality.

Most studies address one side of the question of spatial inequality—that is, how do inequality markers such as those reflected in economic, sociodemographic, and other statuses vary across places? A somewhat different question entails place making or the creation of poor or prosperous regions, through uneven development processes. Although research exists on persistently poor regions such as Appalachia and the rural South, it tends to focus on their unique attributes as opposed to how uneven development unfolds at the subnational scale as a whole. Regional convergence and divergence are not given the attention accorded in other disciplines, such as geography or even economics, as in the new economic geography (Krugman 1991).

The most systematic knowledge about determinants of subnational inequality centers on the private sector. Nearly all studies include measures of industries and employment, either as determinants of focus or control variables (for a review, see Lobao et al. 1999). Far less attention has been given to institutional determinants such as the state and civic society.

Conceptualization of places is limited. Places are often treated in a taken-for-granted manner, as simple aggregate containers. Secondary data, necessary to most studies, inherently limits conceptualization of place processes. The action of elites, governments, and citizens cannot be directly examined. Places in effect become black boxes, where attributes may be read-off from secondary data, but internal operations remain invisible. These issues are compounded because subnational research often involves territorial units whose political-economic operation is little documented. For example, while quantitative studies using secondary data of cities, neighborhoods, and nation-states inherently suffer from the same limitations, large literatures confer scholarly legitimacy for employing these geographic units. By contrast, states, counties, and labor markets remain gray areas, in need of justification.

The remaining sections of this paper build from the observations above, that a need exists to: develop a better conceptualization of inequality processes at the subnational scale; go beyond conventional economic determinants and attend to institutional arrangements, particularly the role of the state; and address the conceptualization of place units. We draw from our own work, jointly and with others, to identify how some these gaps in subnational research may be addressed.

Conceptualizing Inequality at the Subnational Scale

Advancing research requires a common understanding of why inequalities arise across subnational space. In the absence of holistic theory, we approach this problem in our own work through a framework based on sociological principles and existing empirical work. Studying inequality across a nation's territory calls for general frameworks, beyond those aimed at the city and neighborhood, that address principles of stratification. Stratification theorists have long recognized that the organization of the economy sets the level of economic growth and that social actors struggle over its distribution (Lenski 1966). Inequalities arise from and are mediated by the institutionalized relationships emerging from struggles among actors such as capital, labor, the state, and citizens. These insights, staples of stratification, political sociology, and economic sociology, are applicable on the ground to explain subnational inequality. Empirical studies often implicitly recognize these points as well. We do not seek to reinvent the wheel of uneven development or to rehash work by geographers, but to try to understand from a sociological perspective who gets what where. Our framework builds from an amalgam of our own

(Bloomquist and Hooks 1992; Hooks 1994; Hooks et al. 2004; Lobao 1990; Lobao and Hooks 2003; Lobao et al. 1999) and other research. In brief, we see subnational variations in poverty and prosperity as related to:

1. *Economic structure or the ways in which surplus is accumulated from economic activities.* Different types of industries, firms, and jobs result in different levels of economic growth and also affect the degree to which benefits of growth are distributed. That is, industries, firms, and job positions vary in their rewards for employees and in their multiplier-effects for regions. For example, durable manufacturing, such as steel and automotives, tends to be associated with greater economic well-being of both workers and regions.
2. *Institutional arrangements between key social actors: capital, labor, the state, and citizens.* By institutional arrangements, we refer to the relationships established between social actors via customary social practices, laws, and organizations regulating economic growth and distribution of social benefits. Since sustenance of populations comes from two sources, the private sector and state, citizens center their claims on concessions from employers and the state. Employers have differential stakes in supporting and capacities to support the work force at certain material levels. Workers possess different resources, such as education, skill levels, professional associations, and unions, to press for material demands from employers. Citizens, too, possess different resources, including a vibrant civic society and social climate empowering of women and racial/ethnic groups, that enable them to press for concessions from the state or capital. Finally, the state varies in intensity of support for its own interests and the interests of capitalists vis-à-vis the interests of workers and citizens. Research at the subnational scale tends to recognize the importance of institutional arrangements but gives them little systematic attention. For example, variables that could tap institutional arrangements, such as government and state policy measures, union membership, voting rates, and race and gender inequality measures, are either not routinely included in quantitative studies or serve mainly as control variables, as opposed to being centrally theorized.
    Thus, we see economic structure and institutional arrangements as major determinants of subnational inequality, for they set the social wage or levels at which a population is able to reproduce itself. There are also space-time paths and contingencies in the above relationships; these involve particular attributes of the places being studied.
3. *Spatial situation and site factors.* The situation or external position of places in the national and global political economy varies, affecting populations' well-being. For example, federal policy may be deployed to benefit some places over others. Glocalization or the interaction of global with local forces also creates place variations. In turn, places have distinct site or

internal characteristics, such as natural amenities, infrastructure, population attributes and other ecological features which confer differential
advantages.
4. *Past history of economic structure, institutional arrangements, spatial factors.*
The history of social forces and other attributes above is embedded in place.
This history sets in motion the potential for path dependency in development processes and to cumulative, uneven development across places.

   In sum, we see the interplay of economic structure, institutional arrangements, spatial factors, and past history as creating present inequalities across
subnational space. This view is grounded in sociology's stratification heritage
and also builds from economic and political sociological insights about the
private sector and state as allocators of inequality. Finally, it recognizes key
social forces delineated by both macro-level theory as well as empirical work.
This framework is not a replacement for deeper theorizing. Rather, we see it
as useful for synthesizing extant work, highlighting substantive gaps, and connecting subnational research to broader frameworks on inequality—all
needed tasks toward developing more holistic theory.

THE STATE AND INEQUALITY: NEOLIBERALISM, PRISONS, AND ENVIRONMENTAL INJUSTICE

Too frequently, research on the determinants of subnational inequality looks
only at economic structure and pays little attention to the state. While subnational researchers themselves neglect the state, this is compounded on the
opposite end, as discussed by Leicht and Jenkins in this volume, because
political sociologists largely ignore the subnational scale. Our research has
examined the state and subnational processes in several areas.
   Since the 1980s, the United States has undergone fundamental shifts
in the state. Governments at all levels reduce support for citizens at large,
become more punitive to the poor, and act more on behalf of private sector business interests, while the federal government devolves greater
responsibilities to states and locales. This package of changes has been
characterized as the "rollout of neo-liberalism" (Peck and Tickell 2002).
The degree to which the neo-liberal agenda has unfolded and its social
consequences are the subject of broad social science debate. In sociology,
excluding some studies on welfare reform, this debate occurs mainly at the
cross-national or nation-state scale (Esping-Andersen 1990; O'Connor et
al. 1999), when much of it may be more appropriately addressed subnationally. Brenner (2001, 2004) notes that neoliberalism is an assault
against established scales of regulation, which ratchets down responsibilities from federal to lower governments to create minimalist government
nationwide. What do these changes mean for the public good and how do

they inform sociology? Our research has sought answers by focusing on subnational populations.

A central issue in social scientific debates about the state is whether a stronger public sector and social safety net help or harm populations. Rhetoric over this topic fuels the shift toward neoliberal social policy but empirical evidence remains scant. The neoliberal school, grounded in neoclassical economics, contends that where government is leaner and meaner, economic development flourishes and incomes will be higher. Political sociologists, taking Marxist and Weberian approaches, tend to believe otherwise: where the public sector and social safety net are stronger, incomes should be higher and income inequality lower (Piven and Cloward 1997). To evaluate these claims, we look at how government operates on the ground across subnational populations. Neoliberal justifications for limited government exist precisely because communities and families across the nation are asserted to benefit. We examined the effects of public sector employment and social welfare programs, using data for counties for the 1970 to 1990 period (Lobao and Hooks 2003). Our findings do not support neoliberal views that a leaner and meaner government has beneficial effects. Rather, economic well-being of the population at large declines where social programs are less generous to poor residents. Federal employment and social programs reduce income inequality and, to some degree, promote growth. Our findings dispute neoliberal claims and show that a more progressive state improves well-being.

Another state-society shift, the rise of the penal state, is often attributed to a growing punitive stance toward the poor under the neoliberal rollout. Between 1980 and 1998, the U.S. prison population increased by almost 400% and prison construction expanded accordingly (Hooks et al. 2004). Despite sociologists' interest in growing rates of incarceration, little research explores its subnational effects. As states and localities struggle to attract new employment, prisons are often a key component of economic development schemes, particularly in poor rural areas. Critics as well as advocates of prison construction share the assumption that prisons contribute to economic growth. Using data on all existing and new prisons in the United States since 1960, we found no evidence that prisons stimulated growth from 1969 to 1994. In fact, for poorer, rural counties, where prisons are most likely to be touted, the presence of a prison impeded growth compared to similar counties without one. Rather than improving conditions, prisons reinforce longstanding patterns of spatial inequality.

A third way in which we have addressed the state is through its role in environmental inequalities and environmental racism (Hooks and Smith 2004). Political and environmental sociology neglect the war-making role of the federal state and how it may result in serious environmental degradation across subnational territory. Studies of environmental racism also typically focus on housing markets in urban areas, viewing capitalist production as the causal determinant of why poor and minority people reside closer to sites of environmental pollution. Hooks and Smith (2004) focus on the impacts of militarism outside cities, across broad regions of the national territory. They introduce the concept of the "treadmill of destruction" to explain how the state's past history of racial discrimination intersects with contemporary military activities—rather than capitalism—to create a tragic spatial inequality: unexploded ordnance is now located on and near Native American lands.

In sum, research questions significant for sociology at large are centered at the subnational scale. By neglecting this scale, sociology misses an opportunity to interrogate its theoretical perspectives and to understand new and different forms of inequality.

UNDERSTANDING PLACES: WHAT DO COUNTIES DO, FOR INSTANCE?

As we noted, the places studied in subnational research typically fall outside sociology's familiar urban territory and may be given limited interrogation. This is often the case in research employing states and counties. These units have appealing methodological attributes. Unlike cities or labor markets, their boundaries remain relatively stable over time, making them useful in longitudinal research. A wealth of secondary data is available for them, and the fact that they cover rural as well as urban areas makes for a more complete picture of subnational inequality. These attributes also lead researchers to use states and counties for convenience sake and to underestimate their conceptual significance. Both units, however, are increasingly important for understanding subnational inequality. The chapter by Leicht and Jenkins in this volume addresses states and here we draw from our work on counties.

Counties incorporate more people than do municipal governments, which are commonly studied. Counties are the fastest growing general purpose governments. From 1980 to 1997, employment, a common indicator of size, grew by 31 percent for county governments. In the same period, employment grew by 26 percent for states and 8 percent for municipalities, while federal employment declined by 3 percent (Lobao and Kraybill 2005). Federal economic development, environmental, health, and social programs are typically delivered through county-based offices. Federal programs do not have spatially uniform effects, partly because delivery systems vary by counties' political culture (Kodras 1997). Most Americans live in the 15 states where the county determines welfare program rules and/or operates welfare-related services (Lobao and Kraybill 2005). Counties' political importance was evident in the 2000 and 2004 presidential elections, where decisions about counting absentee ballots, operating polling places, and selecting voting machines drew national concern.

Counties' growing role makes them a fertile site for studying spatial inequality. Yet many recent changes cannot be studied with existing data, including the Census of Governments, which provides limited information about activities directly undertaken by counties. To study recent state-society changes, Lobao and collaborators conducted a nationwide survey of county governments in 2001. We focused on economic development and public service provision. We found that county governments provide an array of services that regulate local economic development, enhance human capital, and serve social safety net functions.

We also questioned the degree to which decentralization is occurring and its effects (Lobao and Kraybill 2005). Are subnational governments engaged in a race to the bottom, a response expected by both critics and advocates of the neoliberal rollout? Little generalizable evidence exists on this issue. As federal government decentralizes and cut backs on responsibilities, states and localities may be reluctant or unable to absorb costs of social supports, leading to aggregate cutbacks and minimalist government nationwide, both hopes of a neoliberal policy agenda. These changes are believed to go hand in hand with an established trend, state and local activism to attract outside business (Eisinger 1988). Thus, analysts widely assume that subnational governments are pursuing a trade-off course between redistribution and growth activities: cutting back on social welfare and other public services while increasing private sector business development. We found no support for a trade-off course. Rather, counties appear to be increasing both social service and business development activities. Our findings reflect the broad process of decentralization, with counties assuming a greater role for citizens as well as business. However, they bear the cost of this activism through increased financial pressure. We also find marked spatial variations: poor and remote rural counties report less engagement in public service and economic development activities, and greater financial stress than other counties. Decentralization thus is spatially uneven, with poorer and rural counties falling further behind.

Our research shows that counties are more than population containers. As governmental units, they actively shape growth and redistribution, and thus patterns of subnational inequality.

CONCLUSIONS

Research on subnational inequality has broad significance for sociology. Its overriding contribution is to situate the disciplines' big questions about power and privilege within the heart of its spatial knowledge gap, the subnational scale. To advance the sociology of subnational inequality, much remains to be done and we briefly outline some directions.

First, efforts to create a more coherent field of subnational inequality are needed. Research from spatially-oriented traditions such as demography and rural sociology and from inequality-oriented traditions of stratification, political sociology, and economic sociology provide overlapping conceptual and empirical literatures. These traditions highlight the need for multifaceted attention to: social groups experiencing different types of inequalities; social institutions allocating resources; actors such as capital, labor, the state, and citizens; and spatial processes. Conceptual approaches that recognize this variety of social forces and draw together the traditions above are needed.

Second, advancing subnational research will entail modifications in how we build from theory. As noted earlier, research tends to center on how a single or few conceptual determinants, usually economic structure, affect inequality. Other approaches make broader theoretical headway. These include: synthetic approaches and competitive tests among different theories; spatial extensions of aspatial or macro-level theory; and approaches that seek to develop general principles about stratification at the subnational scale. Relatedly, most research centers on theorizing one side of the spatial inequality question, the distribution of inequalities across subnational populations. A shortcoming of sociology is its limited attention to theorizing how poor or prosperous regions themselves become created through uneven development processes (Lobao 2004).

Third, conceptualization of place units merits greater attention. To understand inequality across space, one must understand how places come to have their distinguishing attributes. And to fully understand particular places, a comparative approach is necessary. Thus, the place-in-society and the society-in-place approaches are complementary and where both are developed, as in the urban and cross-national literature, a deeper, richer spatial inequality tradition emerges. Greater attention to conceptualizing the attributes of place units coupled with comparative analyses is important to building a more coherent approach to subnational inequality.

Fourth, a number of empirical gaps need to be sorted out. States and counties still remain largely black boxes in terms of their political-economic operation. We have not given much attention to tracing the specific pathways by which state and market institutions affect inequality. Dependency on secondary data limits the scope of research questions and understanding of regional processes (Tickamyer 1996). Quantitative studies face a number of empirical concerns, such as spatial autocorrelation (Voss et al. 2005) and endogeneity in regional processes (Weber et al. 2005). Research is not routinized to the point where there is broad consensus over how to appropriately address these concerns.

Fifth, there is a need to address emerging and overlooked research questions. We know little about topics not conventionally part of the sociology heritage, such as the Denver and Aspen effects where growth is combined with inequality, and about various types of health, governmental and other noneconomic inequalities. Complex inequalities of race/ethnicity and gender remain insufficiently explored (McCall 2001). Research on the state, still the major institution concerned with redistribution, is limited to select topics, most recently, welfare reform. Casting a broader net, such as on the spatial effects of neoliberal policy, would broaden sociology's social justice and theoretical agenda. Research also needs to go beyond customary focus on the poor and disenfranchised to give comparable attention to the elites in the public and private sector who create jobs and oversee public policy.

Sixth, we must continue to interrogate sociology's spatial inequality traditions and learn from other disciplines, particularly geography. While sociologists recognize the importance of studying inequality at the urban, national, and cross-national scales, there is less recognition that scales of social action are fluid and take on different importance over time. We have much to learn from geographers' deliberations on spatial scales, as Del Casino and Jones point out in this volume.

Finally, we should work toward a larger project—developing a better understanding of the spatial dynamics of inequality and, more progressively, a sociologically-cast geography of social justice. This will entail greater recognition of the theoretical and empirical commonalities among sociology's spatial inequality traditions, as well as moving beyond fixing the study of inequality at any particular scale. Given the contemporary U.S. environment, social polarization can be expected to deepen relative to the past at all spatial scales. Sociology is uniquely positioned to contribute to the understanding of continuing spatial inequalities and the social justice responses they entail.

NOTES

1. Subnational research often employs local place units of observation. But its scale of interest involves understanding why and how relationships work out differently across a nation, which entails generalizing beyond individual localities and local-level actors and processes.

2. In geography, there is extensive debate about how subnational processes are to be studied (Agnew 2000). While the discipline once had a vibrant tradition in the geography of poverty that addressed subnational inequality (Kodras 1990; Kodras and Jones 1991), this tradition waned in the early 1990s as interest turned to the geography of production. Some analysts argue the postmodern turn in geography also has contributed to less interest in social structural inequalities (Storper 2001) and to more criticism of quantitative research on inequality (Poon 2003). On the other hand, in recent years, a literature on "social exclusion" has developed (Mohan 2002), most of it centering on poverty and other inequalities in cities. Glasmeier (2002, 2006) argues forcefully for geographers to give greater attention to subnational inequality, especially its quantitative documentation.

3. For example, research in stratification (Wilson 1987), economic sociology (Granovetter 1973; Portes 1998), and political sociology (Logan and Molotch 1987)

takes the city as a touchstone for theory building. Similarly, the cross-national scale has been used to theoretically inform and extend theories of stratification (Lenski 1966), economic sociology (Evans 1995), and political sociology (Epsing-Anderson 1990).

REFERENCES

Agnew, John. 2000. "From the Political Economy of Regions to Regional Political Economy." *Progress in Human Geography* 24:101–110.

Beggs, John J. 1995. "The Institutional Environment: Implications for Race and Gender Inequality in the U.S. Labor Market." *American Sociological Review* 60:612–633.

Bloomquist, Leonard E. and Gregory Hooks. 1992. "The Legacy of World War II for Regional Growth and Decline: The Cumulative Effects of Wartime Investment on U.S. Manufacturing, 1947–1972." *Social Forces* 71:303–338.

Bloomquist, Leonard. E. and Gene F. Summers. 1982. "Organization of Production and Community Income Distributions." *American Sociological Review* 47:325–338.

Brenner, Neil. 2001. "The Limits to Scale? Methodological Reflections on Scalar Construction." *Progress in Human Geography* 25:591–614.

———. 2004. *New State Spaces: Urban Governance and the Rescaling of Statehood.* New York: Oxford.

Brooks-Gunn, Jeanne, Greg Duncan, and J. Lawrence Aber, eds. 2000. *Neighborhood Poverty: Context and Consequences for Children.* Volume 1. New York: Russell Sage Foundation.

Brown, David L. 2002. "Migration and Community: Social Networks in a Multi-Level World." *Rural Sociology* 67:1–23.

Brown, David A. and Thomas A. Hirschl. 1995. "Household Poverty in Rural and Metropolitan Core Areas of the United States." *Rural Sociology* 60:44–66.

Brown, David L. and Marlene A. Lee. 1999. "Persisting Inequality between Metropolitan and Nonmetropolitan America: Implications for Theory and Policy." Pp. 151–167 in *A Nation Divided*, edited by Phyllis Moen, Donna Dempster-McClain, and Henry A. Walker. Ithaca, NY: Cornell University Press.

Browne, Irene and Joya Misra. 2003. "The Intersection of Gender and Race in the Labor Market." *Annual Review of Sociology* 29:487–513.

Bunker, Stephen. 1985. *Underdeveloping the Amazon.* Chicago: University of Illinois Press.

Bunker Stephen and Paul Ciccantell. 2005. *Globalization and the Race for Resources.* Baltimore: Johns Hopkins University Press.

Cardoso, Fernando Henrique and Enzo Faletto. 1979. *Dependency and Development in Latin America.* Berkeley: University of California Press.

Champion, Tony and Graeme Hugo. 2004. *New Forms of Urbanization: Beyond the Urban-Rural Dichotomy*. Burlington, VT: Ashgate.

Charles, Camille Zubrinsky. 2003. "The Dynamics of Racial Residential Segregation." *Annual Review of Sociology* 29:167–207.

Chase-Dunn, Christopher and Peter Grimes. 1995. "World-Systems Analysis." *Annual Review of Sociology* 21:387–417.

Chen, Xiangming. 2005. *As Borders Bend: Transnational Spaces on the Pacific Rim*. Lanham, MD: Rowman and Littlefield.

Cotter, David A. 2002. "Poor People in Poor Places: Local Opportunity Structure and Household Poverty." *Rural Sociology* 67:534–555.

Cotter, David A., JoAnne DeFiore, Joan M. Hermsen, Brenda M. Kowalewski, and Reeve Vanneman. 1997. "All Women Benefit: The Macro-Level Effect of Occupational Integration on Gender Earnings Inequality." *American Sociological Review* 62:714–734.

Cox, Kevin R. 1997. "Introduction: Globalization and Its Politics in Question." Pp. 1–18 in *Spaces of Globalization: Reasserting the Power of the Local*, edited by Kevin R. Cox. New York: Guildford Press.

Drier, Peter, John Mollenkopf, and Todd Swanstrom. 2001. *Place Matters: Metropolitics for the Twenty-First Century*. Lawrence, KS: University of Kansas Press.

Duncan, Cynthia. 1999. *Worlds Apart: Why Poverty Persists in Rural America*. New Haven: Yale University Press.

Eisinger, Peter K. 1988. *The Rise of the Entrepreneurial State*. Madison: University of Wisconsin.

Entwisle, Barbara, John B. Casterline, and Hussein A.-A. Sayed. 1989. "Villages as Contexts for Contraceptive Behavior in Rural Egypt." *American Sociological Review* 54:1019–1034.

Esping-Andersen, Gosta. 1990. *The Three Worlds of Welfare Capitalism*. Princeton, NJ: Princeton University Press.

Evans, Peter. 1995. *Embedded Autonomy: States and Industrial Transformation*. Princeton, NJ: Princeton University Press.

Falk, William W., Michael D. Schulman, and Ann R. Tickamyer, eds. 2003. *Communities of Work: Rural Restructuring in Local and Global Contexts*. Athens, OH: Ohio University Press.

Feagin, Joe R. 1998. *The New Urban Paradigm: Critical Perspectives on the City*. Lanham, MD: Rowman and Littlefield.

Fernandez, Roberto M. and Celina Su. 2004. "Space in the Study of Labor Markets." *Annual Review of Sociology* 30:45–569.

Firebaugh, Glenn. 2003. *The New Geography of Global Income Inequality*. Cambridge, MA: Harvard University Press.

Fosset, Mark A. and Therese M. Seibert. 1997. *Long Time Coming: Racial Inequality in Southern Nonmetropolitan Areas*. Boulder, CO: Westview Press.

Frank, Andre Gunder. 1967. *Capitalism and Underdevelopment in Latin America*. New York: Monthly Review Press.

Frank, Thomas. 2004. *What's the Matter with Kansas? How Conservative Won the Heart of America*. New York: Metropolitan Books.

Frazier, John W., Florence M. Margai, and Eugene Tettey-Fio. 2003. *Race and Place: Equity Issues in Urban America*. Boulder: Westview Press.

Freudenburg, William R. and Robert Gramling. 1994. *Oil in Troubled Waters: Perceptions, Politics, and the Battle Over Offshore Drilling*. Albany: State University of New York Press.

Glasmeier, Amy K. 2002. "One Nation Pulling Apart: The Basis of Persistent Poverty in the USA." *Progress in Human Geography* 26:155–173.

———. 2006. *Poverty in America: One Nation, Pulling Apart 1960–2003*. New York: Routledge.

Gottdiener, Mark. 1994. *The New Urban Sociology*. New York: McGraw-Hill.

Gough, Jamie. 2004. "Changing Scale as Changing Class Relations: Variety and Contradiction in the Politics of Scale." *Political Geography* 23:185–201.

Granovetter, Michael S. 1973. "The Strength of Weak Ties." *American Journal of Sociology* 78:1360–1380.

Grant, Don. S. and Wallace, Michael. 1994. "The Political Economy of Manufacturing Growth and Decline Across the American States, 1970–1985." *Social Forces* 73:33–63.

Harvey, David. 1989. *The Urban Experience*. Oxford: Blackwell.

———. 1996. *Justice, Nature, and the Geography of Difference*. Cambridge, MA: Basil Blackwell.

Hooks, Gregory. 1994. "Regional Processes in the Hegemonic Nation: Political, Economic, and Military Influences in the Use of Geographic Space." *American Sociological Review* 59:746–772.

Hooks, Gregory, Clayton Mosher, Thomas Rotolo and Linda Lobao. 2004. "The Prison Industry: Carceral Expansion and Employment in U.S. Counties, 1996–1994." *Social Science Quarterly* 85:37–57.

Hooks, Gegory and Chad L. Smith. 2004. "The Treadmill of Destruction: National Sacrifice Areas and Native Americans." *American Sociological Review* 69:558–575.

Horton, Haywood. 1999. "Critical Demography: The Paradigm of the Future?" *Sociological Forum* 14:363–367.

Huffman, Matt L. and Philip N. Cohen. 2004. "Racial Wage Inequality: Job Segregation and Devaluation across U.S. Labor Markets." *American Journal of Sociology* 109:902–936.

Jargowsky, Paul A. 1997. *Poverty and Place: Ghettos, Barrios, and the American City*. New York: Russell Sage Foundation.

Jorgenson, Andrew K. 2003. "Consumption and Environmental Degradation: A Cross-National Analysis of the Ecological Footprint." *Social Problems* 50:374–394.

Kandel, William and David L. Brown, eds. 2006. *Population Change and Rural Society.* New York: Springer.

Kodras, Janet E. 1997. "Restructuring the State: Devolution, Privatization, and the Geographic Redistribution of Power and Capacity in Governance." Pp. 79–96 in *State Devolution in America*, edited by Lynn Staeheli, Janet Kodras, and Colin Flint. Thousand Oaks, CA: Sage.

Kodras, Janet E. and John Paul Jones III. 1991. "A Contextual Examination of the Feminization of Poverty." *Geoforum* 22:159–171.

Krugman, Paul. 1991. *Geography and Trade.* Cambridge, MA: MIT Press.

Leicht, Kevin. T. and J. Craig Jenkins. 1994. "Three Strategies of State Economic Development: Entrepreneurial, Industrial Recruitment, and Deregulation Policies in the American States." *Economic Development Quarterly.* 8:256–269.

Lenski, Gerhard. 1966. *Power and Privilege: A Theory of Social Stratification.* New York: McGraw Hill.

Lenz, Gabriel. 2004. "The Consequences of Income Inequality for Redistributive Policy in the United States." Pp. 797–820 in *Social Inequality*, edited by Kathryn S. Neckerman. New York: Russell Sage Foundation.

Lichter, Daniel, Diane K. McLaughlin, and David Ribar. 1997. "Welfare and the Rise in Female Headed Families." *American Journal of Sociology* 103:112–143.

Lobao, Linda M. 1990. *Locality and Inequality.* Albany: State University of New York Press.

———. 1996. "A Sociology of the Periphery Versus a Peripheral Sociology: Rural Sociology and the Dimension of Space." *Rural Sociology* 61:77–102.

———. 2004. "Continuity and Change in Place Stratification: Spatial Inequality and Middle-Range Territorial Units." *Rural Sociology* 69:1–30.

Lobao, Linda M. and Lawrence A. Brown. 1998. "Development Context, Regional Differences Among Young Women, and Fertility: The Ecuadorean Amazon." *Social Forces* 76:814–849.

Lobao, Linda M. and Gregory Hooks. 2003. "Public Employment, Welfare Transfers, and Economic Well-Being Across Local Populations: Does Lean and Mean Government Benefit the Masses?" *Social Forces* 82:519–556.

Lobao, Linda M. and David Kraybill. 2005. "The Emerging Roles of County Governments in Metropolitan and Nonmetropolitan America." *Economic Development Quarterly* 19:245–259.

Lobao, Linda M., Jamie Rulli and Lawrence A. Brown. 1999. "Macro-Level Theory and Local-Level Inequality: Industrial Structure, Institutional Arrangements, and the Political Economy of Redistribution, 1970 and 1990." *Annals of the Association of American Geographers* 89:571–601.

Logan, John R. and Harvey L. Molotch. 1987. *Urban Fortunes: The Political Economy of Place*. Berkeley: University of California Press.

Logan, John R., Brain J. Stults, and Reynolds Farely. 2004. "Segregation of Minorities in the Metropolis: Two Decades of Change." *Demography* 41:1–22.

Lorence, Jon and Joel Nelson. 1993. "Industrial Restructuring and Metropolitan Earnings Inequality, 1970–1980." *Research in Social Stratification and Mobility* 12:145–184.

Lyson, Thomas and William Falk. 1993. *Forgotten Places: Uneven Development and the Underclass in Rural America*. Lawrence, KS: University of Kansas Press.

Markusen, Ann. 2001. "Regions as Loci of Conflict and Change: The Contributions of Ben Harrison to Regional Economic Development." *Economic Development Quarterly* 15:291–298.

Massey, Doreen. 1994. *Space, Place, and Gender*. Minneapolis: University of Minnesota Press.

Massey, Douglas and Nancy A. Denton. 1993. *American Apartheid: Segregation and the Making of the Underclass*. Cambridge, MA: Harvard University Press.

McCall, Leslie. 2001. *Complex Inequality: Gender, Class and Race in the New Economy*. New York: Routledge.

McGranahan, David A. 1980. "The Spatial Structure of Income Distribution in Rural Regions." *American Sociological Review* 45:313–324.

McLaughlin, Diane K. and C. Shannon Stokes. 2002. "Income Inequality and Mortality in U.S. Counties: Does Minority Racial Composition Matter?" *American Journal of Public Health* 92: 99–104.

McLaughlin, Diane K., Erica L.Gardner, and Daniel T. Lichter. 1999. "Economic Restructuring and Changing Prevalence of Female-headed Families in America." *Rural Sociology* 64:394–416.

McMichael. 2000. *Development and Social Change*. Thousand Oaks, CA: Pine Forge Press.

Mencken, F. Carson. 2000. "Federal Spending and Economic Growth in Appalachian Counties." *Rural Sociology* 65:126–147.

Mohan, John. 2002. "Geographies of Welfare and Social Exclusion: Dimensions, Consequences, and Methods." *Progress in Human Geography* 26:65–75.

Moller, Stephanie, Evelyne Huber, John D. Stephens, David Bradley, and Francois Nielsen. 2003. "Determinants of Relative Poverty in Advanced Capitalist Democracies." *American Sociological Review* 68:22–51.

Molotch, Harvey, William Freudenburg, and Krista E. Paulsen. 2000. "History Repeats Itself, but How? City Character, Urban Tradition, and the Accomplishment of Place." *American Sociological Review* 65:791–823.

Neckerman, Kathryn, ed. *Social Inequality*. 2004. New York: Russell Sage Foundation.

Nielsen, Francois and Arthur S. Alderson. 1997. "The Kuznets Curve and the Great U-Turn: Income Inequality in U.S. Counties, 1970 to 1990." *American Sociological Review* 62:12–33.

Orfield, Myron. 1997. *Metropolitics: A Regional Agenda for the Community and Stability*. Washington, DC: Brookings Institutions Press.

Orum, Anthony M. and Xiangming Chen. 2003. *The World of Cities: Places in Comparative and Historical Perspective*. Malden, MA: Basil Blackwell.

O'Connor, Julia, Ann Shola Orloff, and Sheila Shaver. 1999. *States, Markets, and Families: Gender Liberalism, and Social Policy in Australia, Canada, Great Britain, and the United States*. Cambridge, UK: Cambridge University Press.

O'Connor, Alice, Chris Tilly, and Lawrence D. Bobo, eds. 2003. *Urban Inequality: Evidence from Four Cities*. New York: Russell Sage Foundation.

Peck, Jamie. 1996. *Work-Place: The Social Regulation of Labor Markets*. New York: Guilford Press.

———. 2001. *WorkFare States*. New York: Guilford Press.

Peck, Jamie and Adam Tickell. 2002. "Neoliberalizing Space." *Antipode* 34:380–404.

Piven, Frances Fox and Richard A. Cloward. 1997. *The Breaking of the American Social Compact*. New York: New Press.

Poon, Jessie E. 2003. "Quantitative Methods: Producing Quantitative Methods Narratives." *Progress in Human Geography* 27:753–762.

Portes, Alejandro. 1998. "Social Capital: Its Origins and Applications in Modern Sociology." *Annual Review of Sociology* 24:1–24.

Rudel, Thomas. 2002. "Paths of Destruction and Regeneration: Globalization and Forests in the Tropics." *Rural Sociology* 67:622–636.

Rural Sociological Task Force on Persistent Poverty. 1993. *Persistent Poverty in Rural America*. Boulder: Westview Press.

Saenz, Rogelio. 1997. "Ethnic Concentration and Chicano Poverty: A Comparative Approach." *Social Science Research* 26:205–228.

Saenz, Rogelio and John K. Thomas. 1991. "Minority Poverty in Nonmetropolitan Texas." *Rural Sociology* 56:204–223.

Salamon, Sonya. 2003. *Newcomers to Old Towns: Suburbanization of the Heartland*. Chicago: University of Chicago Press.

Sampson, Robert J., Jeffrey D. Morenoff, and Thomas Gannon-Rowley. 2002. "Assessing 'Neighborhood Effect': Social Processes and New Directions in Research." *Annual Review of Sociology* 28:443–478.

Sassen, Sakia. 2000. *Cities in a World Economy*. Thousand Oaks, CA: Pine Forge Press.

———, ed. 2002. *Global Networks, Linked Cities*. New York: Routledge.

Singelmann, Joachim, Forrest A. Deseran, F. Carson Mencken, and Jiang Hong Li. 1993. "What Drives Labor Market Growth?" Pp. 125–142 in *Inequalities in Labor Market Areas*, edited by Joachim Singelmann and Forrest A. Deseran. Boulder: Westview Press.

Small, Mario Luis and Katherine Newman. 2001. "Urban Poverty after the Truly Disadvantaged: The Rediscovery of the Family, the Neighborhood, and Culture." *Annual Review of Sociology* 27:23–45.

Smith, Neil. 2003. "Remaking Scale: Competition and Cooperation in Pre-National and Post-National Europe." Pp. 227–238 in *State/Space: A Reader*, edited by Neil Brenner, Bob Jessop, Martin Jones, and Gordon MacLeod. Malden, MA: Blackwell.

Soja, Edward. 1989. *Post-Modern Geographies: The Reassertion of Space in Critical Social Theory*. London: Verso.

Soule, Sarah A. and Yvonne Zylan. 1997. "Runaway Train? The Diffusion of State-Level Reform in ADC/AFDC Eligibility Requirements, 1950–1967." *American Journal of Sociology* 103:733–762.

South, Scott J. and Steven F. Messner. 2000. "Crime and Demography: Multiple Linkages, Reciprocal Relations." *Annual Review of Sociology* 26:83–106.

Storper, Michael. 2001. "The Poverty of Radical Theory Today: From the False Promises of Marxism to the Mirage of the Cultural Turn." *International Journal of Urban and Regional Research* 25:155–179.

Swyngedouw, Erik. 1997. "Neither Global nor Local: Glocalization and Politics of Scale." Pp. 137–166 in *Spaces of Globalization: Reasserting the Power of the Local*, edited by Kevin R. Cox. New York: Guilford Press.

Taylor, Peter J. 1999. "Places, Spaces, and Macy's: Place-Space Tensions in the Political Geography of Modernities." *Progress in Human Geography* 23:7–26.

Tickamyer, Ann. 1996. "Sex, Lies, and Statistics: Can Rural Sociology Survive Restructuring?" *Rural Sociology* 61:5–24.

Tolbert, Charles., Thomas T. Lyson, and Michael Irwin. 1998. "Local Capitalism, Civic Engagement, and Socioeconomic Well-Being." *Social Forces* 77:401–428.

Tolnay, Stewart E., Glenn Deane, and E. M. Beck. 1996. "Vicarious Violence: Spatial Effects on Southern Lynchings, 1890–1919." *American Journal of Sociology* 102:788–815.

Tomaskovic-Devey. 1987. "Labor Markets, Industrial Structure, and Poverty: A Theoretical Discussion and Empirical Example." *Rural Sociology* 52:56–74.

Van der Lippe, Tanja and Liset van Dijk. 2002. "Comparative Research on Women's Employment." *Annual Review of Sociology* 28:221–214.

Wallerstein, Immanuel. 1979. *The Capitalist World Economy*. Cambridge: Cambridge University Press.

Walton, John. 1993. "Urban Sociology: The Contribution and Limits of Political Economy." *Annual Review of Sociology* 19:301–320.

Weber, Bruce, Lief Jensen, Kathleen Miller, Jane Mosley, and Monica Fisher. 2005. "A Critical Review of Rural Poverty Literature: Is there Truly a Rural Effect?" *International Regional Science Review* 28:381–414.

Wilson, William J. 1987. *The Truly Disadvantaged: The Inner City, the Underclass, and Public Policy*. Chicago: University of Chicago Press.

Winson, Anthony. 1997. "Does Class Consciousness Exist in Rural Communities? The Impact of Restructuring and Plant Shutdowns in Rural Canada." *Rural Sociology* 62:429–453.

Voss, Paul. 2007. "Demography as a Spatial Social Science." *Population Research and Policy Review* 26. Forthcoming.

Voss, Paul, Katherine Curtis White, and Roger Hammer. 2006. "Explorations in Spatial Demography." Pp. 407–429 in *Population Change and Rural Society*, edited by William Kandel and David Brown. New York: Springer.

Zukin, Sharon. 1991. *Landscapes of Power*. Berkeley: University of California Press.

THREE

New and Unexplored Opportunities

Developing a Spatial Perspective
for Political Sociology

KEVIN T. LEICHT
J. CRAIG JENKINS

POLITICAL SOCIOLOGY HAS a wide array of theoretical and methodological tools for explaining political processes and their consequences. These
tools provide potent new techniques for addressing global inequalities tied to
differential access to power and resources. From the latest developments in
state theory to studies of social movements, from the use of more advanced
quantitative techniques to the development and systemization of qualitative,
comparative social science, political sociology is the place where new techniques and ideas find fertile ground for development.

The major exception to the growth in sophistication of political sociology is the relative neglect of issues of space. For our purposes, the term *space*
refers to *specific territorial locations that concrete actors occupy.* Territorial locations in the form of land units represent the most basic form of location in
space, and one most fundamental to the nation-state system that defines the
analytical terrain for political sociology. Other definitions of space refer to
the location and naming of political actors with broadly similar values and
beliefs (political parties, lobbyists, social movements, civil services) and
classes of actors seeking similar functional goals (passing an Equal Rights
Amendment, rationalizing tax collection, overthrowing an existing government, or driving out a superpower). Space is a central descriptive dimension

for common understandings of social inequality, as the everyday labeling of "distressed" and "privileged" communities, "first-world" and "less-developed" nations, and "rust belt" and "sun belt" regions illustrate.

We draw on literature on organizations, especially new institutional theory (Powell and DiMaggio 1991), to discuss mechanisms for theoretically addressing space and its potential effects. New institutional theory has difficulty dealing with territorial space and instead focuses on organizational fields and similarities of market location and industry, or structural equivalence (Burt 1987; see Scott 1995).[1] But new institutional theory provides important theoretical tools for understanding the interaction of organizations and political units across space. We believe that a cross-fertilization of ideas from new institutional theory is a useful starting point for elucidating spatial processes in political sociology.

The relative neglect of issues of space is all the more ironic because the foundations of political sociology rest on the study of states (i.e., territories where exclusive control is asserted, backed by the potential use of force, and recognized as such in an international system). Many current debates in political sociology center on the declining (or persistent) centrality of states as controllers of specific territories in an increasingly globalized system of exchange. With a few exceptions, analysts study what they view as parallel internal developments leading to convergent social patterns across space. They almost never imagine that this convergence might be due to interaction (the exchange of ideas and coercive threats and actions between similarly situated actors), mimicry (borrowing action repertoires and organizational ideas from other actors), or interdependence (actual connections between spatial units that limit, constrain, or enable different forms of action) organized across space. But, as analysts of globalization and international interdependence have suggested, this assumption is often highly misleading and obscures the central question.

Discussions of space also lead to questions about units of analysis and spatial scales. To date, a vast majority of research in political sociology has dealt with nation-states as political entities. But the incorporation of a spatial perspective into theorizing and research would lead us to question this primacy, as there are an array of other subnational actors like states, provinces, territories, and cities, each with their own government and political actors, each nested within larger political entities and subject to institutional pressures that can be followed, ignored, or (in some cases) defied. And nation-states themselves are increasingly subject to superordinate international governmental (IGOs) and nongovernmental organizations (INGOs) that confer and withdraw legitimacy and resources based on their evaluations of the behaviors and intentions of state actors (e.g., United Nations, World Trade Organization, International Monetary Fund, and the EU).

Our aim is to discuss the role that a spatial perspective can play in improving contemporary research in political sociology. The role of space in political sociology is theoretical and substantive and not simply a question of measurement error. It also has substantive implications for how real societies operate. As we demonstrate, systematically incorporating spatial analysis into the core of political sociology will create new insights, alter our theories, and change our substantive conclusions.

ANALYZING STATES IN SYSTEMS OF STATES: THREE ANALYTICAL FLAWS

There are three basic, overarching problems with the way space is dealt with in political sociology. Our presentation will address each problem and suggest why they are theoretically and methodologically important for future research.

Neglecting Space Altogether

One major problem with much research in political sociology is that it does-n't deal with issues of space at all. National governments, social movements, and political actors are analyzed as if they were not connected to others attempting to do the same or similar things or others actively seeking to thwart their efforts. Classic examples can be seen in almost all comparative historical accounts of welfare state development (Esping-Anderson 1990; Orloff 1993, 2002; Wilensky 1975). Comparative historical analyses using comparative methods (either Boolean algebraic methods or other methods of systematic comparison) rarely include as variables or elements of the political units the spatial connections between ideas, agents, states, or institutions. Instead, the internal characteristics, actions, and events aiding the development of a specific welfare state are compared to the internal characteristics, actions and events aiding the development of another welfare state. The pairing of similar internal causes with similar outcomes might lead to the recognition of different typologies of welfare state development (Esping-Anderson 1990), but the determinants rarely expand to incorporate developments outside of the units being compared, including the relationship between the sampled units themselves.

The same could be said of all but the most recent writings on social revolutions (Moore 1966; Skocpol 1979, 1994). Theoretical developments in the study of revolutions discuss the role that states play in systems of states and, in particular, the role of war in reducing state's domestic repressive power. These factors are important, but they are not the sum total of influences communicated between states in a nation-state system. Revolutionaries borrow ideas, frames, and tactical knowledge from similarly situated movements in other countries. Moreover, as shown by Conell and Cohn (1995) in their analysis of French strikes and by Holden (1986) in a study of international airline hijackings, insurgent actors are often inspired by victories of spatially proximate, like-minded actors (Strang and Soule 1998).

State managers borrow and reject ideas for dealing with protestors and insurgent groups from the actions (or inactions) of state managers elsewhere. Military elites seem to be the most ruthlessly comparative of all state managers, searching out their performance networks for innovations, claims to resources, and methods of repression and control. These comparisons and the evaluations of civilian and military leaders following from them almost certainly affect the role existing militaries play in propping up or helping to overthrow existing regimes in revolutionary scenarios.[2]

ACTORS ACT, BUT WHERE DO THEIR IDEAS COME FROM?

A second problem with existing research in political sociology is the lack of general theoretical discussion of the source of actors' political ideas. Most contemporary theories in political sociology (for example, social movement theory, institutional theories, and state theories) employ concepts of active human agency as a major factor determining political outcomes. Yet part of what active agents do is take into account the behavior of other active agents who occupy the same social structural positions. This interaction suggests that the study of networks and network connections across space, including shared cultural linkages (i.e., shared values, norms, and beliefs), has the same value in more macro-oriented political sociology as it has in studies of interpersonal and firm interactions (Burt 1987). Political agents actively interact with and manipulate their immediate environment by invoking solutions, repertoires, and action frames that have worked for others in similar circumstances.

This borrowing does not imply that agents don't have distinctive interests of their own. Instead, similarities and differences across circumstances, and the ability to communicate and store information about actions and events, means that very few political agents have to cook up new and innovative responses to their problems from nothing. Obviously, rapidly expanding scholarship in comparative politics and the growth of nongovernmental organizations, social movement diffusion, and international academics, scholars, and activists have accelerated this trend over the past fifty years, but relatively new developments in sociology focusing on human agency require that theories and methods for studying spatial influences move to a central place in most analysis of political phenomena.

Two examples of this communicative process will serve to illustrate the point. The Vietnam War was and continues to be a rich source of political institutional lessons for potential revolutionary actors, professional militaries in advanced Western nations, policy analysts in Washington think tanks, and terrorist organizations seeking to score political points (among others). From the standpoint of state managers in the United States at least, the outcome was so negative that "Vietnam" is a term that invokes a common set of institutional understandings about current and potential military confrontations.

More importantly than the events themselves are the institutionalized ways that "Vietnam" and what it represents has been used. Virtually every revolutionary and dissident movement knows the lessons Vietnam has for them—organize loosely, never allow yourself to be cornered, never confront your more powerful opponent in an open fight, and make it so expensive for them to deal with you that they'll go away or collapse. Similarly, those representing superpower interests have grown weary of "another Vietnam" which their opponents promised if a violent confrontation ensues. This dynamic is a giant spatialized institutional dilemma for any nation-state confronting an insurgent movement—*unlike the insurgent movement, the nation-state has to control space, but the insurgent movement's actions make it impossible for the nation-state to declare "victory" and come home.* Regardless of the eventual outcome, a thorough analysis comparing the relative success of the North Vietnamese with that of the Iraqi-based insurgency against the U.S. military will no doubt draw from this institutionalized action repertoire (Tilly 2003). In short, "Vietnam" has come to represent a set of institutionalized tactics, countertactics, and events that are to be avoided by some and embraced by others.

A second example comes through the concept of social movement framing, that is, the active adoption of available cultural themes to highlight the problems and potential solutions that social movements address (Snow and Benford 1988). Framing theory has been criticized for overplaying the extent to which individual social movement leaders can adopt and manipulate prevailing cultural frames (see Benford 1997). Further, research on social movements has avoided asking tough questions about the source of social movement frames, the full spectrum of political action, the actors that are involved, and the roles external actors play in the development and limitations of social movement activity (Burstein and Linton 2002). It is clear that social movements borrow frames, tactics, repertoires, and identities from geographically and temporally proximate movements with processes tending to diffuse outward from the center, creating protest cycles (Tarrow 1989). But this point often has been neglected in actual analyses and theoretical discussions.

We would argue that one of the answers to this puzzle lies in spatial relationships and connections between social movement actors, state officials, opinion makers, movement opponents, local political cultures, and competing and complementary movement activities in other contexts. Almost no strategy for framing a social movement's claims is invented from whole cloth by movement activists. Nor is the acceptance or rejection of the movement's frame totally in the hands of activists or movement oppo-nents. Further, it is not as if the public casts votes through their television sets (like the Neilsen ratings) regarding which social movement frame is most convincing and which is not. Instead, movement frames impress some key actors and turn off others.

THE EXCLUSIVE FOCUS ON THE NATION-STATE: DOESN'T ANY OTHER TERRITORIAL ACTOR DO ANYTHING?

A third problem is that political sociology has assumed the primacy and crit-icality of the nation-state as the central territorial unit of analysis. This focus is in part due to the international-comparative focus of many traditional research problems in political sociology. Studies of the welfare state (with a few recent exceptions we discuss below) focus on the historical development of welfare states of various types, where *state* refers to the guiding institutional structures housed in national governments and legislation. Analyses of global inequality take as their point of departure the position of nation-states in sys-tems of global inequality (Firebaugh 2003; Wallerstein 2004), and research on social revolutions has focused on the relative position and weakness of nation-states as a key component of revolutionary processes and outcomes (Goldstone 1991; Skocpol 1994).

To a great degree this excellent research on welfare states and revolu-tions has been the paradigm-defining activity of political sociology over the past thirty years, so the unit of analysis has taken on a taken-for-granted sta-tus as the place where the action is. In addition to analyzing political processes as if they were indigenous and ignoring spatial processes, we think there is ample reason (detailed below) to doubt that the nation-state is always the best place to focus research.

A small but growing body of research moves beyond the use of the nation-state as the unit of analysis or uses data on national actors in ways that bring new insights into the regional and local production of social inequality. Hooks' work (Hooks 1994; Hooks and Bloomquist 1992) examines the impact of national policy choices (the location of defense department invest-ments during World War II) on local economic well-being in U.S. counties. His analyses explicitly find a relationship between defense department deci-sions regarding industrial investments associated with war and the relative well-being of manufacturing, aircraft, and steel industries during the post-War era up to the 1990s. Amenta and colleagues (Amenta 1998; Amenta and Halfmann 2000; Amenta and Poulsen 1996) develop and test an institutional politics theory of the liberalization of public social provision in the American states during the New Deal. They find that clean administrative states staffed by progressive political actors freed from the constraints of patronage-ori-ented parties were more likely to pass generous old age and WPA wage packages. Grant, Wallace, and Brady (Brady and Wallace 2000; Grant 1995; Grant and Wallace 1994) explicitly take space into account by theorizing the existence of a spatialized social structure of accumulation and focusing on growing competition between local places for new economic development following the economic stagnation of the 1970s. Their analyses use the 48 American states as units of analysis and suggest that local competition for employment growth, new business formation, and foreign direct investment have had detrimental effects on labor markets for workers. With the exception of Hooks (for an expanded analysis, see also Lobao and Hooks 2003), the relationship between units is theoretically present through increased competition between local spaces and cultural ties between local and national elites, but connections between places and their effects are not explicitly modeled quantitatively or qualitatively.

More explicit modeling of spatial processes occurs in the promising work of Tolnay (Tolnay and Beck 1992; Tolnay, Deane, and Beck 1996), Soule (Soule and Zylan 1997; Zylan and Soule 2000), Myers (1997), and Renzulli and Roscigno (2004). Tolnay and colleagues use county-level data from ten southeastern U.S. states, showing that lynchings in adjacent southern counties are negatively associated with lynchings in target counties. They suggest that lynching has a terror-like quality that altered the behavior of local blacks and whites exposed to it. They also find that lynchings increased black outmigration, which threatened the segmented labor markets constructed by the southern racial state.

Soule and Zylan (1997; see also Zylan and Soule 2000) examine the diffusion of welfare reform measures from 1950 to 1967 and state welfare retrenchment from 1989 to 1995. They explicitly discuss the institutional forces producing conformity between states: "we argue that, as state actors attempt to puzzle out solutions to problems that arise within their institutional domains . . . they may look outward to other states considering the same problems—particularly to states that are institutionally or culturally linked to their own" (1997:735). Soule and Zylan model diffusion using models advanced by Tuma, focusing on states with direct connections and cultural linkages across units. They find considerable effects of "first mover" actions by states traditionally identified as innovators in the provision of new government services and these effects drive state welfare reform and welfare retrenchment.

In a reanalysis of the urban riots of the 1960s, Myers (1997) shows that the propensity to riot was enhanced by geographic distance from cities where riots had recently occurred. While shared grievances mattered, the diffusion of riots was spatially conditioned rather than being due simply to a general climate or media reporting as was assumed by Spilerman's earlier work (1976).

Our final example is Renzulli and Roscigno's analysis (2004) of the adoption of charter school legislation and the founding of charter schools in the

U.S. states. Initiated by school reformers during the 1970s and 1980s, the adoption of legislation authorizing charter schools did not occur until the early 1990s. Between 1991 and 1999, most of the states in the United States adopted some form of charter school legislation. Pointing to the performance networks of school administrators, politicians, and school reformers, geographic adjacency was a central factor in the adoption of charter school legislation, almost equivalent to the intrastate features (teachers union strength, private school strength, and percent of nonwhite students) that accelerated this process. States adopting moderate reform bills were more likely to be adjacent to states with strong reform laws, but region (e.g., northeast, middle Atlantic) proved more important in determining the number of charter schools that were subsequently founded.

   This small but growing body of research, of which our own research is a part, points to more general observations about developing a spatial perspective for political sociology. First, subnational units (cities, counties, provinces, and breakaway quasi republics) have political actors and agendas of their own. They do not just do what national governments tell them to do, even when national governments attempt to dictate and control local and regional activities. Subnational units often have independent powers to formulate policies, implement (or not implement) national policies, or to give national political mandates distinctly local and regional flavors. Yet, with a few notable exceptions, the actions of nested political units are undertheorized. It is especially difficult to theorize about subnational unit interactions when nation-state research does not possess coherent theories about the institutional field of nation-states or theorizes that all political and economic outcomes result from internal dynamics.

   Second, there is ample reason to doubt that late 20th- and early 21st-century political dynamics are driven exclusively by interactions between independent nation-states. Recent scholarship on global inequality and integration (Castells 1998; Giddens 2000) suggests that, if anything, the dynamics of global inequality and inequalities tied to space have more profound consequences for regions and peoples within nation-states than do purely internal structures of nation-states. The development of world cities, global communication chains, and worldwide immigration have produced numerous locations where the first world is in direct contact with the fourth world.

   Regardless of its theoretical utility, it is no longer true that the world is divided neatly into core and peripheral nation-states with a semiperiphery in the middle, with social inequality and political power uniquely ranked from top to bottom. Instead, parts of the core and periphery exist within almost all but the smallest, most fortunate (or unfortunate) nation-states, and the nation-state system now includes a "fourth world" of states and regions providing nothing of value to the newly integrated and globalized market economy (Castells 1998).

Further, the relatively recent global politics of identity, and the striving for recognition and rights among distinctive linguistic, ethnic, and racial groups, rarely if ever pits one nation-state against another (Castells 1998: Blauner 2001). Instead, linguistic and ethnic minorities in segregated regions of nation-states press for autonomy and political rights, sometimes in concert with fellow ethnics in a global diaspora and others in neighboring states. While it is true that nation-states respond to these claims with different combinations of repression, concession, and recognition, the claims do not originate with nation-states and rarely involve conflicts between organized militaries of adjacent states. We seem to be witnessing an end to international war as traditionally understood and a gradual displacement of civil war by more diffuse, locally organized and geographically interdependent violence (Mueller 2004).

Research into the problems of growing global inequalities and globally integrated economies must face the central contradiction of an economic system with less and less regard for specific spaces and places coexisting among people who have a high stake in the economic and political developments of specific spaces and places (Held 2004; Mueller 2004). But it is not only nation-states that represent the spaces and places people wish to defend. People also have stakes in communities, states, provinces, and regions whose economic and political regimes have very real and direct effects on their lives. None of these observations make nation-states irrelevant to political sociology. But they indicate the need to identify concrete spatial interdependencies and mechanisms through which diffusion, political interaction, and power are actually organized.

NEW INSTITUTIONAL THEORIES
OF ORGANIZATIONS: A USEFUL STARTING
POINT FOR SPATIALIZING POLITICAL SOCIOLOGY

To be effective, a spatialized political sociology needs to develop a theory of spatial influence that specifies plausible connections between political actors and units. We think that new institutional theory in organizations provides a starting point for the analysis of spatial and network effects in political sociology.

New institutional accounts of organizations attempt to explain why organizational structures and activities coalesce around a fixed set of well-defined types (Scott 1995). Standard new institutional accounts point to three mechanisms for the production of organizational isomorphism or conformity: (1) *coercive pressures* from external constituencies with the power to alter resource flows and certify organizational activities as legitimate or illegitimate; (2) *normative pressures* from networks of key organizational decision makers who exchange ideas about trends and common responses to problems;

and (3) *mimetic pressures* resulting from borrowing solutions from other organizations that seem to work in a specific context. The end result, regardless of the specific set of pressures identified, is a set of institutionalized ways of organizing specific actions on the part of organizations. In organizational research, new institutional theory has been used to explain the convergence of organizational types in diverse organizational fields, from life insurance to beer brewing (Carroll and Hannan 1995). New institutional accounts often are combined with population ecology explanations for the development and establishment of specific organizational fields (Hannan and Freeman 1989).

The real problem with expanding this perspective into political sociology is that we already have an institutional perspective associated with state theory and its variants (Amenta 1998; Hicks 1999; Huber and Stephens 2001). This perspective draws on older notions of institutions as established organizational units with bureaucracies, officials, rules, and resources devoted to expanding institutional mandates. In the latest version of this institutional perspective, institutional actors shape and channel the influences of extra-institutional actors (classes, social movements, etc.) as these actors attempt to steer a specific political outcome (unemployment insurance, welfare provision, etc.) in their favor. Institutional structures, such as constitutional centralization, reformist political parties, strong social democratic parties, and bureaucratic strength, are seen as creating institutional effects. Institutional precedents operate as "paths," opening the way to subsequent changes in policy (Pierson 1994). The latest versions of our own work draw from and add to this perspective (Jenkins, Leicht, and Wendt 2006).

There are three problems with this political institutional perspective from the standpoint of taking space seriously. First, institutions are almost exclusively identified with government bureaucracies and structures, far narrower than the conception portrayed in new institutional theories of organizations or from the concept of institutions as classically defined in sociology (Stinchcombe 1997). Second, for all of the talk about capacities, the sophistication of government institutions and state managers never seems to expand to the purview of the environment outside of the governing unit. Institutional capacity either ceases at the border or all influences from outside the political unit are reflected in the internal developments that are the proximate causes of the institutional response. Third, even though political institutional theory identifies some plausible mechanisms for explaining the influence of political actors and units, it does not specifically incorporate space into the analysis of institutional influences.

While recent institutional developments in political sociology clearly are sophisticated advancements over their predecessors, this narrow conception of institutions and their capacities deprives political sociology of comparative rigor. Institutional responses to common problems, the very definition of which problems are comparable or not, and the spread of the collective action repertoires of the responses themselves are within the purview of all collective actors, including social movements, guerrilla armies, insurgents, peaceful protesters, organized labor movements, airline hijackers, and arms dealers. But our point is more fundamental than this—*part of what constitutes "capacity" in any of these situations is the ability to determine which situations across time and space are comparable, to weed out effective from ineffective responses to problems that are similar to the present one, and to collect information on these prior and current situations.* Apart from the ability to do this, it is not really clear what institutional capacities actually are independent from the identity of a given group or organization. To claim that these processes are completely enclosed in the internal dynamics of units strikes us as an empirical question that must be answered with more careful research rather than as an a priori assumption.

THE PROBLEM OF METHODOLOGICAL INDEPENDENCE IN SPATIAL POLITICAL SOCIOLOGY

A problem intimately related to viewing states as institutional actors taking each other's behavior into account is methodological. Most methodologies for engaging in comparative analyses of political processes assume that cases are independent units. Boolean algebraic analyses rarely take into account the connections between states as a component of the analysis of structural trajectories. Quantitative analyses assume this independence as a component of most regression-based estimation techniques and most inferential statistics. This issue is compounded by the nesting of smaller governmental units in larger ecological units and the possible influence the larger unit has on the smaller ones (states and provinces within nations, cities and MSAs within states and nations, counties within states and nations, etc.).

In variable-based quantitative analyses, analysts usually assemble data at a specific unit of analysis and then analyze the units as cases, with relationships between variables representing the process producing a specific political or economic outcome. Almost all use some variant of regression techniques with linear models where the relationship between dependent and independent variables is assumed to be linear in parameters, if not in the variables themselves:

$$Y = X\beta + e \tag{1}$$

But this model assumes that the cases being analyzed are independent, that no systematic correlation exists between the error term, e and Y, and that error terms are not correlated across cases. The model further assumes no omitted variables Z that are correlated with X and with the outcome variable Y (i.e., the model specification is correct with no omitted variables).

Apart from the fact that detecting omitted variables in quantitative analysis is often difficult, relationships in political sociology are almost certainly affected by institutional processes involving space and time. These processes become more likely (1) as our theories of active agency in response to environmental stimuli grow and (2) as we suspect that a specific political process is embedded within a larger dynamic affecting the units in our analysis (counties, states, social movements within countries, etc.). As a consequence, researchers are faced with both a statistical inference problem and a question of theoretical importance.

Land and Deane (1992; see also Doreian 1980; Ord 1975) follow in the footsteps of other statisticians and social scientists in suggesting that these connections should be part of the modeling. Without accounting for the diffusion process (or the relationship between units across space and time), statistical estimates of model coefficients will be biased and inefficient. The general formulation of all spatial effects models is specified by:

$$Y = \rho Wy + X\beta + e \tag{2}$$

Where Y is the dependent variable affected by an independent variable X, β is a vector of slope parameters and e is the random disturbance term with an expected value of 0 and constant variance (σ^2_e). Most importantly for our purposes, W is an n-by-n matrix of weights describing the relationship between the units of analysis, and y is a dependent variable n-by-n matrix for the units. (Both W and y have a zero principal diagonal, indicating that the relationship between a given unit and itself is zero.) ρ is the spatial effects coefficient that measures the relationship between the value of Y in a given geographical unit with y in other areas or units. According to Doreian (1980) the coefficients for the exogenous variables X in equation (2) without the spatial effects term are biased upward.

A variety of methods have been proposed for estimating spatial effects, including maximum likelihood methods (Doreian 1980; Ord 1975) and a generalized-population-potential method (Roncek and Montgomery 1984). The problem with all computational methods not treating y as endogenous is that the same process producing the dependent variable for a given unit Y is likely to produce the value of y in related geographic units. In practical terms this means the endogenous y is almost certainly correlated with the error term for the equation, e. Treating the endogenous spatial effect y as an instrumental variable alleviates this problem.

While we view these methods of estimating models with spatial and network effects as important and valuable, we believe their substantive potential has yet to be tapped, especially for political sociology. In our minds these spatial analytical methods, still relatively new to sociology, provide a means for substantively addressing spatial processes as theoretically and empirically interesting in and of themselves, in addition to making for cleaner statistical estimation. This is not simply a question of spatial autocorrelation of errors, as it is typically conceptualized; it is a question of capturing real sociopolitical processes. Often we lack clear measures of the spatial linkages that are operating but that deficiency recommends further work on identifying and measuring such mechanisms.

Specifically, models with spatial and network-effect terms allow researchers to make explicit the relationships between units and ways in which political-institutional processes across units occur. In our mind, spatial and network effects are substantively interesting. The ways they are modeled and the resulting pattern of coefficients they produce can tell us a lot about the mechanisms that spread political-institutional influences across space.

THE IMPLICATIONS OF NEOINSTITUTIONAL
THEORY AND METHODOLOGICAL DEVELOPMENTS
FOR DEALING WITH SPACE

So what are the implications of our perspective on spatial analysis for quantitative macro-political sociology? First, in most contexts where political actors are active decision makers, the functional form of the spatial process (the configuration of the W matrix) is a substantive issue to be addressed. In analyses of spatial units in the United States using states or counties, the W matrix often ties specific geographic units to adjacent units (whose effects are captured through the instrumental variable technique outlined above) or distance matrices that weight adjacent geographic units by the inverse of the distance between a given unit and all other units in the analysis. But other functional forms of W are possible as well. We discuss several below.

One possibility for specifying the relationship between geographic units would be through *input-output matrices* specifying the connections between units relevant to a specific political process. For example, states and governments are often influenced by specific in- and out-migration patterns. The movements of specific populations of people with specific socioeconomic characteristics, job skills, cultural and religious traits, and demographic profiles may affect the actions political actors take and the repertoires of actions available to social movements. In socioeconomic models the movement of specific goods and services (value-added imports and exports, raw material imports and exports, etc.) may identify specific places as central to or distant from the "core" of a network of interactions. This position in a migration and trade network may affect which political mimetic influences are seen as plausible, which set of political actors from outside the unit are viewed as important, and which set of political units will have coercive power. Ideally, from the standpoint of supporting or disproving normative isomorphic effects, it would be good to have information on attendance and nonattendance at public meetings by political actors, attendance at protest functions outside of specific political jurisdictions, and other forms of elite and social movement activist cross-fertilization. Instead of assuming that proximity captures the relevant performance networks, researchers would directly measure these reference groups. All of these ideas can be incorporated into estimates of spatial effects in quantitative models of political processes.

Another possibility is to take a more activist conception of neoinstitutional influence and attempt to explicitly account for strategic responses to institutional pressures. Oliver (1991), in particular, speaks of five different strategic responses to institutional pressures, each of which would be detectable in political actors' behaviors. Environmental stimuli can compel actors to (1) acquiesce, (2) compromise, (3) avoid, (4) defy, or (5) manipulate their environments. Of these, only acquiescence involves passively responding to institutional pressures by following norms taken for granted, the standard assumption used by political sociologists working with spatial data.

One of the key tasks for a spatial political sociology is to figure out the sources of external political pressure, the connections between them and specific political decision makers, and then the agentic response by these decision makers. In quantitative analyses, the agentic response is (in all likelihood) the dependent variable in the analysis. In qualitative comparative analyses of specific cases, the agentic response might be a crucial element of the outcome of interest, but researchers may be as interested in accounts of why a specific agentic response was picked from an array of possible alternatives.

This is where typologies like Oliver's (1991) come in handy. Acquiescence involves *following* taken-for-granted norms, mimicking other models of institutional action that have worked for others, and obeying rules and accepted norms as these are defined by the actions of other units or a superordinate unit (a national government, the United Nations, IMF, World Bank, NATO, EU, etc.). Ambiguity and structural equivalence may or may not be an element in this process. Analysts may be interested in why specific actors chose to take well-worn paths and what information from the institutional environment convinced them this was the right choice. But acquiescence is detectible—a specific set of political actors starts doing what actors in other units do. Compromise involves *balancing* the expectations of multiple environmental influences, placating, and negotiating with institutional stakeholders over the appropriateness or inappropriateness of specific actions. Here analysts might be interested in why some environmental actors are placated while others are taken seriously and negotiated with. They might also be interested in an historical counterfactual comparison with likely outcomes in the absence of this particular configuration of active negotiation and superficial placation. Avoidance involves *disguising* non-conformity, *loosening* institutional linkages, and *changing* one's reference goals and activities. In effect, a specific institutional agent says, "those rules are there, but they don't apply to me because I'm not in that reference group." This strikes us as most directly analogous to a framing problem as active agents define (in the affirmative) who the institutional reference group will be and (perhaps more importantly) who they are emphatically *not* like. Defiance takes avoidance one step further as active agents *ignore, contest,* and *assault* institutionalized rules and norms. Here, agents attempt to replace one set of institutional norms with another set of norms they define for themselves and for the rest of the reference group. Manipulation is the most active response as agents attempt to *shape* institutional values and criteria, *co-opt* other influential institutional actors, and *dominate and control* institutional constituents and rule-making bodies. All of these are potentially detectible sources of institutional influence that a spatial analysis in political sociology would have to address.

Once the influence process across space is specified, then an additional modeling issue becomes important—to what extent does a properly specified quantitative model account for theoretically grounded spatial effects, and in what contexts do spatial effects constitute truly unique sources of variation over and above processes internal to the geographic units of analysis? In most political sociology until very recently, the strong assumption was that responses to the external environment were completely mediated by the proximate causes and institutional configurations within each unit. In this case, there would be no spatially grounded residual variation for a quantitative model to explain once the properly specified variables from each unit were included in the analysis. Instead, we suggest another, more difficult strategy that takes space more seriously as a potential force affecting agent behavior in political sociology.

First, think about and theoretically spell out the sources of institutional influence on the specific actors and outcomes of interest. Which actors have control over the outcome? Where are these people located? What structure of incentives do they face? What ideological and collective action frames do they use? Second, how do those sources of influence play out across political space? Is there a way to precisely link those theoretical processes to specific units, actors, and agents? Third, empirically, how much of a difference do these institutional connections make? Quantitatively, this partly comes down to how large the coefficient is. In a qualitative, comparative historical analysis, do these institutional influences alter the pathways of development of specific programs, policies, and actions? Finally, does any specification of agent capacity and activity within the unit reduce the size of the institutional influence? If so, this suggests agents are actively responding to institutional influences through buffering and bridging activities of the kind Oliver (1991) describes.

The real, unsolved issue is the meaning of significant spatial effects once institutional configurations and actions within each unit have been controlled. The outcomes here vary anywhere from further investigations into omitted variables that might explain the result (i.e., reduce the size of the spatial coefficient) to arguments for mimetic isomorphism and acquiescence.

SPATIAL SOCIOLOGY IN OUR RESEARCH AGENDA

Our own research agenda over the past ten years (Jenkins and Leicht 1996; Jenkins, Leicht, and Jaynes 2006a; Jenkins, Leicht, and Jaynes 2006b; Jenkins, Leicht, and Wendt 2006; Leicht and Jenkins 1994; Leicht and Jenkins 1998) deals explicitly with issues requiring the consideration of space and the incorporation of space into the very process we study.

Specifically, we have been interested in the development and impact of U.S. state economic development programs. These programs are part of the (now) long-term move toward "new federalism" in the United States—moving decision making about key social and economic policies to the state level and permitting a myriad of locally-based experiments in policy innovation with only broad sets of guidelines provided by the federal government. From the reimbursement rates for Medicare and Medicaid, to payment levels for welfare recipients, to post-1996 experiments in welfare reform, to the development and funding of schools and educational policies, state and local governments have been front and center in the development of new policy innovations in the United States.

There is perhaps no place within political sociology where the development and use of spatial analysis techniques and theories can have a greater impact than in the study of state economic development policies. States increasingly compete for jobs, plants, research and development facilities, and other footloose capitalist enterprises that are part of the new spatialized production regime (Grant and Wallace 1994). In this competition, state governments pay close attention to what others are doing and publicly express fears about falling behind in the race for new sources of economic development. In short, this is an area with intense competition and intense institutional pressure to appear to be a player in the competitive game involving state managers, labor representatives, and local economic elites.

Our studies (Jenkins and Leicht 1996; Jenkins, Leicht, and Wendt 2006; Leicht and Jenkins 1998) point to constellations of advanced state capacities, active political labor movements, and business representatives that we term the "new mezocorporatism" as major sources of new entrepreneurial and industrial recruitment initiatives by states. The absence of this constellation of political actors tends to promote a race to the bottom—attacks on organized labor and fair employment practices often associated with a "get poor" strategy of economic development (see also Canak and Miller 1990). Overall, our results suggest that a distinctive brand of neocorporatism has developed in the United States that exploits the interest aggregation and local-state capacities in an environment where the fragmentation and relatively limited capacities of the federal government prevent the development of a coherent, nondefense-oriented industrial policy.

Most importantly, from the standpoint of addressing space as an issue in political sociology, our research program employs the Land and Deane method for addressing spatial autocorrelation, and we have estimated effects using matrices accounting for adjacent states and matrices connecting each state with all others using highway mileage between capitols (i.e., a 48-by-48 matrix of mileage distances). Our results reveal not only a major and generalized ratcheting process in which the number of programs of different types increases year by year, but considerable spatial similarities in the adoption of entrepreneurial and industrial recruitment programs not accounted for by the internal dynamics of specific states.

We argue that the remaining spatial effects after we control for political actors and state capacities are the result of direct mimetic pressure—the simple desire to copy the activity of other states in an attempt to keep up in the race for promoting economic development in specific geographic areas. Mimetic pressure, in institutional theory, is the most passive and least agentic type of institutional force, and in our case the instrumental variable ($y*$) represents the ability of a given state's political-institutional constellation to predict the economic development program adoption of adjacent states. In short, we estimate both the intrastate factors and the diffusion networks through which policies come into place.

This perspective and a broader, neoinstitutional perspective focused on governments of smaller unit scale has major implications for a new spatial perspective of political sociology. Presently, we are expanding our research to address issues of job creation and the production of high- and low-quality jobs (Jenkins, Leicht, and Jaynes 2006a; Jenkins, Leicht, and Jaynes 2006b). This research is also distinctively spatial. Not only do economic development programs affect the production and growth of jobs in specific locations, but they combine with specific locational advantages to drastically enhance spatial inequality in the states.

But other possibilities would inform a new focus in political sociology on government units and social actors competing with, or avoiding economic and political competitions with, similarly situated units and actors. Some examples would include studies of shifts and changes in transfer payments from the federal to state and local governments, changes in and shifts in Medicare and Medicaid rules affecting the health and well-being of people in specific locales, changes in the spread and efficacy of different types of welfare reform proposals, and changes in the symbolic politics of regions involving long-term changes in the desirability and political influences of specific regions over national political agendas. Each would involve the search for common and overlapping actors, common socialization experiences of elites, competitions for jobs and tax revenues, attempts to change identities and perceptions of desirability through media outlets, and other established and potentially revolutionary measures to change the economic and social hierarchy of specific places. All of these competitions involve governments and actors below the national level and exist in a context where there is a growing contradiction between an economic system that does not care about place and concrete cultures and actors who do. In developing this spatial agenda, the closer one can get to identifying the specific spatial linkage mechanism, the more compelling the analysis will be.

CONCLUSION

Our paper has attempted to make the case for incorporating space and spatial concepts into political sociology. These moves are justified because theories are increasingly interested in the active agents that promote or impede specific political processes.

But the reasons for incorporating space and spatial processes in political sociology are as much a response to the empirical world political sociologists seek to explain as reflecting theoretical developments in the subdiscipline. There is a growing disjuncture in the 21st century between globalization, a process where production of different types of goods and services can take place anytime and anywhere, and the concrete human need to be rooted in specific communities in defined geographic space with economic, social, and political opportunities tied to where people actually live. Ultimately, globalization will not lead to "global citizens" who no longer have connections or roots in specific places, exchanging these allegiances for some amorphous world village. They will not do this because it is inherently alien to human community and ways of life. Instead, locally-based communities will seek to harness their collective energies to bring economic development, jobs, and economic growth to their specific spot on the globe or to push away that development so they are not sucked in to a globalized economy where they surrender autonomy to amorphous economic forces over which they have no control.

This general disjuncture and the responses of political and economic agents to it defines the central set of questions for political sociology in the 21st century. From the standpoint of our paper, these questions are spatial. We suggest that neoinstitutional organizational theory is a plausible place to start looking for ways to explain influences across space in political sociology. We have also suggested that many of the key current and future questions for political sociology involve government and spatial units defined below the nation-state level. As social inequality, life chances, and political representation become local and regionalized, and as the world's people gain further access to news, advice, and histories of other governments, social movements, and cultural identity strategies, the need for a truly spatialized political sociology will grow, and the ability to explain political phenomena exclusively through institutional political developments internal to specific units will shrink. The real question before us is whether political sociology will answer this call and develop potent new tools for explaining the growing geographic dispersal of basic political rights and life chances.

NOTES

1. In their defense, neoinstitutional theorists often deal with symbolic space in ways that are important, nuanced, and have implications for the study of space in political sociology. The ability and willingness of organizations to define themselves as part of (or separate from) a particular institutional environment is not completely tied up in definitions enforced by people in adjacent locations (organizations in the same city, street, etc.). They include organizations in the same market and organizations in competition for the same resources from the external environment.

2. In a more prosaic example, Knoke (1982) traced how geographic proximity and common networks promoted the diffusion of municipal reform from a single city (Galveston, Texas) throughout the United States.

REFERENCES

Amenta, Edwin. 1998. *Bold Relief: Institutional Politics and the Origins of American Social Policy*. Princeton, NJ: Princeton University Press.

Amenta, Edwin and Drew Halfmann. 2000. "Wage Wars: Institutional Politics, WPA Wages, and the Struggle for U.S. Social Policy." *American Sociological Review* 65:506–528.

Amenta, Edwin and Jane D. Poulsen. 1996. "Social Politics in Context: The Institutional Politics Theory and Social Spending at the End of the New Deal." *Social Forces* 75:33–60.

Benford, Robert D. 1997. "An Insider's Critique of the Social Movement Framing Perspective." *Sociological Inquiry* 67:

Blauner, Bob. 2001. *Still Big News: Racial Oppression in America*. Philadelphia, PA: Temple University Press.

Brady, David and Michael Wallace. 2000. "Spatialization, Foreign Direct Investment, and Labor Outcomes in the American States, 1978–1996." *Social Forces* 79:67–105.

Burstein, Paul and April Linton. 2002. "The Impact of Political Parties, Interest Groups and Social Movement Organizations on Public Policy." *Social Forces* 81:380–408.

Burt, Ronald S. 1987. "Social Contagion and Innovation: Cohesion Versus Structural Equivalence." *American Journal of Sociology* 92:1287–1335.

Canak, William and Berkeley Miller. 1990. "Gumbo Politics: Unions, Business and Louisiana Right-to-Work Legislation." *Industrial and Labor Relations Review* 43:258–271.

Carroll, Glenn R. and Michael T. Hannan. 1995. *Organizations in Industry: Strategy, Structure, and Selection*. New York: Oxford University Press.

Castells, M. 1998. *The End of Millenium*. Oxford, UK: Blackwell Publishers

Conell, Carol and Samuel Cohn. 1995. "Learning From Other People's Actions: Environmental Variation and Diffusion in French Coal Mining Strikes, 1890–1935." *American Journal of Sociology* 101:366–403.

Doreian, Patrick. 1980. "Linear Models with Spatially Distributed Data: Spatial Disturbances or Spatial Effects?" *Sociological Methods and Research* 9:29–60.

Esping-Andersen, Gosta. 1990. *The Three Worlds of Welfare Capitalism*. Cambridge: Polity.

Firebaugh, Glenn. 2003. *The New Geography of Global Income Inequality*. Cambridge, MA: Harvard University Press.

Giddens, Anthony. 2000. *Runaway World: How Globalization is Shaping Our Lives*. New York: Routledge.

Goldstone, Jack A. 1991. *Revolution and Rebellion in the Early Modern World*. Berkeley: University of California Press.

Grant, Don Sherman, II. 1995. "The Political Economy of Business Failures across the American States, 1970–1985: The Impact of Reagan's New Federalism." *American Sociological Review* 60:851–873.

Grant, Don Sherman, II and Michael Wallace. 1994. "The Political Economy of Manufacturing Growth and Decline across the American States, 1970–1985." *Social Forces* 73:33–63.

Hannan, Michael T. and John Freeman. 1989. *Organizational Ecology*. Cambridge, MA: Harvard University Press.

Held, David. 2004. *Global Covenant: The Social Democratic Alternative to the Washington Consensus*. Cambridge: Polity.

Hicks, Alexander. 1999. *Social Democracy and Welfare Capitalism*. Ithaca, NY: Cornell University Press.

Holden, R. T. 1986. "The Contagiousness of Aircraft Hijackings." *American Journal of Sociology* 91:800–837.

Hooks, Gregory. 1994. "Regional Processes in the Hegemonic Nation: Political, Economic, and Military Influences on the Use of Geographic Space." *American Sociological Review* 59:746–772.

Hooks, Gregory and Leonard E. Bloomquist. 1992. "The Legacy of World War II for Regional Growth and Decline: The Cumulative Effects of Wartime Investments on U.S. Manufacturing, 1947–1972." *Social Forces* 71:303–337.

Huber, Evelyne and John D. Stephens. 2001. *The Development and Crisis of the Welfare State*. Chicago: University of Chicago Press.

Jenkins, J. Craig and Kevin T. Leicht. 1996. "Direct Intervention by the Subnational State: The Development of Public Venture Capital Programs in the American States." *Social Problems* 43:306–326.

Jenkins, J. Craig, Kevin T. Leicht and Arthur Jaynes. 2006a. "Do High Technology Policies Work? High Technology Industry Employment Growth in U.S. Metropolitan Areas, 1988–1998." *Social Forces* 85:283–314.

Jenkins, J. Craig, Kevin T. Leicht, and Arthur Jaynes. 2006b. "How to Become a High Tech Growth Pole." Department of Sociology, Ohio State University and University of Iowa. Unpublished manuscript.

Jenkins, J. Craig, Kevin T. Leicht, and Heather Wendt. 2006. "Class Forces, Political Institutions, and State Intervention: Subnational Economic Development Policy in the U.S., 1971–1990." *American Journal of Sociology* 111:1122–1180.

Knoke, David. 1982. "The Spread of Municipal Reform: Temporal, Spatial and Social Dynamics." *American Journal of Sociology* 87:1314–1339.

Land, Kenneth C. and Glenn Deane. 1992. "On the Large-Sample Estimation of Regression Models with Spatial or Network Effects Terms." *Sociological Methodology* 22:221–248.

Leicht, Kevin T. and J. Craig Jenkins. 1994. "Three Strategies of State Economic Development: Entrepreneurial, Industrial Recruitment and Deregulation Policies in the American States." *Economic Development Quarterly* 8:256–270.

Leicht, Kevin T. and J. Craig Jenkins. 1998. "Political Resources and Direct State Intervention: The Adoption of Public Venture Capital Programs in the American States, 1974–1990." *Social Forces* 76:1323–1345.

Lobao, Linda and Gregory Hooks. 2003. "Public Employment, Welfare Transfers, and Economic Well-Being Across Local Populations: Does Lean and Mean Government Benefit the Masses?" *Social Forces* 82:519–556.

Moore, Barrington. 1966. *Social Origins of Dictatorship and Democracy*. Boston: Beacon Press.

Mueller, John. 2004. *The Remnants of War*. Ithaca, NY: Cornell University Press.

Myers, Daniel J. 1997. "Racial Rioting in the 1960s: An Event History Analysis of Local Conditions." *American Sociological Review* 62:94–112.

Oliver, Christine. 1991. "Strategic Responses to Institutional Processes." *Academy of Management Review*. 16:145–179.

Ord, Keith. 1975. "Estimation Methods for Models of Spatial Interaction." *Journal of the American Statistical Association* 70:120–126.

Orloff, Ann Shola. 1993. *The Politics of Pensions: A Comparative Analysis of Britain, Canada, and the United States*. Madison, WI: University of Wisconsin Press.

———. 2002. *Women's Employment and Welfare Regimes: Globalization, Export Orientation, and Social Policy in Europe and North America*. Geneva: United Nations Institute for Social Development.

Pierson, Paul. 1994. *Dismantling the Welfare State: Reagan, Thatcher, and the Politics of Retrenchment*. New York: Cambridge University Press.

Powell, Walter and Paul DiMaggio, eds. 1991. *The New Institutionalism in Organizational Analysis*. Chicago: University of Chicago Press.

Renzulli, Linda A. and Vincent J. Roscigno. 2005. "Charter School Policy, Implementation, and Diffusion Across the U.S." *Sociology of Education* 78:344–365.

Roncek, Dennis W. and Andrew Montgomery. 1984. "Spatial Autocorrelation: Diagnoses and Remedies in Large Samples." Presented at the annual meeting of the Midwest Sociological Society, Des Moines, IA.

Scott, W. Richard. 1995. *Institutions and Organizations*. Thousand Oaks, CA: Sage.

Skocpol, Theda. 1979. *States and Social Revolutions: A Comparative Analysis of France, Russia, and China*. Cambridge, UK: Cambridge University Press.

———. 1994. *Social Revolutions in the Modern World*. Cambridge, UK: Cambridge University Press.

Snow, David and Robert Benford. 1988. "Ideology, Frame Resonance, and Participant Mobilization." Pp. 197–217 in *From Structure to Action: Social Movement Participation Across Cultures*, edited by Bert Klandermans, Hanspeter Kriesi, and Sidney Tarrow. Greenwich, CT: JAI.

Soule, Sarah A. and Yvonne Zylan. 1997. "Runaway Train? The Diffusion of State-Level Reform in ADC/AFDC Eligibility Requirements, 1950–1967." *American Journal of Sociology* 103:733–762.

Spilerman, Seymour. 1976. "Structural Characteristics of Cities and the Severity of Racial Disorders." *American Sociological Review* 41:771–793.

Stinchcombe, Arthur. 1997. "On the Virtues of the Old Institutionalism." *Annual Review of Sociology* 23:1–18.

Strang, David and Sarah A. Soule. 1998. "Diffusion in Organizations and Social Movements: From Hybrid Corn to Poison Pills." *Annual Review of Sociology* 24:265–290.

Tarrow, Sidney. 1989. *Democracy and Disorder: Protest and Politics in Italy, 1965–1975*. New York: Oxford University Press.

Tilly, Charles. 2003. *The Politics of Collective Violence*. Cambridge, UK: Cambridge University Press.

Tolnay, Stewart E. and E. M. Beck 1992. "Racial Violence and Black Migration in the American South, 1910 to 1930." *American Sociological Review* 57:103–116.

Tolnay, Stewart E., Glenn Deane, and E. M. Beck. 1996. "Vicarious Violence: Spatial Effects on Southern Lynchings, 1890–1919." *American Journal of Sociology* 102:788–815.

Wallerstein, Immanuel. 2004. *World-Systems Analysis: An Introduction*. Durham, NC: Duke University Press.

Wilensky, Harold. 1975. *The Welfare State and Equality: Structural and Ideological Roots of Public Expenditure*. Berkeley: University of California Press.

Zylan, Yvonne and Sarah Soule. 2000. "Ending Welfare As We Know It (Again): Welfare State Retrenchment, 1989–1995." *Social Forces* 79:623–652.

FOUR

Territories of Inequality

An Essay on the Measurement and Analysis of Inequality in Grounded Place Settings

MICHAEL D. IRWIN

SOCIOLOGY AS A DISCIPLINE began with a core interest in the relationship between space and social organization (Burgess 1925; Cooley 1894; McKenzie 1927; Sorokin and Zimmerman 1929; Von Thünen [1826] 1966; Weber 1889). In the early to mid-20th century, substantive work turned to measurement issues (Alexander 1954; Berry and Pred 1961; Harris and Ullman 1945; Hoover 1948; Losch 1938; Vance and Sutker 1954) but this concern faded by the mid-1960s. However, in the last decade the proliferation of Geographic Information Systems (GIS) software, the release of census (and other) geographically aggregated data on the Web, and the diffusion of spatial statistics have driven the proliferation of territorially based analysis. This has encouraged sociology's traditional interest in the relationship between space and society to reemerge, albeit along 21st-century social science themes.

Unlike earlier work that stressed the spatial aspects of social equilibrium and functional integration underlying spatial differentiation (Hawley 1981, 1986), much current work focuses upon social inequalities associated with place (specific territorially bounded units of investigation) and with space (the general influences of social relations across territories) (Castells 1989; Mencken and Singelmann 1998; Nielsen and Alderson 1997; Tolbert, Lyson, and Irwin 1998). Empirical investigation of contemporary sociospatial inequality necessarily confronts both issues.

This chapter discusses the methodological construction of places by examining U.S. census geographic units widely used in empirical research. In this discussion, I explain how different place units capture the ecological concept of community, as it is often used in studies of neighborhoods, cities, and other regions. Here, community is understood to include direct and indirect territorially-bounded social elements affecting individuals. While such elements may include local place identification and sentiments, my focus involves material elements of social organization, such as economic and population attributes that coalesce in a particular territory. In this sense, a community is a material reflection of society associated with territory.

Different territorial units lend themselves to alternative ways of conceptualizing community and the adequacy of unit measurement will differ depending upon the underlying social concepts guiding the research questions. However, the match between concept and measurement is inevitably imperfect and may raise important questions of validity to be addressed in analytic designs. In this chapter, I review techniques for assessing, adjusting, and reconstructing territorial units to address such issues. New approaches such as GIS and spatial statistics allow researchers to structure their analyses to better control for the match between underlying concepts and existing territorial units. These approaches ground our understandings of community, spatial inequality, and other sociological concepts in more appropriate empirical measures of spatial processes and place units.

THE USE OF TERRITORIAL UNITS IN SOCIAL SCIENCE

Spatial dimensions to social organization arise because society exists upon and across the land. Even where physical barriers to interaction are minimal, spatial boundaries often mark social divisions and delimit the overall nature and frequency of daily interactions. For either reason, there are distances beyond which regular daily social interaction do not extend. Where these barriers occur, social organization coalesces into cohesive sociospatial units and the structure of human activity is more oriented within a geography than outside a geography (White and Mueser 1988). This cohesive unit character justifies the use of certain sociospatial units for summarizing aspects of social organization. As objects of study, they represent superindividual social units with emergent characteristics. For instance, a place may be characterized as racially segregated or diverse, rich or poor. These place characteristics have tangible effects upon individuals that transcend personal characteristics. An individual raised in a poor, segregated, African American neighborhood has fewer opportunities than an individual raised in a wealthy, white, professional neighborhood.

For this reason, analyses at the individual level often use classifications of places, such as urban-rural or metropolitan-nonmetropolitan location, as contextual attributes of individuals assumed to represent place characteristics. However, such classifications are only as good as the match between territorial units and actual spatial cohesion of social organization. The choice of territorial units to represent social concepts is as much a theoretical issue as an empirical one. Different theoretical assumptions lead to different notions of the boundaries of social cohesion and to different spatial units for analysis. Consider sociology's classical theorists. Marx (1867) focused on national units to understand the nature of capitalism. He recognized that as the geographic scope of production and consumption expands, so does the geographic scope of competition. This expanded geographic competition for capital drew together the common interests of capitalists within an area. In this sense, economic interaction became the bounding force in differentiating individual societies from each other. Conversely, Weber's (1889) view of trade and transportation as external limitations on internal forms of social organization led him to focus on more tightly bounded spatial units. Here cultural cohesion became the mechanism for place formation in space. The city particularly was a central arena of social interaction and agreements arising from trade relations (Weber [1921] 1978a:1218–1219).

Ecological approaches have an interest in other place-based units. These approaches stress that social-organizational linkages are inextricably interwoven with space through transportation and communications technology (Hawley 1981, 1986). Organizational functions locate in places providing maximum access to and control of interarea flows of products and information. This gives rise to regional geographical formations such as metropolitan areas, the bounds of which readily supersede governmental spatial jurisdictions associated with cities, states, and nations (McKenzie 1933). Here the friction of space comprising the material conditions creates social cohesion for place formation.

These examples show that alternative theoretical approaches imply different notions of spatial process and boundaries that lead researchers to focus on different territorial units as places of study. For these reasons, place units used for the analysis of one social process may not be appropriate for another process. Choice of geographic units involves a choice among the competing theoretical notions of how social processes interact in places. Further, these units should be matched to the nature of the social interactions under study.

In the United States, sociospatial data is predominantly presented through census geography. Most researchers use census units as objects of analysis or construct new geographies using census units. The choice of spatial units is the first issue confronting researchers studying sociospatial relationships. The best way to make such a choice is to understand the sociospatial concepts underlying these units. In the next section I discuss these census geographic units and their construction.

SPACE IN PRACTICE: CENSUS GEOGRAPHY

A number of problems plague the match between census units and sociological concepts. Many census units are constructed for convenience of administration and data gathering (U.S. Census Bureau 1994, 2002a). Social characteristics linked conceptually to one type of spatial unit may, for reasons of disclosure or sampling variability, only be reported at a larger, less theoretically appropriate spatial unit. As the population size of the territorial unit increases so does the amount of data available, forcing researchers toward what may be less theoretically-justifiable units for purely pragmatic reasons.

Table 4.1 shows the most commonly used census geographies, listed from largest (the nation, with the most data available) to the smallest (the block, with the least information available but with some 8,205,582 units covering the United States) (U.S. Census Bureau 2002b). The table illustrates selected spatial units with reference to their construction, the type of sociospatial unit they are intended to represent, and related attributes of social life associated with them (U.S. Census Bureau 1994).

In Census reporting, each enumerated unit (person, family, household, housing units, institution, farm, business establishment, employee, occupation, etc) is assigned in space, at a given point in time. Notably the degree to which these units are attached to points in space is variable. Persons move through space daily, while buildings are fixed in location. For this reason, persons are located in space in reference to their buildings, either by residence or workplace.

Census space is divided into geographic tabulation units with either legal/administrative or statistical definition. Legal/administrative identity originates from "legal actions, treaties, statutes, ordinances, resolutions, court decisions, and the like" (U.S. Census Bureau 1994:2–2). These de jure spatial units, therefore, have a political/legal authority over processes within the areas. Statistical units, on the other hand, "evolve from practice, custom, usage, or need" and are usually designed to meet the data user's needs (U.S. Census Bureau 1994:2–2). Here statistical criteria are used to determine boundaries for some underlying notion of a sociospatial concept. These units, and in many respects the sociospatial concepts underlying them, can be arrayed in a hierarchy. Figure 4.1 overlays the hierarchy of census spatial units from housing unit location to society (U.S. Census Bureau 1994). This figure also overlays three major sociospatial conceptual levels (regions, communities, and neighborhoods) for the moment without reference to specific forms of each type (e.g., cities, towns, villages).

The census block is the smallest geography used for public tabulation and is fully nested within any other geographic level, as seen in figure 4.1. Block boundaries are constructed from both visible features (e.g. streets) and governmental boundaries (U.S. Census Bureau 2004a). For the 2000 Census there are 8,269,131 blocks (U.S. Census Bureau 2002b). Blocks aggregate to

TABLE 4.1
Census Geography Definitions and Sociological Concepts

Census Geography	Social Unit	Related Concepts and Categories	Definition
United States	Nation	Society, State	Legal Boundary: All U.S. States and Territories
Regions	Cultural/ Economic Region	Regionalism, Regional Economies	Statistical: Subsets of U.S. States
Divisions	Cultural/ Economic Region	Regionalism, Regional Economies	Statistical: Subsets of U.S. States
States/Territories	Political Units	Regional Political System	Legal Boundary
Metropolitan Area (MSA, PMSA, CMSA)	Social/Cultural/ Economic Region or Community	Metropolitan, Cosmopolitan, Urban, Urban-ism, Suburb, Suburbanism, Nonmetropolitan	Statistical: Clusters of Counties around Large Urban Area
Local Labor Market	Social/Cultural/ Economic Region or Community	Local Labor Market, Economic Region	Statistical: Clusters of Counties Based on Commuting
Commuting Zone	Social/Cultural/ Economic Region or Community	Local Labor Market, Economic Region	Statistical: Clusters of Counties Based on Commuting
Micropolitan	Social/Cultural/ Economic Region or Community	Urban, Urbanism, Suburb, Suburbanism, Nonmetropolitan	Statistical: Subsets of Counties around Medium Urban Area

(continued on next page)

TABLE 4.1 (*continued*)

Census Geography	Social Unit	Related Concepts and Categories	Definition
Urban Area	Social/Cultural/ Economic Region or Community	Metropolitan, Cosmopolitan, Urban, Urbanism, Suburb, Suburbanism, Nonmetropolitan	Statistical: Population Density of Block Groups
Urban Cluster	Community: Cities and Towns	Urban, Urbanism, Rural, Ruralism	Statistical: Population Density of Block Groups
County	Community Area	Varies by Context	Legal Boundary
Census Designated Place	Community: Cities, Towns, Villages, Hamlets	Urban, Urbanism, Rural, Ruralism	Statistical: Population and Economic Concentration
Incorporated Place	Community: Cities, Towns, Villages, Hamlets	Urban, Urbanism, Rural, Ruralism	Legal Boundary
Minor Civil Division (MCD)	Community: Towns, Villages, Hamlets, Neighborhoods	Social District	Legal Boundary
ZIP Code Areas (ZCTAs)	Community: Towns, Villages, Hamlets, Neighborhoods	Social District	Administrative Boundary
Tracts	Community: Towns, Villages, Hamlets, Neighborhoods	Social District	Statistical: Population Minimum

(*continued on next page*)

TABLE 4.1 (*continued*)

Census Geography	Social Unit	Related Concepts and Categories	Definition
Block Groups	Community: Villages, Hamlets, Neighborhoods	Social Districts	Statistical: Population Minimum
Blocks	Community: Hamlets, Neighborhoods	Social District	Statistical: Population Minimum
Housing Unit	Household, Family	Dwelling, Place of Residence	De facto
Commercial Building	Business, Firm, Activity	Workplace	De facto

Source: Bureau of the Census (1994), Table 2–1 Geographic Entities of the 1990 Census.

block group and generally contain between 300 and 3,000 people, with an optimum size of 1,500 people. Block groups are the lowest geography for which sample data are presented. For the 2000 census there are 211,827 block groups. Sets of block groups comprise Census tracts. Tracts (and the equivalent block numbering areas) are designed for an optimal size of 4,000 people and typically have between 1,500 and 8,000 people. Census tracts were originally designed to identify relatively homogeneous socioeconomic groups, although in many cases the original social cohesion used to bound tracts no longer pertain (U.S. Census Bureau 2002a). There are 66,438 tracts in the 2000 Census (U.S. Census Bureau 2002b, 2004b).

Counties (or statistical equivalents) are used as a building block for other census territories (such as metropolitan areas) as well as for researcher-defined regions (local labor markets, economic areas, etc.). Counties are legal/administrative areas constructed originally around minimal population criteria as part of state government formation. There were 3,141 counties in 2000. Additionally, in some states incorporated places are legally separated from (and function as) counties. These "independent cities" are treated by the Census Bureau as equivalent to counties, although they are cities in their own right (U.S. Census Bureau 2002c).

A metropolitan area (MA) is defined as a large population nucleus together with adjacent counties that have a high degree of economic and

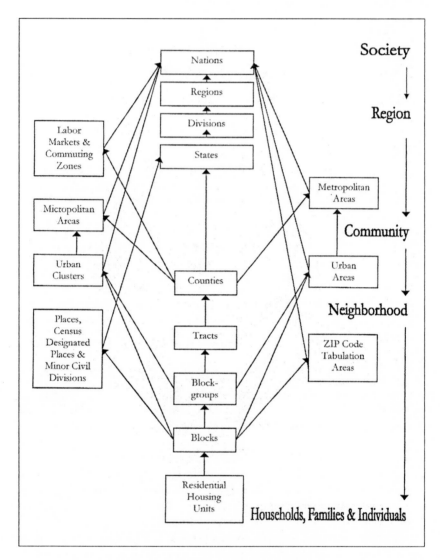

FIGURE 4.1. Hierarchy of Census Geography
Definitions and Sociological Concepts

social integration with that urban area. MA collectively refers to three categories of metropolitan statistical areas: consolidated metropolitan statistical areas (CMSAs); primary metropolitan statistical areas (PMSAs); and
MSAs. An MA must have a population of at least 50,000 in a single urbanized area and a total MA population must be at least 100,000 (75,000 in

New England). According to the 2000 Census, there are 362 MAs (U.S. Census Bureau 2002b).

For 2000, micropolitan areas have been added as a socioeconomic region surrounding smaller urban areas. Each micropolitan statistical area must have at least one urban cluster of at least 10,000 but less than 50,000. The county (or counties) in which at least 50 percent of the population resides within urban areas of 10,000 or more, or that contain at least 5,000 people residing within a single urban area of 10,000 or more population, is identified as a "central county" (counties). According to the 2000 Census, there are 560 micropolitan areas (U.S. Census Bureau 2002a).

Collectively, a micropolitan and metropolitan area is referred to as a "core-based statistical area" (CBSA). CBSA regions include adjacent counties if they meet requirements of commuting to or from the central counties. A county qualifies as an outlying county of a CBSA region under either of two conditions. Either at least 25 percent of employed residents must work in the central county or counties of the region or at least 25 percent of employment in the county must be by those residing in the central county or counties of the region, although few micropolitan areas are multicounty regions.

The "incorporated place" captures notions of cities, towns, villages, etc., operationalized as a type of governmental unit, incorporated under state law as a city, town, township, borough, or village. According to the 2000 Census, there are 19,452 incorporated places (U.S. Census Bureau 2002a). A geographic entity serving as the statistical counterpart of an incorporated place for the purpose of presenting census data is a "census designated place" (CDP). Local places not within formally-incorporated place boundaries, however, are identifiable to the community population by local names or identity and are defined cooperatively with state, local, or tribal officials based on Census Bureau guidelines (U.S. Census Bureau 2004c). According to the 2000 Census, there are 5,698 CDPs (U.S. Census Bureau 2002b). In addition, "minor civil divisions" (MCDs) are identified by a variety of terms and are often treated as townships, villages, etc. However, MCDs may also include areas with governmental and/or administrative functions. Examples of such areas include American Indian reservations, assessment districts, election districts, towns, and townships.

Two other statistical definitions of urban units are widely used. An "urbanized area" (UA) is a settled area with a population of at least 50,000 and is also used to define the core city of an MA. The geographic core of block groups or blocks must have a population density of at least 1,000 people per square mile, and adjacent block groups and blocks must have at least 500 people per square mile. "Urban cluster" (UC) is used to define micropolitan areas. These city areas consist of a geographic core of block groups or blocks with a population density of at least 1,000 people per square mile, and adjacent block groups and blocks with at least 500 people per square mile that together encompass a population of at least 2,500 people, but fewer than 50,000.

The "ZIP code tabulation area" (ZCTA) is a statistical entity developed by the Census Bureau to approximate the delivery area for a U.S. Postal Service five-digit or three-digit ZIP Code in the U.S. and Puerto Rico. A ZCTA is an aggregation of census blocks with the same predominant ZIP code associated with the mailing addresses in the Census Bureau's master address file. The Postal Service's delivery areas have been adjusted to encompass whole census blocks so the Census Bureau can tabulate census data for the ZCTAs. Thus ZCTAs do not necessarily match ZIP code geography (including the ZIP code areas used by Economic Censuses). Conversely, ZCTAs do not include all ZIP codes used for mail delivery (U.S. Census Bureau 2002c). According to the 2000 Census, there are 31,913 five digit ZCTAs aggregated to 1,135 three digit ZCTAs (U.S. Census Bureau 2002b).

The census hierarchy has clearly defined nested geographies and clearly separated divisions within these hierarchies. The sociospatial concepts overlaying the census units do not have distinct separations and figure 4.1 shows potential overlap among major categories' conceptual levels. Conceptual distinctions are most clear at the upper and lower levels of this hierarchy. However, depending upon the theoretical approach used, regions are not distinct from communities (Hawley 1950) and communities are not distinct from neighborhoods (Jacobs 1961). Since there is conceptual overlap, the theoretical meaning attached to each empirical unit is likewise ambiguous. This overlap is not simply resolvable empirically, since the problem is conceptual in nature. Conversely, the identification of these statistical units influences individual notions of region, community, and neighborhood. As White (1987:9) states, "Once the statistical geography is established, it becomes a sort of de facto social system, since all subsequent analysis proceeds from this set of boundaries." In this way, statistical identification may result in the formation of place identification.

MATCHING THEORY AND PRACTICE: SPATIAL CATEGORIES OF SOCIAL LIFE AND CENSUS UNITS

Simply making a decision among spatial units does not sidestep a number of practical measurement issues. As an example, take three categories of social life with spatial referents: urban, metropolitan, and rural. Perhaps the most central unit is the city, since many of the remaining spatial units are defined in reference to it. The city is a type of community associated with specific characteristics: a nonagricultural economy, large numbers of people concentrated in a relatively small space with distinctive institutional characteristics.

"Urban" refers to the class of characteristics associated with cities while "urbanism" refers to the class of cultural characteristics of social life distinct to urban places. Rural space is generally defined in relationship to the city. It includes all space not part of cities and may include countryside, villages, and towns. In this sense, "rural" is not truly a discrete spatial unit, clearly bounded in space. Nevertheless, like the city, the social organization of rural space has distinctive institutional and cultural attributes that constitute a distinctive class of social organization.

The largest cities comprise a different type of city, with overarching social and economic influence extending well beyond its political or geographic boundaries. This type of city, the metropolis, is characterized by cosmopolitan attributes, with distinctive urban institutions and services. These cosmopolitan and metropolitan characteristics influence the central city's suburban hinterland (rural and adjacent towns and cities). Thus the "metropolis" is a spatial unit, built on the conception of the city, but it extends the concepts of urbanization and urbanism beyond city boundaries. All space within the metropolis not part of the central city is suburban and may include large cities as well as low-density residential areas.

Similarly, nonmetropolitan space is defined as all areas outside of metropolitan areas. It is residual, as is rural space. Unlike the concept of rural, however, it is not clear that "nonmetropolitan" represents a distinct class of social life. In nonmetropolitan space, social organization may be urban or rural and may contain cities or countryside.

From these conceptual definitions we can see that the categories of social life—urban, metropolitan, and rural—are not mutually exclusive. Further, we see that several important categories of social life conceptually related to space—suburban, rural, and nonmetropolitan—have no true spatial boundaries but are defined only by default.

As categories these may be adequate for description. We may cross-classify nonmetropolitan space with rural space to evaluate aspects of rural nonmetropolitan social organization (Butler and Beale 1994). In doing this, however, we are by no means evaluating rural community or nonmetropolitan community. "Community" implies the cohesive character of a unit that coalesces in spatial boundaries. Such categories have neither. Thus, while there is a rich sociological literature using these concepts and social categories, most analyses, either in aggregate or as individual context, are using poorly operationalized measures.

Improving this literature requires the study of the discrete spatial referents of community as units of analysis to match theoretical notions of community with appropriate measures, and understanding the spatial processes creating the spatial dimensions of such phenomenon as sociospatial inequality. To do so, the next section discusses spatial relationships associated with four census geographies—ZIP codes, tracts, block groups, and counties—

along three types of sociospatial inequality—spatial divisions in community wealth, racial diversity, and occupational homogeneity.

ANALYZING PLACE IN SPACE: SPATIAL AUTOCORRELATION AND UNIT CHOICE

It is often noted that everything is related to everything else. In a sense this is the problem presented by spatial autocorrelation—aspects of one place may be influenced by aspects of another. While interrelationships may be pervasive we can also add the caveat that places close to one another are generally more interrelated than those distant from one another (Tobler 1970; Johnson et al. 2001). The problem in analyzing place is how much space moderates or increases these interrelationships (Haining 1990).

As an example, table 4.2 presents three dimensions of inequality for different territories across two different geographic scopes—a global (comparing across a state) and a local (comparing across a metropolitan area). Specifically, for the state of Pennsylvania, table 4.2 presents inequality across counties and across ZIP codes (ZCTA) while for the Pittsburgh MA inequality is contrasted for ZCTAs, tracts, and block groups. These four territories (counties, ZCTAs, tracts, and block groups) are geographic units often used to define spatial inequality. Many studies have noted that choice of units determines the degree of apparent inequality across space (Farley and Frey 1994; Jargowsky 1994; Keller 1968; Tauber and Tauber 1965). This is the modifiable areal unit problem, where results may differ under different levels of unit aggregation or boundary change. White (1987:6–8) chooses tracts to contrast residential homogeneity yet notes that spatial differentiation may well exist within these areas. Ellen (2000:77–79) similarly focuses on tracts on theoretical grounds but shows that racial homogeneity varies somewhat differently among block groups within tracts. Larger territories, commuting zones, are used to depict segregation by Beggs et al. (1997), and Fischer et al. (2004) contrast levels of various dimensions of spatial inequality across regions, metropolitan areas, cities, suburbs, places, and tracts. This latter study finds that spatial inequality varies considerably by both geographic unit and the specific dimension of inequality, while Beggs et al. (1997) demonstrate that cross-area interactions influence our understanding of racial inequality even across multicounty regions. Below I exam both effects, unit choice and spatial influences, by contrasting three dimensions of social inequality often associated with communities and neighborhoods (per capita personal income, percent white, and percent professional and managerial employment). Table 4.2 provides descriptive statistics for this analysis.

All units cover the contiguous space and population respectively for Pennsylvania and for the Pittsburgh MA. Differences in averages for personal income, percent white, and percent professional and managerial employment

TABLE 4.2
Descriptive Statistics for State of Pennsylvania and Pittsburgh Metropolitan Area by Census Unit, 2000

Type of Unit N	Statistic	Area in Square Miles	Population	Personal Income	Percent White	Percent Professional and Managerial
County (Total in State) N=67	Mean	1,732.45	183,299	$18,388	94.04%	57.51%
	Median	1,697.70	90,366	$17,224	96.48%	58.56%
	Std. Dev.	701.16	265,443	$ 3,412	7.52%	3.89%
ZCTA (Total in State) N=1731	Mean	54.86	5,803	$18,784	94.96%	57.85%
	Median	26.70	1,661	$17,012	98.45%	57.14%
	Std. Dev.	76.15	9,947	$ 8,571	11.72%	10.72%
ZCTA (Total in MA) N=290	Mean	32.29	7,886	$19,049	93.49%	59.66%
	Median	10.60	2,471	$17,326	97.50%	59.22%
	Std. Dev.	46.42	10,569	$ 7,016	11.83%	10.72%
Tract (Total in MA) N=704	Mean	17.06	3,350	$20,342	86.36%	63.61%
	Median	25.86	3,147	$18,670	95.47%	62.64%
	Std. Dev.	40.53	1,688	$ 8,406	22.76%	9.34%
Block Group (Total in MA) N=1990	Mean	6.04	1,185	$20,302	88.09%	63.11%
	Median	10.76	1,064	$18,436	96.34%	63.22%
	Std. Dev.	12.80	547	$ 8,722	21.47%	10.40%

result from differences in the way the population is parceled in space. Overall, averages for all three indicators are similar, with somewhat lower levels for personal income and for percent professional and managerial found within the Pittsburgh MA for ZCTAs. Spatial inequality in the patterning of these dimensions is apparent, however. Spatial autocorrelation analysis quantifies the degree of spatial patterning in these variables by modeling interrelationships among places using a spatial weights or connection matrix and then examining the similarity of places close to or far away from one another as measured by this matrix (Griffith 2003). More formally, spatial autocorrelation tests the match between locational similarity and similarity along a dimension of interest (Anselin, Syabri, and Kho 2006). Table 4.3 presents one statistic, global Moran's I, to test this correlation between distance (defined in different ways) and three dimensions of inequality (Anselin 2003).

Moran's I indicates the degree of overall correlation between distance among places and each dimension of spatial inequality. Interpreted as the degree of spatial clustering for each dimension, Moran's I varies from 0 (no spatial relationship), with positive values indicating a high degree of spatial clustering and negative values indicating an inverse pattern of spatial clustering (high values in one area are associated with low values in nearby areas). Central to this measure is the way we think about spatial relationships among places, and there are several alternative ways to model closeness among places.

Table 4.3 presents five alternative ways to look at spatial interrelations among places. Rook adjacency, queen adjacency (immediate and higher order), nearest-neighbor distance, and distance. Rook adjacency defines a matrix of connections (where 1= connection between two places and 0= no connection) as any two places with a common border. Queen adjacency defines this matrix as including both common borders and common points. These two matrixes both model spatial influence through direct connections. Two other measures take account of indirect influences. Queen adjacency may be extended to include not only areas with common borders or points, but areas with common points with those adjacent places. Thus, a second tier of geographic influence is assumed. Distance-weight matrixes use the distance between the centroids (latitude and longitude coordinates) of each place to define a continuous notion of spatial influence. Here spatial influence weights are based on a minimum distance band around each place that ensures each observation has at least one neighbor (Anselin 2003: 95). Finally, nearest-neighbor approaches use distance matrixes as defined above, but hold influence to a set number of nearby places (Anselin 2004).

Looking across these five methods, we see that the Moran's spatial influence indicator is highest among the immediate contiguity-based measures, rook, queen first order, and nearest neighbors. The measures examining the influence of more distant areas (queen second order and distance) have lower levels of Moran's I. Together these numbers indicate that most of the spatial influence on place inequality comes from the immediately surrounding areas.

TABLE 4.3
Spatial Autocorrelation Indicators by County, ZIP Code Area, Tract and Block-Group

				Moran's I			
Variable	Type of Unit	Rook	Queen 1st Order	Queen 2nd Order	Distance Weight	Nearest Neighbor (5 Units)
Personal Income						
Global (State)	County (PA)	0.5154	0.5116	0.3464	0.4755	0.4369
Global (State)	ZCTA (PA)	0.3937	0.3914	0.3142	0.3945	0.2829
Local (MA)	ZCTA	0.2665	0.2725	0.2181	0.2303	0.3176
Local (MA)	Tract	0.4839	0.4752	0.3279	0.0758	0.4832
Local (MA)	Block Group	0.5336	0.5239	0.3781	0.1431	0.4997
Percent White						
Global (State)	County (PA)	0.2833	0.2809	0.2220	0.2666	0.2973
Global (State)	ZCTA (PA)	0.5220	0.5167	0.4229	0.5220	0.3029
Local (MA)	ZCTA	0.3283	0.3292	0.2644	0.3283	0.4116
Local (MA)	Tract	0.6573	0.6572	0.4937	0.1320	0.6754
Local (MA)	Block Group	0.7587	0.7520	0.5999	0.2175	0.7669
Percent Professional and Managerial						
Global (State)	County (PA)	0.3776	0.3718	0.1921	0.3138	0.3398
Global (State)	ZCTA (PA)	0.2244	0.2249	0.1968	0.2244	0.1853
Local (MA)	ZCTA	0.2068	0.2133	0.1648	0.2408	0.2408
Local (MA)	Tract	0.4942	0.4870	0.3655	0.1498	0.4767
Local (MA)	Block Group	0.4858	0.4786	0.3955	0.1948	0.4686

At the state level, personal income and percent managerial and professional have the highest degree of spatial clustering for counties and lower apparent spatial clustering for ZCTAs. However, spatial clustering is more apparent for percent white at the ZIP code geography than among counties. In terms of global spatial patterns, some dimensions of inequality are better captured by counties, others by the smaller ZCTA geography.

At the local Pittsburgh MA level, for all three indicators of spatial inequality, Moran's I levels are generally highest for block groups and lowest for ZCTAs. Spatial influence across levels of inequality for tracts are very close to levels for block groups and in a few cases slightly exceed the block group Moran's I index. These levels of spatial influence are highest for percent white and lowest for managerial and professional employment.

The results of table 4.3 indicate clear spatial patterns in neighborhood inequality within the Pittsburgh MA and show that these patterns tend to be very localized. Nearby neighborhoods, however we define them, tend to have similar levels of inequality and are dissimilar from distant neighborhoods. This clustering of inequality levels in space is as strong among tracts as among the smaller block group units, suggesting that little information is gained by analyzing at the more local block group level. In contrast, low levels for Moran's I among ZCTAs shows that this geography masks spatial patterns of inequality among neighborhoods. Table 4.3, therefore, would lead a researcher towards a tract level when analyzing neighborhood social inequality. ZCTAs mask spatial inequality while block groups may provide too much geographic specificity.

However, these tests only examine the distribution of these three dimensions of inequality across space. Of greater interest to most researchers is the specification of relationships underlying place inequality (Anselin and Bera 1998). The extension of univariate interarea influence to the multivariate case complicates the analysis in two ways. First, if levels of the dependent variable are spatially correlated, then errors in predictions of that variable are also likely to be interrelated across space, violating the OLS regression assumption that our error terms are uncorrelated across observations. Adjustments for this problem are termed "spatial error models." Second, if factors in one area (either dependent or independent variables) influence outcomes in a nearby area, we violate the OLS assumption of independence among observations. Adjustments for this problem are termed "spatial lag models." The first problem can lead to inefficient estimates while the second can lead to both inefficient estimates and biased estimators. To illustrate these models we show the degree to which variation in personal income among areas is predicted by our other two forms of spatial inequality, racial homogeneity (percent white) and occupational homogeneity (percent professional and managerial).

A queen first order matrix was used in all cases to model spatial interrelationships. Turning first to the statewide (global) comparisons in table 4.4, we see that county models have higher explained variance than do ZCTAs across all methods. ZCTAs are likely capturing variance in these dimensions of inequality across Pennsylvania that is aggregated out at the county level, and in these highly simplified models, less of this variance is explained. Of greater importance is that adjustments for spatial autocorrelation in the lag and error models dramatically increase explained variance for ZIP code geography and also increase R^2 in the county model.

In table 4.5, we view corresponding contrasts in OLS regression with both spatial lag and spatial error models, for each geographic unit in the Pittsburgh MA. Note first that both spatial models (error and lag) improve variance explained over the OLS models. Some of the variance associated with the relationships in these models is due to cross-unit effects. However, both spatial lag and error models increase explained variance equally. Turning to comparisons among the three geographic units, we see that, for spatial lag models, the lag coefficient is significant across all types of units, but highest (.55) for block groups. The equivalent statistics for spatial error, the error coefficient or lamda (.68), is also highest for block groups.

In general, spatial lag model estimates for percent white and percent professional and managerial employment are lowered by taking account of interplace influences. Spatial error model estimates for percent white are higher than OLS estimates for ZCTAs and block groups and about the same for tracts, while professional and managerial employment estimates are uniformly lower for spatial error models than for OLS models.

These very simple models certainly do not constitute an explanation of the spatial clustering (and thus spatial inequality) of personal income. However, they do illustrate that types of inequality are interrelated and that there are clear spatial patterns to these interrelationships. Inequality (as defined here) in one area leads to inequality in nearby areas. Further, taking account of these spatial patterns through spatial error and spatial lag models alters estimates from simple OLS inferences.

This finding echoes conclusions stated by Beggs et al. (1997:86) that failure to specify such spatial processes creates specification errors in models of spatial inequality that ultimately harm both theory and policy. The models used here are by no means sufficiently specified to thoroughly predict patterns of income inequality. However, the variations of estimates in tables 4.4 and 4.5 do illustrate how inference can change when spatial controls and underlying models of spatial relationships are included.

Similarly, the choice of geography leads to very different estimates and therefore inferences. Choice of ZCTAs as geographic units might lead a researcher to conclude that neighborhood racial characteristics and occupational characteristics had slight to moderate effects upon variation in neighborhood wealth. Using tracts or block groups leads one to conclude these factors are highly predictive of neighborhood income. Simply maximizing

TABLE 4.4

Global (State) Comparisons of Regressions of Personal Income on Percent White and Percent Professional/Managerial by County and ZCTA for Pennsylvania

Type of Unit	Variable	Coefficient	t-test	Probability	R-Sq	DF
County						
OLS	CONSTANT	−3286.18	−4.96	0.00	0.66	64
	Percent White	80.47	2.04	0.05		
	Percent Professional	791.55	10.35	0.00		
Spatial Lag (ML)	CONSTANT	−5174.60	−9.26	0.00	0.82	63
	Percent White	198.47	6.50	0.00		
	Percent Professional	667.78	11.71	0.00		
	Lag Coefficient	0.63	7.08	0.00		
Spatial Error (ML)	CONSTANT	−36659.53	−7.65	0.00	0.82	64
	Percent White	192.85	7.08	0.00		
	Percent Professional	615.75	10.76	0.00		
	Error Coefficient	0.80	10.76	0.00		

(continued on next page)

TABLE 4.4 (continued)

Type of Unit	Variable	Coefficient	t-test	Probability	R-Sq	DF
ZCTA						
OLS	CONSTANT	-2672.52	-2.87	0.08	0.19	1731
	Percent White	44.77	3.49	0.00		
	Percent Professional	297.85	19.66	0.00		
Spatial Lag (ML)	CONSTANT	-6662.11	-4.68	0.00	0.30	1730
	Percent White	60.13	5.07	0.00		
	Percent Professional	239.72	17.01	0.00		
	Lag Coefficient	0.33	15.86	0.00		
Spatial Error (ML)	CONSTANT	-1644.15	-1.07	0.28	0.36	1731
	Percent White	104.86	7.26	0.00		
	Percent Professional	177.71	12.38	0.00		
	Error Coefficient	0.51	22.44	0.00		

TABLE 4.5

Local (Metropolitan Area) Comparisons of Regressions of Personal Income on Percent White and Percent Professional/Managerial by ZCTA, Tract, and Block Group for Pittsburgh

Type of Unit	Variable	Coefficient	t-test	Probability	R-Sq	DF
ZCTA						
OLS	CONSTANT	−7666.76	−1.91	0.06	0.20	287
	Percent White	94.80	2.97	0.00		
	Percent Professional	299.24	8.50	0.00		
Spatial Lag (ML)	CONSTANT	−8496.74	−2.17	0.03	0.24	286
	Percent White	85.66	2.76	0.01		
	Percent Professional	272.36	7.93	0.00		
	Lag Coefficient	0.18	4.20	0.00		
Spatial Error (ML)	CONSTANT	−4421.90	−1.08	0.28	0.25	287
	Percent White	100.19	2.91	0.00		
	Percent Professional	227.26	6.31	0.00		
	Error Coefficient	0.45	7.83	0.00		
Tract						
OLS	CONSTANT	−31007.94	−15.96	0.00	0.50	699
	Percent White	145.28	14.50	0.00		
	Percent Professional	608.62	23.71	0.00		

(continued on next page)

TABLE 4.5 (continued)

Type of Unit	Variable	Coefficient	t-test	Probability	R-Sq	DF
Spatial Lag (ML)	CONSTANT	-2650.45	-15.16	0.00	0.61	698
	Percent White	106.85	11.24	0.00		
	Percent Professional	441.86	17.07	0.00		
	Lag Coefficient	0.47	12.91	0.00		
Spatial Error (ML)	CONSTANT	-21332.42	-9.48	0.00	0.61	699
	Percent White	145.15	10.87	0.00		
	Percent Professional	455.78	15.59	0.00		
	Error Coefficient	0.59	14.41	0.00		
Block Group						
OLS	CONSTANT	-23228.93	-19.30	0.00	0.41	1982
	Percent White	127.99	17.87	0.00		
	Percent Professional	510.23	33.58	0.00		
Spatial Lag (ML)	CONSTANT	-17599.70	-16.91	0.00	0.57	1981
	Percent White	81.00	12.42	0.00		
	Percent Professional	308.75	21.38	0.00		
	Lag Coefficient	0.55	25.72	0.00		
Spatial Error (ML)	CONSTANT	-9657.38	-6.49	0.00	0.57	1982
	Percent White	142.71	13.06	0.00		
	Percent Professional	273.35	16.30	0.00		
	Error Coefficient	0.68	31.08	0.00		

estimates and R^2 does not necessarily indicate a better explanation. If real underlying neighborhoods more closely follow ZCTA boundaries than tract or block group, then it may be true that these dimensions of inequality are weakly associated. Inference ultimately depends upon the concept of neighborhood (or community or region), and from that conception methodology proceeds.

CONCLUSIONS

The use of GIS for data retrieval and description and associated proliferation of spatial statistics has important implications for sociological research. Using geographic information systems necessitates a shift in focus from the spatial context of social organization to a more direct concern with sociospatial units themselves since these methods retrieve and analyze social data as characteristics of discrete spatial areas. These areas are census geographies in almost all sociological research. The utilization of these methods, extrinsically based upon the presentation of social organizational data in the form of actual geographic units, forces researchers to visually confront categories of social life as actual discrete, spatially bounded units. In doing so, the type of unit used and the underlying conceptions of social life attached to that unit are also confronted.

This chapter has shown that the use of territorial units inherently represents an attempt to conceptually bound social organization into spatial systems exhibiting unit character. As each type of unit represents the specific conceptual concerns of the researcher, each is based upon different assumptions about spatial unit character. Examination of the spatial boundaries and organization of these social units are important in order to develop concrete measures of social organization and explicate differences or similarities among them. As more researchers adopt GIS and related methods, and as they apply their methods to different substantive topics and make different theoretical assumptions about the elements constituting sociospatial units, interest in conceptual and methodological attributes of units will increase. Greater interrogation of the territories used to analyze inequality will enhance our fundamental understanding of space, place, and society.

REFERENCES

Alexander, John W. 1954. "The Basic Nonbasic Concept of Urban Economic Functions." *Economic Geography* 30:246–261.

Anselin, Luc. 2003. *GeoDa 0.9 User's Guide*. Spatial Analysis Laboratory (SAL). Department of Agricultural and Consumer Economics, University of Illinois, Urbana-Champaign, IL.

———. 2004. *GeoDa 0.95i Release Notes*. Spatial Analysis Laboratory (SAL). Department of Agricultural and Consumer Economics, University of Illinois, Urbana-Champaign, IL.

Anselin, Luc and A. Bera. 1998. "Spatial Dependence in Linear Regression Models with an Introduction to Spatial Econometrics." Pp. 237–289 in *Handbook of Applied Economic Statistics*, edited by A. Ullah and D. E. Giles. New York: Marcel Dekker.

Anselin, Luc, Ibnu Syabri, and Youngihn Kho. 2006. "GeoDa: An Introduction to Spatial Data Analysis." *Geographical Analysis* 38:5–22.

Beggs, John J., Wayne J. Villemez, and Ruth Arnold. 1997. "Black Population Concentration and Black-White Inequality: Expanding Consideration of Place and Space Effects." *Social Forces* 76:65–91.

Berry, Brian J. L. and Allan Pred. 1961. *Central Place Studies: A Bibliography of Theory and Applications*. Philadelphia, PA: Regional Studies Research Institute.

Burgess, Ernest W. 1925. "The Growth of the City: An Introduction to a Research Project." Pp. 47–62 in *The City*, edited by R. E. Park, E. W. Burgess, and R. D. McKenzie. Chicago: University of Chicago Press.

Butler, Margaret A. and Calvin L. Beale. 1994. *Rural-Urban Continuum Codes for Metro and Nonmetro Counties, 1993*. U.S. Department of Agriculture, Economic Research Service Staff Report No. 9425 (September). Beltsville, MD.

Castells, Manuel. 1989. *The Informational City: Information Technology, Economic Restructuring, and the Urban-Regional Process*. New York: Basil Blackwell.

Cooley, Charles H. 1894. "The Theory of Transportation." *Publications of the American Economic Association* 9:312–322.

Ellen, Ingrid Gould. 2000. *Sharing America's Neighborhoods: The Prospects for Stable Racial Integration*. Cambridge, MA: Harvard University Press.

Farley, Reynolds and and William Frey 1994. "Changes in the Segregation of Whites From Blacks During the 1980s: Small Steps Towards a More Integrated Sociology." *American Sociological Review* 59:23–45.

Fischer, Claude S., Gretchen Stockmayer, John Stiles, and Michael Hout. 2004. "Distinguishing the Geographic Levels and Social Dimensions of U.S. Metropolitan Segregation, 1960–2000." *Demography* 41:37–59.

Griffith, Daniel A. 2003. *Spatial Autocorrelation and Spatial Filtering: Gaining Understanding Through Theory and Scientific Visualization*. New York: Springer.

Haining, Robert. 1990. *Spatial Data Analysis in the Social and Environmental Sciences*. Cambridge, MA: Cambridge University Press.

Harris, C. D. and E. L. Ullman. 1945. "The Nature of Cities." *The Annals of the American Academy of Political and Social Science* 242:7–17.

Hawley, Amos H. 1950. *Human Ecology: A Theory of Community Structure*. New York: Ronald Press.

———. 1981. *Urban Society: An Ecological Approach*. New York: John Wiley and Sons.

———. 1986. *Human Ecology: A Theoretical Essay*. Chicago: University of Chicago Press.

Hoover, Edgar M. 1948. *The Location of Economic Activity*. New York: McGraw-Hill.

Jacobs, Jane. 1961. *The Death and Life of Great American Cities*. New York: Vintage.

Jargowsky, Paul. 1994. "Ghetto Poverty Among Blacks in the 1980s." *Journal of Policy Analysis and Management* 13:288–310.

Johnson, Kevin, Jay M. Ver Hoef, Konstantin Krivoruchko, and Neil Lucas. 2001. *Using ArcGIS Geostatistical Analyst*. Redlands, CA: ESRI.

Keller, Suzanne. 1968. *The Urban Neighborhood: A Sociological Perspective*. New York: Random House.

Lösch, August. 1938. "The Nature of Economic Regions." *Southern Economics Journal* 5:71–78.

Marx, Karl. [1867] 1977. *Capital*. Translated by Ben Fowkes. New York: Vintage.

McKenzie, Roderick D. 1927. "Spatial Distance and Community Organization Patterns." *Social Forces* 5:623–638.

McKenzie, Roderick D. 1933. *The Metropolitan Community*. New York: McGraw-Hill.

Mencken, F. Carson and Joachim Singelmann. 1998. "Socioeconomic Performance and Nonmetropolitan Areas During the 1980s." *Sociological Quarterly* 39:215–38.

Nielsen, Francois and Arthur S. Alderson. 1997. "The Kuznets Curve and the Great U-Turn: Income Inequality in U.S. Counties, 1970 to 1990." *American Sociological Review* 62:12–33.

Sorokin, Petirim and Carl C. Zimmerman. 1929. *Principles of Rural-Urban Sociology*. New York: Henry Holt and Co.

Tauber, Karl and Alma Tauber. 1965. *Negroes in Cities: Residential Segregation and Neighborhood Change*. Chicago: Aldine.

Tobler, Waldo. 1970. "A Computer Movie Simulating Urban Growth in the Detroit Region." *Economic Geography* 46:234–240.

Tolbert, Charles T., Thomas A. Lyson, and Michael D. Irwin. 1998. "Local Capitalism, Civic Engagement, and Socioeconomic Well-Being." *Social Forces* 102:401–428.

U.S. Census Bureau. 1994. *Geographic Areas Reference Manual (1990)*. Washington, DC: U.S. Department of Commerce.

———. 2002a. *Appendix A. Census 2000 Geographic Terms and Concepts*. Retrieved April 6, 2005 (http://www.census.gov/geo/www/tiger/glossry2.pdt).

———. 2002b. *Census 2000 Tabulation Geographic Entity Counts*. Retrieved April 6, 2005 (http://www.census.gov/geo/www/tallies/tallyindex.html).

———. 2002c. *Reference Resources for Understanding Census Bureau Geography*. Retrieved April 6, 2005 (http://www.census.gov/geo/www/reference.html).

———. 2002d. *Census 2000 Urban and Rural Classification*. Retrieved April 6, 2005 (http://www.census.gov/geo/www/ua/ua_2K.html).

———. 2004a *Census 2000 Statistical Areas Boundary Criteria*. Retrieved April 6, 2005 (http://www.census.gov/geo/www/psapage.html).

———. 2004b *U.S. Census Bureau's Guide to Census Tract Resources*. Retrieved April 6, 2005 (http://www.census.gov/geo/www/tractez.html).

———. 2004c. *Geographic Programs Involving Local Participation for Census 2000*. Retrieved April 6, 2005 (http://www.census.gov/geo/www/partnership.html).

Vance, Rupert B. and Sara S. Sutker. 1954. "Metropolitan Dominance and Integration." Pp. 114–132 in *The Urban South*, edited by R. B. Vance and N. J. Demereth. Chapel Hill, NC: The University of North Carolina Press.

Von Thünen, Johann H. [1826] 1966. *Von Thünen's Isolated State*. Translated by C. M. Watenburg. London: Pergamom Press Ltd.

Weber, Max. 1889. *Zur Geschichte der Handelsgesellshaften im Mittelalter [On the History of Trading Companies in the Middle Ages]*. Stuttgart, Germany: F. Enke.

Weber, Max. [1921] 1978a. "The City (Non-Legitimate Domination)." Pp. 1212–1372 in *Economy and Society: An Outline of Interpretive Sociology*, edited by G. Roth and C. Wittich. Translated by Ephraim Fischoff et al. 2 vols. Berkeley: University of California Press.

White, Michael J., 1987. *American Neighborhoods and Residential Differentiation*. New York: Russell Sage Foundation.

White, Michael J. and Peter R. Mueser. 1988. "Implications of Boundary Choice for the Measurement of Residential Mobility." *Demography* 25:443–459.

PART II

Studies of Spatial Inequality

FIVE

The Spatial Politics of Public Policy

Devolution, Development, and Welfare Reform

ANN R. TICKAMYER
JULIE ANNE WHITE
BARRY L. TADLOCK
DEBRA A. HENDERSON

AT THE END of the last century, the U.S. embarked on a large-scale social experiment to restructure the welfare system. The passage of the Personal Responsibility and Work Opportunity Reconciliation Act (PRWORA) by the U.S. Congress in 1996 marked an enormous shift in the institutional arrangements of social welfare policy, affecting the form and structure of the safety net, the relative power and autonomy of different political units, and of course, the fortunes of individuals, families, and communities who were the focus. Although the full meaning and impact of welfare reform is still unfolding, this massive restructuring of public policy provides social scientists, policy analysts, and policymakers with a rare opportunity to research the effects of this social experiment and its policy outcomes and implications. One particularly important component is relatively little scrutinized or understood—the role of spatial inequalities and their influence on public policy. In particular, the story of welfare reform is partly about its variable capacity to accomplish its goals across place and space. Its advent permits researchers to scrutinize the capacity for welfare reform in different geopolitical units across space and the construction of new forms of difference and inequality. Most importantly, it permits an assessment of an increasingly popular political theory underlying the decision to overhaul this safety net.

Here we briefly describe the history, theory, and politics of welfare reform as the background for examining how spatial inequality shapes the process and outcomes. We illustrate using results from a comparative case study of devolution and welfare reform in selected Ohio counties representing regional and rural-urban diversity. The example of welfare reform demonstrates the importance of scrutinizing spatial inequality in studying public policy by addressing a series of questions: How do places vary in their ability to implement welfare reform? What are the impacts of spatial variations on individuals, families, and communities within and across regions and the metro/nonmetro divide? How does devolution affect welfare reform outcomes and which political factors shape these results? Overall, what are the spatial politics of welfare reform policy? We focus on the *spatial politics* of welfare reform because intriguing contradictions, ironies, and lessons exist for both the study of poverty, social welfare policy, and the processes of spatial inequality, and because few studies have looked at the conjunction of the two topics.

THE RESTRUCTURED WELFARE SYSTEM

The two primary components of welfare reform were to move welfare recipients from cash assistance into paid employment and to replace federal authority with "local control." Thus PRWORA marked the end of long-standing entitlement programs guaranteeing access to public assistance for all means qualified recipients, substituting time-limited cash assistance combined with incentives to encourage self-sufficiency through labor force attachment. The primary program of cash assistance, Aid to Families with Dependent Children (AFDC), was replaced with TANF (Temporary Assistance to Needy Families), with emphasis on "temporary," creating a maximum lifetime eligibility of five years. The power to design, implement, and administer new programs was devolved to state and local governments, including the power to set more stringent requirements and time limits than PRWORA specified.

These changes were the culmination of two political trends. There was broad popular support for the view that the welfare system created a series of moral hazards for poor people that included dependency and deviance at public expense. There was also growing belief that federal control over the welfare system was a failure and that more local forms of control would result in more efficient and effective programs that could be tailored to local needs and would be more democratic. Devolution is part of a larger political movement—New Federalism, a strand of neoliberal political theory seeking to downsize government, reduce its jurisdiction through deregulation and privatization, and substitute market forces and voluntary action for government mandates (Conlan 1998; Lobao and Hooks 2003).

Debate about welfare reform generally ignored spatial variation although these have long been a hallmark of both the distribution of poverty and the generosity of the safety net (Soss et al. 2001). Nevertheless, deep-seated spatial assumptions lurked behind the political discourse. For example, substantial evidence exists that in popular perception, poverty means urban ghetto poverty associated primarily with African Americans and other race and ethnic minorities. Further, the stigma attached to welfare and the aversion to supporting safety-net programs that provided the impetus for welfare reform arises partly from the coded racism embedded in these views (Schram, Soss, and Fording 2003; Weir 1999).

Similarly, the national and urban bias of welfare reform policy is manifest in the lack of attention to spatial variation in the numerous impact studies attempting to assess its success or failure (CLASP 2001; Jones et al. 2003; Loprest 1999; Moffitt 2002). There are studies that document state differences in policy and program formation (Burt, Pindus, and Capizzano 2000; Lieberman and Shaw 2000; Nathan and Gais 2001; Soss et al. 2001), but little effort has been made to determine whether spatial factors influence outcomes. Some national-level research distinguishes between metropolitan and nonmetropolitan locations where differences are few, most likely because of the lack of adequate geographic detail (Lichter and Jayakody 2002; Weber et al. 2002). The metro/nonmetro distinction obscures variation within each of these categories, most notably the difference between central city and suburban locations and between adjacent and nonadjacent rural locations.

The most comprehensive review of existing studies either permitting finer geographic distinction or comparing research conducted in different locations shows that the biggest differences are not between rural and urban or metro and nonmetro but between disadvantaged places within metro and nonmetro places compared to more affluent areas in each. Specifically, central cities and nonadjacent rural counties share similar problems in contrast to suburban and adjacent rural counties (Fisher and Weber 2002). Limited evidence suggests caseload declines have occurred disproportionately in the suburban areas with cases becoming more concentrated in central urban places and rural counties (Katz and Allen 2001; Weber 2001). Residents of both remote rural and central city locations groups face similar barriers to employment including lack of jobs, transportation, and child care (Fisher and Weber 2002). Numerous questions remain about spatial variation in devolution and welfare reform outcomes.

Both implicitly in the emphasis on devolution as one of the components of the restructured system and explicitly in the claims that local control would end a top-down, "one size fits all" approach to public policy, the potential for spatial difference was incorporated into welfare reform legislation. Yet, somewhat paradoxically, spatial variation in what is an inherently spatial process receives little systematic scrutiny. Thus, to what extent devolution actually fulfills this expectation remains an open question as are the degree and forms of spatial variation. The result is a contradiction between the politics and the actual outcomes of welfare reform. On the one hand, public policy was and is debated and formulated on a national basis with a strong urban bias. On the other, these debates were partly a response to a spatialized political landscape with devolution supplying both a rationale and a means to reinforce and recreate spatial difference and inequalities.

SPATIAL INEQUALITIES:
A COMPARATIVE CASE STUDY APPROACH

Most subnational research adopts a "society-in-place" approach and focuses on regional variation, urban problems, or global comparisons of metropolitan and nonmetropolitan locales. While the use of ecological units such as cities, counties, and labor markets spanning the entire nation or subsuming very broad territorial and geographic designations, such as metro-nonmetro or south-nonsouth, is an improvement over analyses that ignore spatial variation, these analyses remain limited in their ability to identify and explain patterns of spatial inequality. The need to use ecological units for which comparable data are already available or can be generated places severe constraints on both the geography and the processes that can be scrutinized. Results confirm broad variation and patterns in spatial inequalities, but the limits on units and measures are as likely to hide as much as they illuminate.

Alternatively, the "place-in-society" approach—place-based case studies—emphasizes the contextual meaning of particular locales, both as formative influences on local social and economic well-being or as a means to uncover the social construction of place itself. Case studies focusing on the characteristics of a particular place, the historical development of local social structure and process, and the changing fortunes of a place and its inhabitants are a long tradition in social science research and help illuminate the way that local patterns of inequality are constructed and maintained. Studies of regional identity, culture, political economy, and livelihood practices (Billings and Blee 2000; Duncan 1999; Falk, Schulman, and Tickamyer 2003; Lyson and Falk 1993) demonstrate the ways that local systems and processes of inequality are produced and reproduced. This focus on local place, however, has limited application and less generalizability for understanding variation across space.

Although examples of mixed models exist, researchers interested in spatial inequalities have typically opted for either large-scale aggregate approaches or small-scale case studies. The former are dependent on the vagaries of existing data collected for administrative units designed for historical and political purposes not necessarily coinciding with theoretically generated hypotheses. The latter are dependent on the possibly interesting but ultimately idiosyncratic details of specific local histories and the ensuing difficulties of sorting larger lessons from the particular configuration. This choice mirrors the conceptual distinction between space and place, with "space" representing the abstraction of territorial units that can be compared in scale and characteristics and "place" representing the particular locale or setting with ensuing geography, material form, and meaning (Gieryn 2000; Tickamyer 2000). Researchers can use spatial units as a proxy for other processes such as industrial structures, creating settings that bundle other variables to examine their relationships, or they can focus on the construction, meanings, and outcomes of particular locales with their emphasis on local history and development.

As a means of bridging these different approaches to the meaning and analysis of spatial processes, we advocate greater use of case comparative methods combining place and space. This requires carefully selected place-based case studies in a comparative framework permitting systematic examination of similarities and differences in structures, processes, and practices of interest, using subnational units either exclusively or embedded within larger regions as the units of analysis. While quite prevalent in cross-national and urban research—robust traditions of research exist on social and economic inequality in a variety of venues including historical comparative studies of economic development (and underdevelopment), urban research, globalization, and the emerging study of its urban centers—and to a lesser extent in rural and community research, the case comparative approach is less common for other subnational units. These studies have identified key variations in processes and outcomes for constructing, maintaining, and (to a lesser extent) dismantling spatial inequalities. We argue for the importance of place in explaining spatial inequality, but with emphasis on systematic comparisons across places. Without place, studies of spatial inequality become yet one more example of the tendency to totalize, globalize, and universalize social relations, except that they substitute aggregate units for individuals. Without a comparative approach, place-based studies remain a local narrative.

WELFARE REFORM IN OHIO

To address questions about spatial inequalities in the implementation, impacts, and politics of welfare reform, we draw on multi-year case comparative research on the impacts of welfare reform in selected Ohio communities. Ohio presents an interesting site for case studies of welfare reform. First, it is generally viewed as a highly urbanized, industrial state; in fact, its 88 counties run the gamut from urban rust belt in the north through midwestern agrarian to a region of Appalachian poverty and economic distress in the southeast, the focus of this study. Second, Ohio is one of 13 states to devolve responsibility for welfare reform directly to the county, permitting scrutiny of local variation in the politics and implementation of welfare reform. In this paper we investigate the spatial politics of welfare reform, looking at how decisions were made and responded to across space and place, focusing on both rural/urban and Appalachian/non-Appalachian comparisons.

This research analyzes data collected in ten Ohio counties—four in Appalachian and six in non-Appalachian counties. The data include existing statistics, participation and observations in state and local activities related to welfare reform over a four-year period, and both quantitative and qualitative primary data collection from a multitude of sources (see Tickamyer et al. 2000, 2002, 2003; White et al. 2003). The research originated as a longitudinal study of the impact of welfare reform in Appalachian Ohio, a twenty-nine-county region in southeastern Ohio characterized historically by high poverty and unemployment rates, low levels of human capital and economic development, isolation from larger labor markets, and a lack of infrastructure capable of attracting new investment. After collecting baseline data on employment, poverty, and case loads and interviewing the county directors of the human service agencies for all 29 counties, we selected for more intensive scrutiny four counties representing similar levels of poverty and underdevelopment, but varying degrees of rurality and institutional capacity of local government structures and agencies. Counties are the appropriate unit for this type of study since in Ohio they serve as the primary administrative unit for local government and services. In fact, they have a dual role as the administrative arm of the state and a locally elected government to respond to local issues (Tadlock et al. 2005). Even in heavily urban areas of the largest metropolitan centers with an overlapping city government, the county is the primary provider of social services.

We conducted interviews, surveys, and focus groups with recipients, local employers, case managers, county commissioners, and other key informants beginning in 1999 and extending to the present. In the spring and summer of 2002, we added six non-Appalachian counties—two large urban counties, two suburban counties, and two rural counties—to extend our comparisons beyond rural and Appalachian places. We interviewed Directors of Jobs and Family Services, county commissioners, and key informants among nonprofit providers of social services and conducted focus groups with case managers in the six non-Appalachian counties to match data collected in the original case study area. While the data from the non-Appalachian counties cannot match the breadth or provide the longitudinal depth of the data from the original counties, they enable us to make more extensive cross-region comparisons.

FINDINGS

A number of themes emerge from this research demonstrating the inherent spatiality of devolution and welfare reform as well as specific rural-urban and regional effects. In particular, our results address issues of whether devolution actually provides greater local responsiveness and control; whether county variation in capacity to implement welfare reform is associated with different spatial characteristics and locations; and whether responses and impacts reflect both rural-urban and regional differences. Additionally, the focus on ethnographic detail illustrates the specific ways these differences are manifested.

Devolution: Rhetoric Versus Reality of Local Control

The ostensible purpose of devolution to the states and, in the case of Ohio, to the counties was to provide the flexibility and local knowledge to appropriately design and target programs to community needs (Adams and Wilson 2000). One purpose of this research was to determine whether devolution actually increases local control. In our initial interviews very early in the process with the directors of the county human service agencies in the Appalachian region (now Directors of Job and Family Services, DJFS, after a reorganization of the state welfare bureaucracy), most directors were highly positive about prospects for welfare reform (Tickamyer et al. 2002) and particularly gratified by the flexibility and increased resources available to design and implement new programs. This result spanned all counties and directors interviewed, although there was considerable variation in what they actually did with newly available resources. The most innovative and successful in capturing state monies were the higher capacity counties. Three years later, there was also a uniform response, but this time it was characterized by disillusionment, pessimism, and cynicism about current and future prospects for welfare reform. In the interim, the state had reneged on promises of recurring resources for local programs, cut spending, removed much of the former flexibility in programming, and reverted to a system of earmarked funds for programs viewed as either unnecessary or inferior to local versions that could no longer be supported. The prevailing views are expressed by DJFS directors:

> I was optimistic. I realize we have a large job. The silver bullet or part of the success I was hopeful for was not a developed piece. I thought that if you put money in a development and had a community effort and you did all the right things locally that you could convince people at the state level of the worth of making decisions to try to enhance this region and this county in particular. I am not optimistic today about this.
>
> . . . and more and more often when they allocate funds to us they're saying this is how it has to be spent and they're saying, . . . you have to modify your locally-designed program to say what we want it to say. Which virtually means it's not, I mean I just laugh at 'em and say why don't you just send us the money, send us the rules, why even go through the charade of having a local program, you know, a local plan if you dictate to us what has to be in it.

Similarly,

> it's like . . . the emperor has no clothes. Nobody is . . . willing to go
> around and talk about what the reality, the hard realities of this whole situ-
> ation is. Welfare reform is dead. We just haven't got it buried. And that is
> sad. It is dead.

Others referred to the "awful joke," "charade," and the "schizophrenia"
of the state's approach to local control. Directors varied in their interpretations of why the state backed away from the early promises of devolution and
welfare reform. Some thought it merely a byproduct of fiscal crisis and competing pressing political agendas, especially an unresolved school funding
issue that took budget priority. Others believed the state was deliberately
backing away from devolution (even as they took credit for innovative programming from county agencies in congressional testimony) because it felt
threatened by the loss of power and budget control. Either way, whereas previously directors and county commissioners celebrated (or in some cases wor-
ried about) their ability to program creatively and flexibly, they now
bemoaned the loss of autonomy and reversion to prewelfare reform kinds of
earmarks, red tape, and shortage of resources.

SPATIAL DIFFERENCES

While there was consistency across locales in embracing increased local control brought by devolution and then mourning its loss, both the initial expectations and the subsequent reactions had a spatial interpretation and
response, shaped by the politics of region and place in the state. In the interviews with directors, employers, and county commissioners in 1999, still relatively early in welfare reform implementation, there was general agreement
that state and federal policymakers did not understand the needs of rural
communities and had a long history of misunderstanding or ignoring the
needs of Appalachia. The general views were expressed by one commissioner
when he stated,

> a lot of the policies are geared towards the poor urban areas rather than
> the poor rural areas, and I think that's what they deal with because there's
> more people in those areas and . . . Appalachia—in general in our area I
> think there's a misconception and a misunderstanding of a lot of people
> where the dollars should go and how they should be spent. . . .

Similarly, in the words of one human service director, "I don't think they
really address the needs of the Appalachian area when they come up with
these policies. . . ." This lack of political attention made devolution attractive.

Since we did not initially collect data outside the Appalachian Ohio
region, it is not possible to compare these views across the regional boundary

to determine if other areas had similar views about lack of concern for their special problems or even if they perceived other regions to have particular issues. However, in the follow-up interviews with DJFS directors, county commissioners, and even in the focus groups with case workers beyond Appalachian counties, distinct differences in the political response to the retraction of devolutionary power were evident. All regretted its loss. All discussed the various practical measures they had to take including cutting programs, eliminating subcontracted services, reorganizing staff work loads, and, in some few cases, letting personnel go; however, their political responses differed.

In the Appalachian region, directors spoke about the intra-organizational measures they were forced to take, their relations with the county commissioners who were their supervisors, and their relations with various community leaders and officials and even public opinion in general. With one exception, they rarely spoke about larger political action even when directly pressed about what message they would take to the state capital (Columbus) and Washington about welfare reform. They addressed these questions in generalities about maintaining flexibility and funding levels and, more pointedly, about the need to restrain the state from diverting federal TANF funds to other state needs such as educational equity. Only one Appalachian director discussed any larger political response. A director in a high-capacity county from the four-case-study counties indicated a desire to join the lawsuit brought by an urban county against the state's diversion of TANF dollars. This same director organized a meeting of other regional agency directors and officials with the congressional representative for many of the counties in the area. In general, however, there was resigned frustration at their lack of political voice in state politics. In the words of an Appalachian county DJFS director,

> I am just a dumb ole hillbilly, but I can't figure this one out. I am better off trying to communicate with Charleston, West Virginia, than I am Columbus, Ohio. Probably have more success because they will take the time to return my phone call.

This contrasts with the responses of directors in non-Appalachian counties, especially the urban and suburban counties we studied. In these counties, directors invoked their meetings and relationships with various state officials, including the governor, various state legislators, and state level department heads:

> We've supplied both the White House, the office of Department of Health and Human Services at the federal level, the Ohio Department of Job and Family Services as well as our two senators and now we're beginning to work on the congressional delegation with our views on TANF reauthorization.

The comparison with the one meeting with the congressional representative in the Appalachian counties is particularly striking since agency officials' complaints were primarily with the state, giving the congressman little that he could do or promise other than to hear them out. The city with the largest welfare caseload, Cleveland in Cuyahoga County, initiated the lawsuit mentioned above. Political action was directed outward to a much greater extent than in the Appalachian counties.

ACCOUNTABILITY: RESPONSIVENESS TO LOCAL NEEDS

Regional differences are also found in the politics of implementing welfare reform and in client response. Local control in our study counties was always more geared toward elite views of local needs than targeted populations (White et al. 2003). Despite state mandates for county plans for welfare reform to include input from citizens and "consumers of family services," there was very little of the former and virtually none of the latter. The planning process either bypassed citizen input or was unable to generate grassroots interest. Instead, it was largely a technocratic undertaking dominated by human service agency directors and officials and county commissioners, with some technical assistance from the state and from public policy institutes. In the words of a DJFS director,

> We decided that it was important for us to sample public response and participant response in the programs and . . . to try to get ideas. So, about two-and-a-half years ago we started a series of community forums that we held in different parts of the county. . . . And through those community forums which essentially amounted to focus groups that provided some dinner and an opportunity for people, some participants and some community leaders to. . . . When I say community I mean neighborhood leaders to sit down with us and tell us not only what they thought about our agency but what they thought they needed our agency to do in the community, and we've continued those forums in different parts of the county.

The result was a strong belief among elites that the programs implemented truly met local needs, a belief not shared by the targeted population.

Interviews spanning a three-year period with recipients and former recipients from the four county study make it clear that although they support the goals of welfare reform and find positive outcomes in the push for employment, few think the process has been responsive to their needs or those of their communities (Henderson et al. 2002). Areas of disagreement include adequacy of service provision for child care and transportation, as well as the lack of responsiveness of caseworkers to the particular difficulties encountered on a day-to-day basis. Finally, in no county was the human service agency ombudsperson (also a state mandate) someone drawn from the community or from the client pool. In some cases, directors seemed unfamiliar with how this position was filled; most indicated it was an agency staff member.

Again, we don't have comparable early or recipient data from outside the Appalachian region, but our data from agency personnel, community providers, and county officials in the non-Appalachian comparison counties make it appear that there is greater citizen and client involvement in planning, monitoring, and exchanging information in the more urban counties and in the non-Appalachian region, in general. Certainly, circumstantial evidence exists of greater exchange of information among recipients in the urban sites. A common theme among agency personnel was that clients had better knowledge of agency rules and regulations than they did and were even quicker to transmit changes to their networks, sometimes preceding caseworkers in their information about these impending changes. Additionally, the urban counties have a wide array of advocacy agencies ranging from state-supported legal services to various voluntary organizations monitoring agency operations and client rights. Comparable organizations are rare or nonexistent in the poorest rural Appalachian counties, which may count themselves lucky to have a single food pantry.

LOCAL VARIABILITY: DIFFERENCES IN CAPACITY AND RESOURCES

Assessing local capacity is difficult and probably inherently somewhat tautological, especially if the purpose is to juxtapose this measure against outcomes both reflecting and defining capacity. Nevertheless, spatial variation is fundamental to this research, both within and across the regional divide defined by Appalachian and non-Appalachian location. Initially, we selected the Appalachian counties to represent different capacities on the basis of their leadership, human and social capital, levels of infrastructure, and economic development. The small metro county and the formerly rural adjacent, now micropolitan, county are relatively high capacity. They are larger and more urbanized, their agencies are larger, and they have greater local infrastructure as well as human and social capital to draw on, including a larger employment base, institutions of higher education, a better educated population, and more experienced and credentialed leadership. The non-Appalachian counties were also selected to reflect an array of urban, suburban, and rural locations.

As might be expected, larger, more urbanized counties in both regions are wealthier, have lower poverty and unemployment rates, and have higher household incomes. Their agencies are generally larger with more staff, the directors have at least a college education and frequently post-graduate degrees, and there are substantial numbers of social service agencies in the county in addition to state welfare agencies. Table 5.1 shows selected population characteristics and welfare statistics for all ten counties. Comparisons of the ten counties on basic population and socioeconomic factors show

TABLE 5.1
Characteristics of Appalachian and Non-Appalachian Counties[a]

	Appalachian				Non-Appalachian						
	Washington	Athens	Meigs	Vinton	Cuyahoga	Hamilton	Butler	Geauga	Ashland	Knox	Ohio
Beale Code[b]	3	4	6	9	1	1	1	1	4	6	NA
Population	63,251	62,223	23,072	12,806	1,393,845	845,303	332,807	90,895	52,523	54,500	11,353,140
Median household income ($1000)	$33.4	$29.0	$25.2	$26.7	$36.8	$38.8	$43.5	$52.4	$36.4	$34.0	$41.0
Average household size (number of people)	2.45	2.40	2.47	2.59	2.39	2.38	2.61	2.84	2.58	2.56	2.49
Number in poverty	7,002	14,728	4,506	2,529	185,790	94,440	25,175	4,523	4,188	5,195	1,170,698
Percent in poverty	12.3	19.1	20.4	18.7	13.6	11.4	8.1	5.0	8.1	10.1	10.6
Percent of female-headed households with children under 18 in poverty	44.6	47.0	55.2	50.7	36.4	35.3	27.5	16.7	34.4	36.5	34.6
Percent of female-headed households with children under 5 in poverty	64.1	60.5	82.4	62.2	49.8	49.7	43.1	29.2	53.9	46.8	49.2

(continued on next page)

TABLE 5.1 (continued)

	Appalachian				Non-Appalachian						Ohio
	Washington	Athens	Meigs	Vinton	Cuyahoga	Hamilton	Butler	Geauga	Ashland	Knox	
Percent with less than high school degree	11.6	12.8	18.6	20.3	13.9	12.8	12.3	7.3	11.8	12.4	12.6
Percent with high school degree or GED only	43.0	34.2	46.6	47.6	30.0	27.8	33.6	28.1	47.0	42.1	36.1
Employment rate (percent in labor force)	61.6	56.9	54.6	55.7	62.5	65.5	66.6	68.2	64.7	64.2	64.8
Percent employed in service sector	14.3	18.5	15.7	10.8	13.9	14.3	12.6	11.0	13.8	14.6	14.6
Unemployment rate (percent)	4.6	11.1	10.0	9.0	4.6	3.5	3.2	3.2	4.1	4.9	5
2000–2001 PRCDR ($ millions)[c]	9.34	12.02	3.41	1.25	180.75	56.58	26.15	1.73	2.02	3.12	296.37
PRCDR funds per capita	$147.71	$193.20	$147.83	$97.51	$129.68	$66.93	$78.57	$19.07	$38.38	$57.23	$26.35
PRCDR funds per person in poverty	$1,334.33	$816.24	$756.95	$493.75	$972.87	$599.11	$1,038.67	$383.18	$481.31	$600.39	$255.49

[a] All data from http://quickfacts.census.gov (Census 2000) unless otherwise noted
[b] Source: http://www.ers.usda.gov/Data/RuralUrbanContinuumCodes
[c] Source: http://www.ohio.gov/odjfs/owf/prc/prcdr_vol01.pdf

striking differences across them, with Appalachian counties having almost uniformly more depressed economic indicators than any of the others, whether rural or urban and regardless of indicator—income, poverty, employment, or other.

One of the innovative aspects of welfare reform and devolution in Ohio was the program of Prevention, Retention, and Contingency Development Reserve (PRCDR) that was the primary source of discretionary funds for county human service agencies. For an eighteen-month period in 2000 and 2001, large sums of money were made available by the state (from federal TANF monies) for counties to use to advance goals of welfare reform, including reducing assistance rolls and moving recipients from welfare to work. Counties had great discretion in both the amounts and uses for these funds, and wide variation exists in both allocations and programming. Table 5.1 shows the total amounts of PRCDR funds allocated to each county. As might be expected, there are huge differences in the amounts reported for the largest metropolitan counties with both large populations and large numbers of poor persons, including urban Cuyahoga and Hamilton and suburban Butler. If these funds are adjusted for population and for poverty population, however, differences are muted and patterns discernable.

First, the counties with the highest per capita expenditures are two Appalachian counties: Washington and Athens, the high capacity counties. Even Vinton County with the lowest figure in the region exceeds all but Cuyahoga County. On the other hand, adjusted for size of poverty population, there is less clear distinction both between and within the two regions, with Vinton, Ashland, and Geauga having the lowest figures and both regions showing a substantial range between lowest and highest.

Part of this difference comes from difference in uses for these funds. Table 5.2 reports PRCDR allocations in five categories: employment services, family services, domestic violence programs, emergency funds, and community/economic development efforts. Interesting differences emerge. In Appalachian counties the largest percentage is used for family services, compared to employment in the non-Appalachian counties. The figures are almost exactly reversed in the two regions. Emergency funds are also a smaller amount in the Appalachian region (5.73 percent compared to 11.39 percent). On the other hand, a much larger proportion of these monies is allocated to economic development in the Appalachian counties (15 percent versus 5 percent). These differences remain when comparing only rural counties across regions—neither of the rural non-Appalachian counties uses any of these monies for economic development initiatives compared to the relatively large allocation found in the Appalachian counties.

Within the Appalachian region, differences also emerge. In particular, the two most rural counties have a higher allocation to employment and somewhat less to family or emergency services than Washington and Athens. All counties have high investment in economic development, with Athens, the most anomalous county, having the lowest percentage.

To further investigate these differences we compared adjusted expenditures of PRCDR funds by region (Appalachian/non-Appalachian) and by type (rural/urban/suburban) for the ten counties in the study. Figure 5.1 shows that the four Appalachian counties average higher per capita and per poverty population expenditures than the six non-Appalachian counties, and both study areas exceed Ohio averages. Figure 5.2 makes the same comparison for rural, urban, and suburban counties. The two urban counties have higher averages, followed by the six rural counties. The two suburban counties in the study average smaller adjusted expenditures.

Figures 5.3 and 5.4 display the same comparisons for each category of PRCDR funds. These figures illustrate the previous findings of different patterns of fund allocation by place. Among the noteworthy differences are the larger amounts spent on community and economic development in Appalachian and rural counties, and the higher levels of family services in rural, suburban, and Appalachian counties compared to higher employment funds in urban and non-Appalachian locations.

During this time there were large decreases in caseloads for cash assistance in all counties, ranging from 9 to 88 percent reductions and averaging 70.5 percent in Appalachian counties compared to a 50 percent decrease in the other six counties (data not shown). These results confirm the nearly universal finding that welfare reform has had a dramatic impact in reducing assistance rolls, but beyond the regional difference there are no obvious patterns. County variations may reflect differences in policies, administration, or economic environment, all factors emerging in the interviews and focus groups with different groups involved in welfare reform, but none clearly associated with spatial factors.

There are so many reasons for caseload changes, ranging from recipients successfully finding jobs to aggressive sanctioning and case-closing among agency personnel, that it is not possible to draw definitive conclusions from these numbers. However, interviews with recipients in the Appalachian counties spanning a three-year period, starting from before they reached the end of their eligibility until after they no longer qualified for public assistance, suggest differences between counties within this region. Recipients from the two higher capacity counties had a better record of finding and keeping employment than those from the more rural, remote counties. These data are not available for the non-Appalachian counties, although the information collected from interviews and focus groups with agency personnel, county officials, and key informants suggest availability of employment was less an issue in these counties than other barriers, most notability client problems ranging from disabilities to substance abuse.

TABLE 5.2
Prevention, Retention, and Contingency (PRC) and Development Reserve (PRCDR) Funding for 2000–2001

	Employment	Family Services	Domestic Violence	Emergency	Community/ Economic Development	Geographic Area Total
Ohio	$337,567,670	$248,331,384	$8,033,216	$67,882,502	$33,432,666	$695,247,438
Percent of state funds	48.55%	35.72%	1.16%	9.76%	4.81%	100%
Washington	$1,517,345	$5,564,663	$29,600	$523,644	$1,707,705	$9,342,957
Percent of county funds	16.24%	59.56%	0.32%	5.60%	18.28%	100%
Athens	$2,812,000	$6,925,239	$0	$836,000	$1,448,293	$12,021,532
Percent of county funds	23.39%	57.61%	0.00%	6.95%	12.05%	100%
Meigs	$1,077,959	$1,721,850	$0	$96,000	$515,000	$3,410,809
Percent of county funds	31.60%	50.48%	0.00%	2.81%	15.10%	100%
Vinton	$390,000	$570,872	$13,000	$36,000	$238,830	$1,248,702
Percent of county funds	31.23%	45.72%	1.04%	2.88%	19.13%	100%
Appalachian County Total	$5,797,304	$14,782,624	$42,600	$1,491,644	$3,909,828	$26,024,000
Percent of counties (4) funds	22.28%	56.80%	0.16%	5.73%	15.02%	100%

(continued on next page)

TABLE 5.2 (continued)

	Employment	Family Services	Domestic Violence	Emergency	Community/ Economic Development	Geographic Area Total
Cuyahoga	$98,350,501	$46,134,939	$185,000	$27,078,719	$9,001,125	$180,750,284
Percent of county funds	54.41%	25.52%	0.10%	14.98%	4.98%	100%
Hamilton	$38,495,444	$14,183,160	$0	$1,142,117	$2,758,964	$56,579,685
Percent of county funds	68.04%	25.07%	0.00%	2.02%	4.88%	100%
Butler	$12,318,875	$10,979,142	$6,000	$1,850,000	$994,394	$26,148,411
Percent of county funds	47.11%	41.99%	0.02%	7.07%	3.80%	100%
Geauga	$781,660	$883,475	$0	$45,000	$23,000	$1,733,135
Percent of county funds	45.10%	50.98%	0.00%	2.60%	1.33%	100%
Ashland	$610,672	$1,327,068	$0	$78,000	$0	$2,015,740
Percent of county funds	30.30%	65.84%	0.00%	3.87%	0.00%	100%
Knox	$1,993,229	$534,783	$0	$591,000	$0	$3,119,012
Percent of county funds	63.91%	17.15%	0.00%	18.95%	0.00%	100%
Non-Appalachian County Total	$152,550,381	$74,042,567	$191,000	$30,784,836	$12,777,483	$270,346,267
Percent of counties (6) funds	56.43%	27.39%	0.07%	11.39%	4.73%	100%

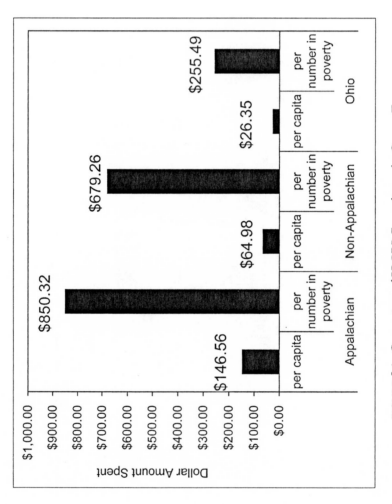

FIGURE 5.1. Comparison of PRCDR Expenditures by County Type

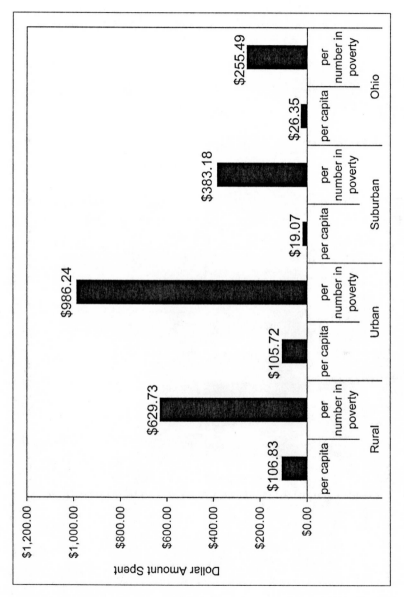

FIGURE 5.2. Comparison of PRCDR Expenditures by Rural-Urban Continuum Codes

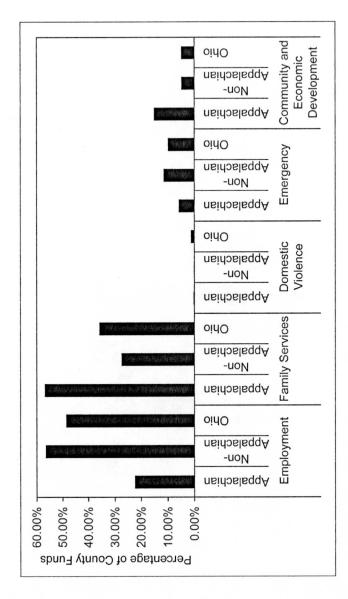

FIGURE 5.3. Comparison of PRCDR Fund Distribution by Appalachian and Non-Appalachian Counties

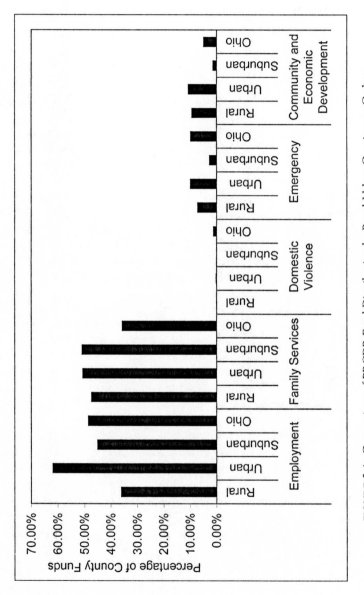

FIGURE 5.4. Comparison of PRCDR Fund Distribution by Rural-Urban Continuum Codes

ECONOMIC DEVELOPMENT AS A RESPONSE TO SPATIAL INEQUALITY

One distinct difference across counties we did not anticipate is the way economic development became incorporated into welfare reform in rural Appalachian counties. The biggest problem of the poorest, most rural and remote counties is the lack of jobs and the even greater scarcity of stable, living-wage jobs with benefits. Therefore, when money was plentiful in the initial stages of welfare reform, and even after funds dried up, many counties emphasized the importance of economic development as part of their mission and devoted a portion of their flexible spending to economic development efforts that might result in new jobs. While such efforts are quite common among rural counties (Dewees et al. 2003), they are a substantial departure from the traditional mission of human service agencies, yet many directors and county officials enthusiastically embraced this task. In fact, as resources and flexibility disappeared and it appeared to many directors that the window of opportunity that initially opened in welfare reform was closing, this was the one area they still pointed to with some pride and optimism, in some cases going so far as to say it was their major source of current job satisfaction. Few of the non-Appalachian and urban officials displayed much interest in economic development efforts, although counties varied in terms of whether they actually allocated resources for this task. For one thing, they did not perceive job availability to be a problem, and at least until very recently it has not been in their communities. Additionally, there are many more specific agencies and avenues for dealing with job creation. Urban officials were much more concerned with client problems such as substance abuse, mental illness, emotional instability, and lack of skills. All except the last item (which was the focus of intense concern among most human service agencies) are problems occasionally referred to among Appalachian agency personnel, but with much less frequency than the structural problems facing their communities and clients.

If we examine variation within the Appalachian study counties, an interesting difference emerges here as well. In the high capacity counties, directors were more concerned with workforce development than economic development. Again, this probably reflects the realities of the available opportunities and employment resources in high versus low capacity counties.

SPATIAL POLITICS OF WELFARE REFORM

Welfare reform has decreased the welfare rolls, but has not necessarily addressed poverty or the needs of the poor, including a growing body of working poor (Blakeslee 2000). This sentiment is equally found in Ohio counties as voiced by food pantry operators who have seen an enormous increase in the demand for their services:

Three years ago the primary reason why someone came in was basically a sort of, was either zero income or some sort of family catastrophe: a fire or death, some other thing you know. Or something as stupid as the refrigerator broke, and that was what we mostly were organized around. Now, what we're doing is we're beginning to see people five, six times a year. And those people are primarily coming in because they simply can't live on what they can earn on their jobs, part-time or otherwise. . . . I attribute that mostly to welfare reform as well you might imagine.

The problem this year revolves around the working poor. Welfare reform has driven up the numbers of people that we're supporting with food.

The prevailing view is summed up by a key informant:

I think it [welfare reform] has failed us terribly. It's gotten people off the rolls, but at what expense? Where are these people? What's the tracking of these folks? There is none. We have less involvement with families. Now you don't know what's happening to those children. It's like now there's hardly any contact with some families and that's not good. That's not good at all. So I see that as a failure because that caseworker isn't going out and saying, "How are you feeding your two children now that you're not getting food stamps?"

These views are most dramatically voiced in rural and Appalachian counties facing numerous structural barriers to making successful welfare-to-work transitions, ranging from lack of jobs to the lack of basic social supports necessary to make employment possible, such as transportation and child care. These problems were clearly seen at a time when the economy was still in a period of expansion, offering little hope for the subsequent period of stagnation, rising unemployment, and state and local budget crises.

The experiment with devolution has wider implications beyond debates about the success or failure of welfare reform to reduce welfare rolls, increase employment, and reduce poverty. The mixed experiences of poor rural communities in managing a devolved welfare system demonstrate a spatial politics to devolution not widely acknowledged despite the fact that devolution is precisely about the politics of local jurisdictions and is justified by the goal of increasing democratic participation and accountability via local control.

In fact, the implication that devolution creates democratic participation is belied by the experience with devolving welfare reform to the states and in this study to the counties. First, there are clearly serious political obstacles to larger, more powerful administrative entities relinquishing control as evidenced by the state's backing off many of its early promises and practices to the counties. Interestingly, there appears to be some similar move in this direction at the national level in the debates over reauthorization, with fears that the federal government will tighten its control over welfare reform. The overwhelming fear of many states is that welfare reform will end up representing another set of unfunded and underfunded mandates in the guise of local control.

Similarly, the relative uniformity of the pattern of elite control across places very different in their access to public goods, economic resources, and social programs suggests that without some means of grass roots empowerment, devolution only replaces one level of elite authority with another. It might be argued that even so, local elites are more attuned to local needs, values, and practices, and therefore it is preferable to place power in their hands. Given the long history of corruption, misrule, patronage, and usurpation of resources by local government officials especially in very poor and isolated places, such as Appalachia, it is difficult to be optimistic about improvement of representation and democratic accountability under a system of devolution that has already demonstrated lack of responsiveness to its poorest citizens.

Finally, the initial premise of devolution is flawed to the extent that it does not take account of initial power and capacity differentials across different locations. Handing over authority and even resources to implement new programming cannot work if the receiving units are so depressed that they do not have the capacity to mobilize for new action. This was the case in the poorest of the rural Appalachian counties, where there was greater reluctance to initiate new programs, less ability to actually do so, and little local capacity to draw on in the effort.

These results provide insights into both theoretical and policy issues surrounding the politics of devolution and welfare reform. The claims for the benefits of devolution advocated by the proponents of New Federalism, policies undergirded by neoliberal political theories, are again brought into question, adding to the growing body of evidence that devolution does not necessarily improve social welfare or equity (Lobao and Hooks 2003) but rather accentuates uneven development across space (Kodras 1997). They also demonstrate the particular ways that subnational (and substate for that matter) units are differentially impacted and the mechanisms by which disadvantage occurs. They reinforce the importance of both rural-urban and regional inequality and, in this case, demonstrate that location in rural Appalachia exacerbates inequality above and beyond standard rural-urban differences. These results suggest the importance of more systematic investigation of regional factors and especially the ways that systems of spatial inequality are embedded in nested and overlapping spatial scales.

The politics of welfare reform suggest that initial spatial inequality not only undermines the ability to successfully implement new public policy, but also reinforces and recreates old inequalities while constructing new ones. At the same time, it also demonstrates conditions under which devolution may have positive impacts and points to the importance of institutional resources and social capital as factors that create a positive climate for local initiatives.

Overall, this research demonstrates the importance of systematic investigation of spatial variation using qualitative, case comparative methods in addition to quantitative spatial analysis.[1]

NOTES

1. The research reported here was funded by Ohio State Legal Services Association and Legal Aid Society of Greater Cincinnati (OSLSA/LASGC) and by grants from the Joyce Foundation, the National Research Initiative of the Cooperative State Research, Education and Extension Service, USDA, Grant #97–35401–4561, and Ohio University.

REFERENCES

Adams, Charles F. and Miriam Wilson. 2000. *Welfare Reform Meets the Devolution Revolution in Ohio*. Albany, NY: Rockefeller Institute.

Billings, Dwight B. and Kathleen M. Blee. 2000. *The Road to Poverty: The Making of Wealth and Hardship in Appalachia*. New York: Cambridge University Press.

Blakeslee, Jan. 2000. "The Three-Panel Survey of Milwaukee Families and the Wisconsin Works Welfare Program: An Update." Retrieved December 11, 2002 (http://www.ssc.wisc.edu/irp/srlist.htm77).

Burt, Martha, Nancy Pindus, and Jeffrey Capizzano. 2000. *The Social Safety Net at the Beginning of Federal Welfare Reform: Organization of and Access to Social Services for Low-Income Families*. Occasional Paper Number 34. Washington, DC: Urban Institute.

Center for Law and Social Policy (CLASP). 2001. "Frequently Asked Questions about Working Welfare Leavers." Washington, D.C. November.

Conlan, Timothy. 1998. *From New Federalism to Devolution: Twenty-Five Years of Intergovernmental Reform*. Washington, DC: Brookings Institution Press.

DeWees, Sarah, Linda Lobao, and Lou Swanson. 2003. "Local Economic Development in an Age of Devolution." *Rural Sociology* 68:182–206.

Duncan, Cynthia M. 1999. *Worlds Apart: Why Poverty Persists in Rural America*. New Haven, CT: Yale University Press.

Falk, William W., Michael D. Schulman, and Ann R. Tickamyer, eds. 2003. *Communities of Work: Rural Restructuring in Local and Global Context*. Athens, OH: Ohio University Press.

Fisher, Monica and Bruce A. Weber. 2002. "The Importance of Place in Welfare Reform: Common Challenges for Central Cities and Remote Rural Areas." The Brookings Institution Center on Urban and Metropolitan Policy and Rural Policy Research Institute, June (http://www.brookings.edu/es/urban/publications/weberfull.pdf).

Gieryn, Thomas F. 2000. "A Space for Place in Sociology." *Annual Review of Sociology* 26:463–496.

Henderson, Debra A., Ann Tickamyer, Julie White, and Barry Tadlock. 2002. "Rural Appalachian Families in the Wake of Welfare Reform." *Family Focus*. National Conference of Family Relations Report 47:F7–F9.

Jones-DeWeever, Avis, Janice Peterson, and Xue Song. 2003. *Before and After Welfare Reform: The Work and Well-Being of Low Income Single Parent Families*. Washington, DC: Institute for Women's Policy Research. Retrieved June 26, 2004 (http://www.iwpr.org/pdf/D454.pdf).

Katz, Bruce and Katherine Allen. 2001. "Cities Matter: Shifting the Focus of Welfare Reform." *Brookings Review* 19:30–33.

Kodras, Janet E. 1997. "Restructuring the State: Devolution, Privatization, and the Geographic Redistribution of Power and Capacity in Governance." Pp. 79–96 in *State Devolution in America: Implications for a Diverse Society*, edited by Lynn A. Staelheli, Janet E. Kodras, and Colin Flint. *Urban Affairs Annual Reviews* 48. Thousand Oaks, CA: Sage Publications.

Lichter, Daniel and Rukmalie Jayakody. 2002. "Welfare Reform: How Do We Measure Success?" *Annual Review of Sociology* 28:117–141.

Lieberman, Robert C. and Greg M. Shaw. 2000. "Looking Inward, Looking Outward: The Politics of State Welfare Innovation under Devolution." *Political Research Quarterly* 53:215–240.

Lobao, Linda and Gregory Hooks. 2003. "Public Employment, Welfare Transfers, and Economic Well-Being across Local Populations: Does a Lean and Mean Government Benefit the Masses?" *Social Forces* 82:519–556.

Loprest, Pamela. 1999. *Families Who Left Welfare: Who Are They and How Are They Doing?* Washington, DC: Urban Institute.

Lyson, Thomas and William Falk. 1993. *Forgotten Places: Uneven Development and the Underclass in Rural America*. Lawrence, KS: University of Kansas.

McCall, Leslie. 2001. *Complex Inequality: Gender, Class, and Race in the New Economy*. New York: Routledge.

Moffitt, Robert A. 2002. *From Welfare to Work: What the Evidence Shows*. Welfare Reform and Beyond. Policy Brief #13. Washington, DC: Brookings Institute.

Nathan, Richard and Thomas Gais. 2001. "Federal and State Roles in Welfare: Is Devolution Working? *Brookings Review* 19:25–29.

Schram, Sanford F., Joe Soss, and Richard C. Fording, eds. 2003. *Race and the Politics of Welfare Reform*. Ann Arbor: University of Michigan.

Soss, Joe, Sanford F. Schram, Thomas P. Vartanian, and Erin O'Brien. 2001. "Setting the Terms of Relief: Explaining State Policy Choices in the Devolution Revolution." *American Journal of Political Science* 45:378–396.

Tadlock, Barry, Ann Tickamyer, Julie White, Debra Henderson, and Benjamin Pearson-Nelson. 2005. "Leadership in an Age of Devolution: County Commnmissioners' Role in the Implementation of Appalachian Ohio's Welfare Reform." *Public Administration Quarterly* 29:32–53.

Tickamyer, Ann R. 2000. "Space Matters! Spatial Inequality in Future Sociology." *Contemporary Sociology* 29:805–813.

Tickamyer, Ann R., Debra A. Henderson, J. A. White, and Barry Tadlock . 2000. "Voices of Welfare Reform: Bureaucratic Rationality vs. the Perceptions of Participants." *Affilia: Journal of Women and Social Work* 15:173–192.

Tickamyer, Ann R., Debra A. Henderson, Barry Tadlock, and Julie White. 2002. "Where All the Counties Are Above Average." Pp. 231–254 in *Rural Dimensions of Welfare Reform: Welfare, Food Assistance, and Poverty*, edited by Bruce A. Weber, Greg J. Duncan, and Leslie A. Whitener. Kalamazoo, MI: W. E. Upjohn Institute.

Tickamyer, Ann R., Barry Tadlock, Debra Henderson, and Julie White. 2003. *Devolution in America: TANF Reauthorization Study. Final Report*. Athens, OH: George Voinovich Center for Leadership and Public Affairs, Ohio University.

Weber, Bruce A. 2001. "Welfare Reform Reauthorization: The Importance of Place." *Poverty Research News* 5:14–15.

Weber, Bruce A., Greg J. Duncan, and Leslie A. Whitener, eds. 2002. *Rural Dimensions of Welfare Reform: Welfare, Food Assistance, and Poverty*. Kalamazoo, MI: W. E. Upjohn Institute.

Weir, Margaret. 1999. "Welfare Reform and the Political Geography of Poverty." Pp. 49–60 in *Welfare Reform: A Race to the Bottom?* edited by Sanford Schram and Samuel H. Beer. Washington, DC: Woodrow Wilson Press.

White, Julie, Ann R. Tickamyer, Debra Henderson, and Barry Tadlock. 2003. "Does Welfare-to-Work Work? Rural Employers Comment." Pp. 240–264 in *Communities of Work*, edited by William Falk, Michael Schulman, and Ann Tickamyer. Athens, OH: Ohio University Press.

SIX

Differential Mortality
Across the United States

The Influence of Place-Based Inequality

DIANE K. McLAUGHLIN
C. SHANNON STOKES
P. JOHNELLE SMITH
ATSUKO NONOYAMA

RISKS OF DEATH have long differed across geographic areas. Historically, cities were less healthy places to live, with much higher mortality rates and lower life expectancy associated with greater urban population densities, poor sanitation, and higher levels of infectious and communicable diseases (Woods 2003). These rural-urban differentials have been reduced over time with most authorities predicting better future health in urban areas due to greater access to health care facilities. Nonetheless, systematic differences in mortality are still found across geographic areas within the United States (Pickle et al. 1996). Despite clear documentation of these spatial variations in mortality and the clear spatial clustering of high (and low) mortality rates, our understanding of why these spatial differentials exist has not advanced much beyond the classic work of Kitagawa and Hauser (1973). The shift in focus to individual explanations in studies of differential mortality has greatly increased our knowledge of individual factors associated with higher mortality risks but has resulted in less emphasis on understanding variations across places and spatial patterns of high and low risks.

Much of the ecological research on mortality is largely descriptive and has focused on correlates of mortality rather than attempting to specify the pathways by which characteristics of local social systems influence health and mortality. We examine aspects of inequality focusing on income inequality as one characteristic of localities that has been hypothesized to influence mortality. Prior ecological research has found a positive relationship between income inequality and mortality across nations, states, metropolitan areas, and counties in the United States, but that research has not gone beyond relatively simple models. We extend prior research, testing hypotheses that link income inequality to mortality by including additional, relatively unexplored measures of local conditions. Based on this perspective, we hypothesize that the relationship between income inequality and mortality will be mediated by other measures of local socioeconomic inequality, social conditions and safety, health service availability, and environmental risks. Such mediation is consistent with these factors constituting, at least in part, mechanisms through which income inequality affects mortality.

Theoretical perspectives explain how inequality within a local, geographically delimited area contributes to understanding broader patterns of inequality in mortality across space. Yet the spatial patterns of mortality suggest that residents of specific geographic places face much higher mortality risks than those in other places and that high (and low) mortality clusters together in space. Thus, inequality within places is inextricably linked to patterns of inequality across space. The strong spatial patterning of mortality rates further indicates the need for attention to spatial relationships and more sophisticated statistical modeling to consider these patterns and relationships. We pay special attention to how spatial inequality is manifest in inequality in mortality across places, as measured by counties in the United States.

SPATIAL INEQUALITY AND MORTALITY RISKS

The positive relationship between income inequality and mortality, such that areas with higher levels of income inequality have higher mortality is well documented (Kawachi et al. 1997; Kawachi and Kennedy 1997; Lynch et al. 1998; McLaughlin and Stokes 2002). The mechanisms by which income inequality influences mortality rates are complex and two major explanations are generally posed. The "reduced investment" perspective suggests that higher levels of income inequality may result in less investment in health, educational, and social services in a locality. A second "psychosocial" perspective argues that those who have lower incomes in areas with high inequality are especially aware of their disadvantage and experience increased feelings of deprivation and isolation (Daly et al. 1998; Wilkinson 1996). These feelings affect physical and mental health potentially increasing mortality among these groups (Haan, Kaplan, and Camacho 1987).

THE REDUCED INVESTMENT PERSPECTIVE

Inequality is an aggregate measure of how equally resources are distributed within a particular place (Lobao 1990) but also can be used to indicate how resources and risks vary across places (Daly et al. 1998; Wilkinson 1996). We draw upon perspectives that explain how local context affects individual well-being because individuals experience much of their lives, interact with others, access services, and are exposed to environmental risks in the local community (Brown 1990; Young and Lyson 2001). One aspect hypothesized to contribute to the failure of communities to provide a full range of economic opportunities, health services, and social support is the level of income inequality. Daly et al. (1998:319) note that "an inequitable income distribution may be associated with a set of economic, political, social and institutional processes that reflect systematic underinvestment in human, physical, health and social infrastructure."

Consistent with this view is the hypothesis relating lower individual and social well-being in local communities to greater inequality (Wilkinson 1991) and evidence of less investment in infrastructure in areas with high inequality (Duncan 1996; LaVeist 1993). This underinvestment especially has consequences for the health of poor and middle-class individuals who lack their own resources to go outside the local area to meet their needs. It represents the material dimension of the inequality link. This rationale is consistent with the strong negative relationships found between socioeconomic status and health or mortality in individual level studies (Feinstein 1993; Williams and Collins 1995).

The presence of health services locally is often viewed as crucial to improving health status and lowering mortality risks of Americans. Although many studies find no effect or a positive relationship of physicians per capita or hospital beds on mortality or health indicators (Miller and Stokes 1978), the availability of health care providers and facilities varies significantly across local communities (Office of Technology Assessment 1990). Less available health care and other services could result from underinvestment due to high income inequality. Alternatively, other forces have influenced the distribution of health care across the United States. Declines in health care availability have occurred with recent hospital closures, especially in rural areas, and continued inability of some areas, especially more rural areas, to attract and retain health care professionals (Morton 2003; Office of Technology Assessment 1990; Zimmerman, McAdams, and Halport 2004). Differential access to available health care for persons of low socioeconomic status, minorities, and rural residents suggests a more complex pathway linking inequality and mortality (Berk et al. 1983; Rowland and Lyons 1989).

Environmental quality reflects any environmental hazards in the local area, such as higher levels of air pollution and exposure to toxic materials from industrial waste sites that may increase mortality rates. Air pollution is detrimental to those with existing respiratory conditions, although support for a causal relationship between particulate matter and mortality is mixed (Bates 2000; Zanobetti and Schwartz 2000). Exposure to chemical toxins in the water, air, and soil can influence a number of organ systems (Kamrin et al. 1994). This type of exposure may be especially problematic for those with wells or springwater systems, which rarely are tested for chemical toxins, although chemical emissions may be less in places with higher reliance on individual water systems (rural and more isolated areas).

The environmental justice literature indicates that environmental risks or hazards (e.g., toxic waste dumps, hazardous waste-producing plants) are more likely to be located in places with low incomes or high minority concentrations (Anderton et al. 1994; Bryant and Mohai 1992), although the evidence is mixed. The location decisions of different production facilities and local development or farming activities (Stokes and Brace 1988) can affect chemical emissions to land and water and particulate matter in the air, adding environmental risks to the broader theoretical model relating local variations in inequality to mortality. While links between environmental risks and mortality are difficult to establish, inequality in different types of environmental risk factors is well documented.

THE PSYCHOSOCIAL PERSPECTIVE

Daly et al. (1998:319) suggest that "inequitable income distribution may directly affect people's perceptions of their social environment, which may in turn have an impact on their health." This idea is consistent with Wilkinson's (1991) assertion that inequality is a major barrier to the development of social ties and well-being in a community and may prevent actions in communities that would improve both social and physical well-being. This link to health and mortality stems from the reduced social capital of highly inequitable communities that results in lower social cohesion, greater perceived inequities in social influence, lower levels of trust, and less willingness to participate in community activities (LaVeist 1993; Putnam 1993). To the extent such forces contribute to mortality separately from income inequality or pose one of the mechanisms by which income inequality influences well-being, it is important to consider the effects of social conditions and safety when examining spatial variations in mortality rates.

The psychosocial perspective requires a focus on local social conditions and safety. The presence of local organizations and institutions that promote social capital, social interaction, and improved social relationships among a population is expected to have positive impacts on health (Putnam 1993; Wilkinson 1991). Conversely, special interest organizations (i.e., those engaged in rent-seeking), social disorganization, high unemployment, and the presence of disadvantaged minority groups are posited to negatively influence local social capital and health.

Although recent reviews have questioned the psychosocial explanation of inequality, the issue is far from settled. Much of the extant research has focused on national, regional, state, and metropolitan units of analysis, which we argue are not the appropriate local contexts to examine the putative effects of inequality regardless of whether they operate through reduced investments or psychosocial factors (Deaton and Lubotsky 2003; Lynch et al. 2004a; Lynch et al. 2004b). Similarly, adding a measure of state income inequality to a model of individual-level mortality risks (Finch 2003) (in addition to being an inappropriate level to measure *local* context) likely conflates the effects of other state policies and characteristics associated with state income inequality.

Brown and Lee (1999:155) argue that "the persistence of spatial inequalities suggests that it is critical to take into account how characteristics of locality modify social and economic processes." Moreover, since geographic differences in social and economic structures, demographic characteristics, and local government are likely to be cumulative over time, it is important that such characteristics be incorporated into our models (Lobao 1996). The factors leading to illnesses in individuals are sometimes different than the factors leading to the incidence of disease among populations (Lynch et al. 2004a). It is essential to study both individuals and populations.

Similarly, while factors related to individuals' health such as income are determined in part by other characteristics of individuals such as education and labor force experience, income inequality is determined by a range of other social system characteristics. In order to understand health at the population level, it is necessary to include these structural determinants. The fact that such determinants are differentially distributed across places suggests that a local conditions approach to cumulative advantages or disadvantages might better inform our understanding of population health. Moreover, logic dictates that the ecological unit of analysis should be one in which most activities of daily living take place since this is the unit in which exposures to health risks of all kinds occur (e.g., occupational, environmental, social, cultural, nutritional). As Murray et al. (2001:211) note, "The smaller the level of aggregation we can achieve, the more likely we are to find groups of individuals with similar health risks."

In this research, we move beyond past ecological models assessing the effects of income inequality on mortality by assessing the extent to which that direct relationship changes as factors identified as pathways or mechanisms by which income inequality influences mortality are introduced. In particular, we include additional indicators of inequality in socioeconomic status within the local area, indicators of social conditions and physical safety, availability of health services, and environmental risk factors. We also consider the geographic clustering of places with similar mortality rates. To the extent places with high mortality also have high levels of income inequality and other health risk factors (e.g., environmental toxins), the influence of these local conditions on mortality rates of local populations needs to be assessed. Identifying places with particularly high (or low) mortality and the factors that are associated with those levels is essential to developing meaningful policy responses that address systemic social and institutional shortcomings at the local, state, and federal levels.

DATA AND METHODS

Examining the relationship between mortality rates and local conditions requires determining an appropriate unit small enough to reflect local social conditions yet large enough to be meaningful for policy. We use counties as the unit of analysis. County governments provide structure and make many decisions related to planning and development, as well as local service provision, or they dictate the structure of smaller units of government (Lobao 1990; Lobao and Hooks 2003). Prior analysis also has revealed that counties are a better unit of analysis than census tracts when measuring income inequality since residential segregation in metropolitan areas tends to minimize income inequality at the smaller, tract level (Soobader and LeClere 1999). Census tracts in nonmetro areas are relatively meaningless as boundaries containing local social systems or units of local decision making. Thus, counties, while not recognized as actual communities, are a valid spatial and decisional unit of analysis for our purposes. Further, in using counties we are able to incorporate all geographic areas in the continental United States, and thus we capture the range in mortality from the largest metropolitan areas to the most rural regions. Given the variability in mortality rates across the United States, it is essential to determine the forces corresponding with high and low mortality rates in local populations.

We use the Compressed Mortality Files from the National Center for Health Statistics (National Center for Health Statistics 2003a, 2003b) as the source for the number of deaths and the population used to calculate mortality rates. We use five years of deaths, from 1996 to 2000 (the most recently available mortality data), to calculate total mortality rates adjusted for age, sex, and race. The 2000 U.S. population is used to standardize the rates. Because of the larger uncertainty in calculating mortality rates for counties with fewer deaths across years, we calculated annual rates and use the inverse of the variance of those rates for each county for the five years of our data to weight the analysis to adjust for heteroscedasticity (McLaughlin and Stokes 2002; Neter, Wasserman, and Kutner 1985). This procedure gives less weight to counties (usually with small populations) whose mortality rates vary more widely. Even with these precautions, three counties were eliminated from the analysis because they had too few or no deaths over the five-year period. These were King and Loving Counties in Texas and Yellowstone County in Montana.

Income inequality and socioeconomic status have been found to be correlated with mortality differentials across places. We identify four other groups of measures related to the theoretical models serving as mechanisms by which income inequality might influence mortality: urbanicity/rurality, social conditions and safety, health care availability, and environmental risks. We use 1990 census data, or data from other sources before 1996, for all of our independent variables so the measurement of the independent variables occurs prior to reported deaths used to construct the dependent variable. This assumes a modest lag in the effects of independent variables on the dependent variable and stability in the relative values of the independent variables over the short time period involved.

Income inequality is measured using categorical household income data from the 1990 U.S. Census of Population and Housing Summary Tape File 3C (U.S. Bureau of the Census 1993). We explored several different measures of income inequality (see Allison 1978 and Kawachi and Kennedy 1997 for relevant descriptions) and found only minimal differences across the measures in the relationship with mortality (McLaughlin and Stokes 2002). We selected the commonly used Gini Coefficient as our measure of household income inequality. A value of one indicates complete inequality and a value of zero perfect equality (each household has an equal share of income). This measure was divided into quartiles and dummy variables for the three highest inequality quartiles were included in the analysis. The use of quartiles allows for a nonlinear relationship between income inequality and mortality and provides a clear indication of that relationship.

Because income and other measures of socioeconomic status have been shown to be important determinants of mortality and because many of these measures are correlated, we submitted six county-level indicators of socioeconomic status to a factor analysis to reduce the number of measures included in the models and thereby minimize potential problems of multicollinearity while retaining as much information as possible. The single factor that resulted, the socioeconomic status factor, includes per capita income (factor loading .91), per capita income squared (.90), percent of persons aged 25 and over with more than a high school education (.77), percent of persons aged 25 and over with a college degree or more (.92), percent of employees in executive, administrative, and managerial positions (.89), and percent of employees in professional positions (.76). Descriptive statistics, factor loadings, and eigenvalues from the principal axis factor analyses are available from the first author.

We conducted additional factor analysis to identify structures in the remaining independent variables and to reduce multicollinearity in the models.

Two factors were identified based on principal axis factoring with orthogonal rotations. Factor one reflects characteristics of *old urban* counties. The following variables load on the old urban factor: log of the population (.86), percent of the population living in urban places (.87), the violent crime rate from 1988 to 1992 (.59), percent of the population without a well (.50), and counties with a super-fund site (.61). The second factor captures *structural disadvantage*. The variables loading on this factor include median household size (.60), the unemployment rate in 1990 (.60), percent of the county population that is black in 1990 (.66), and the percent of the population under age 65 (.57). The names for these fac-tors were based on the variables with the heaviest factor loadings, but we also examined the counties with the highest factor scores on each factor as a check on the naming of the factor.

Data for the majority of the variables in the factor analysis were from the 1990 Census of Population and Housing STF3 Files. Violent crime per 100 population, a measure of safety, was calculated from the 1988 to 1992 Uni-form Crime Reports from the FBI (1993). Whether a Superfund site was located in the county was used as one indicator of environmental risk. These data were from the Web site www.scorecard.org, which lists every county with a Superfund site and the number of sites in the county.

Independent variables from each variable group not loading in the fac-tor analysis were retained as individual explanatory variables in the models. An additional measure of socioeconomic conditions—the percentage of workers employed in farming, forestry, and fishing occupations—provides an indicator of extractive employment in the local economy.

Social conditions and safety can be difficult to measure directly with available secondary data. Following Rupasingha, Goetz, and Freshwater (2000), we construct measures of the types of organizations in counties that could be considered to provide opportunities for social activities to reflect possible social interaction and cohesion. The number of bowling centers, public golf courses, membership sports and recreation clubs, civic and social associations, and religious organizations per 1000 population were identified as Putnam-type establishments. A larger share of these is expected to be asso-ciated with lower mortality. Rent-seeking (Olson-type) special interest orga-nizations have been argued to reduce economic performance and well-being [as cited in Rupasingha et al. 2000] and so are expected to be associated with higher mortality. These are the number of labor organizations, business asso-ciations, professional organizations, and political organizations per 1000 pop-ulation. These measures are constructed from 1990 County Business Patterns data (U.S. Department of Commerce 1993).

Individual-level studies of mortality make a strong case for the impor-tance of religious participation for reduced mortality risks (Hummer et al. 1999), and religious activities provide a forum that helps build networks and relationships of trust and assistance. We use 1990 county-level data from the

Glenmary Research Center (1992) to calculate the percentage of residents in a county who report belonging to any religion. Population mobility and change has been associated with lower social cohesion, so we include a measure of percentage of the population that moved into their current house from 1989 to 1990 as an indicator of population mobility.

Health service availability measures are derived from the Area Resource File (Office of Health Professions Analysis and Research 1993). We use number of active physicians in 1990 per 100,000 population, whether all or part of a county had been designated a health professional shortage area for primary care providers (based on 1989 classification), and the change in hospital beds per 1000 from 1980 to 1990 (1990 value minus 1980 value). Because number of physicians may have a nonlinear relation to mortality (Farmer et al. 1991), we included a physicians-squared term among the indicators.

Environmental risks are measured using chemical emissions to the air, surface water, and land (including underground injections) from industries with standard industrial classification (SIC) codes 20 to 39. These emissions were reported in the Toxic Release Inventory (TRI) Explorer database maintained by the Environmental Protection Agency. The measures were emissions in pounds per square kilometer of area in the county for 1988. While there is difficulty in linking environmental hazards with mortality because exposure to some toxins may require years before any signs of illness develop, we suggest that current environmental hazards reflect the relative levels of emissions in earlier years and so are indicators of prior and continuing exposure for long-time residents.

We begin by estimating weighted least squares regression models of age-sex-race adjusted total mortality for 3,062 counties in the contiguous United States. Three nested models are estimated to show the change in the coefficients for the income inequality quartiles as key variable groups are added to the model. In conducting the analysis, we tested for multicollinearity in the models (Belsley, Kuh, and Welsch 1980). We also estimate the extent of spatial autocorrelation in the dependent variable and given the spatial patterning of mortality we estimate spatial linear models (Anselin and Bera 1998). The presence of spatial autocorrelation can result in biased estimates of standard errors used in hypothesis tests (Odland 1988). The weighted least squares models are estimated using SAS, and the spatial linear models are estimated using Splus linked to ARCView (Kalazny et al. 1998). Unfortunately, we were unable to estimate weighted spatial linear models, so the spatial models do not include the adjustment for heteroscedasticity in the mortality rates.

RESULTS

Descriptive statistics for the dependent and independent variables for all counties in the analysis are given in table 6.1. We report the unweighted

TABLE 6.1

Descriptive Statistics and Weighted Least Squares Regression Models of Age-Sex-Race Adjusted
Total Mortality and Spatial Linear Model of Age-Sex-Race Adjusted Total Mortality (n=3,062 counties)

Variables	Descriptive Statistics[a]	Model 1	Model 2	Model 3	Spatial Linear Model
Age-sex-race adjusted total mortality (per 100,000 population)	845.1 (133.0) 305 to 1761				
Intercept		800.8***	898.5***	976.3***	848.2***
Income inequality-Gini coefficient	.413 (.035) .296 to .550				
Lowest quartile	less than .389	Ref.	Ref.	Ref.	Ref.
Second quartile	.389 to .409	10.9***	12.9***	17.4***	13.4**
Third quartile	.410 to .439	48.8***	29.3***	37.3***	19.3***
Highest quartile	greater than .439	115.3***	62.2***	65.2***	36.9***
Socioeconomic status factor	0 (1.00) −2.0 to 6.1	—	−52.0***	−55.0 ***	−67.3***
Structural disadvantage factor	0 (1.00) −2.1 to 5.6	—	10.6***	18.5***	20.5***
Urbanicity/Rurality					
Old urban area factor	0 (1.00) −2.8 to 6.4	—	3.8***	8.7***	12.2***
Percent population employed in farming, forestry, and fishing	8.1 (8.0) 0.2 to 66.9	—	−11.2***	−9.6***	−5.1***

(continued on next page)

TABLE 6.1 (continued)

Variables	Descriptive Statistics	Model 1	Model 2	Model 3	Spatial Linear Model
Social Conditions and Safety					
Putnam-type establishments/1000 pop.	1.09 (0.54) 0 to 4.35	—	—	−1.4	4.6
Special interest establishments/1000 pop.	0.19 (0.17) 0 to 2.17	—	—	46.7***	23.8*
Percent population church adherents in 1990[b]	59.5 (19.4) 4.0 to 146.1	—	—	−.6***	.1
Percent population moved to current housing unit in 1989–1990	17.7 (5.2) 5.2 to 47.6	—	—	−3.4***	−.2
Health care availability					
Active medical doctors per 100,000 pop.	95.6 (105.9) 0 to 2,052.4	—	—	.1**	.1*
Active medical doctors, squared	—	—	—	−.0+	.0
Primary health care shortage area in 1989	0.53 0 to 1	—	—	−25.9***	−12.9***
Hospital beds (1990 minus 1980)/ 1000 pop.	−0.56 (3.9) −56.4 to 56.5	—	—	−1.0*	−.6

(continued on next page)

TABLE 6.1 (continued)

Variables	Descriptive Statistics	Model 1	Model 2	Model 3	Spatial Linear Model
Environmental risks					
Lbs. of chemicals released to water in land/sq km	754.1 (11544.9) 0 to 5000052.36	—	—	-.0	-.0
Lbs. of chemicals released to air/sq km	703.5 (2961.8) 0 to 67414.0	—	—	.0*	.0
Adjusted R²	—	.136	.427	.521	Rho=.147

Source: Mortality data combine deaths from the 1996 to 2000 Compressed Mortality Files, standardized to 2000 population. Data are from the National Center for Health Statistics Compressed Mortality Files 1989 to 1998 and 1999 to 2000.

[a] Mean, standard deviation, and range shown.

[b] Church adherents are reported by location of the churches, rather than the residence of the people, so some counties have more than 100 percent church adherents.

* p ≤ 0.05   ** p ≤ 0.01   *** p ≤ 0.001   + p ≤ 0.10 (two-tailed tests)

mean, standard deviation, and the minimum and maximum values for each variable. The minimum and maximum reveal the variability of values across counties in the United States. The age-sex-race adjusted total mortality rate has a mean of 845 and standard deviation of 133, with values ranging from 305 to 1761 deaths per 100,000 population.

Figure 6.1 shows the spatial distribution of total mortality across counties in the continental United States based on quintiles of mortality (much more detail on spatial patterns in mortality is available from Pickle et al. 1996). The spatial patterning in mortality is obvious in figure 6.1. Areas of very high mortality are found throughout central and southern Appalachia including much of Ohio, through the black belt of the south, along the Mississippi River from southern Illinois south through most of Louisiana, most of Oklahoma and parts of Texas. Many counties in Missouri also have above average mortality rates. The lowest age-sex-race adjusted mortality rates are found in the midwest, especially in Iowa, Wisconsin, Minnesota, and the Dakotas and throughout the Great Plains and most of the Rocky Mountain west. Exceptions are those counties with Native American reservations. There are clear spatial concentrations of high and low mortality.

Results of the weighted least squares regression models for age-sex-race adjusted total mortality across all counties (n=3,062 counties) are shown in table 6.1. Model 1 gives the simplest model including only the relationship between income inequality and mortality. The gradient of mortality with income inequality is reflected in the estimated coefficients for the inequality quartile dummies. The increase in mortality from the lowest to the highest inequality quartile is 115 deaths per 100,000. Model 2 adds the SES factor, structural disadvantage and old urban factors, and percentage employed in extractive occupations. Adding these covariates almost triples the adjusted R^2 and cuts the gradient from the lowest to highest inequality quartile to 62 deaths per 100,000. A higher score on the SES factor is associated with lower mortality, while higher scores on the structural disadvantage factor and the old urban factor correspond with higher mortality. A higher percentage employed in extractive occupations is associated with lower mortality once other measures of SES are controlled.

The remaining variable groups are added in model 3, resulting in an increase of the adjusted R^2 from .489 to .521. The inequality gradient remained relatively steady at 65 deaths per 100,000 population in model 3, after the addition of controls for social conditions and safety, health care availability, and environmental risks.

In this final, full model, a higher SES score continues to be associated with lower mortality rates, while a higher structural disadvantage score still corresponds with higher mortality rates in a county as does being an old urban county. Extractive employment remains negatively associated with mortality. Consistent with the arguments that special interest establishments

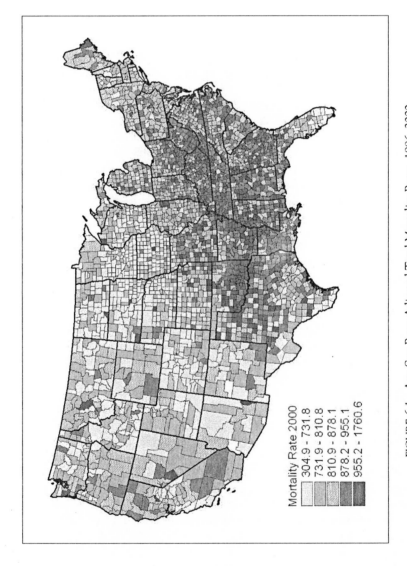

Mortality Rate 2000

☐ 304.9 - 731.8
▨ 731.9 - 810.8
▥ 810.9 - 878.1
▤ 878.2 - 955.1
▓ 955.2 - 1760.6

FIGURE 6.1. Age-Sex-Race Adjusted Total Mortality Rates, 1996–2000.

Source: National Center for Health Statistics (Compressed Mortality File 1989–1998 and 1999–2000)

are associated with lower well-being, counties with larger shares of these establishments have higher mortality rates. As expected, higher church membership in a county is related to lower mortality rates as is a higher level of recent population mobility. The measure of active medical doctors has a nonlinear relationship with mortality rates that first is positively related but then becomes negatively related to mortality. As one would expect, an increase in hospital beds in a county is associated with lower mortality rates. Interestingly, once other measures of county characteristics are controlled, counties designated as primary health care shortage areas have lower mortality rates than other counties.

Emissions of chemicals to land were not associated with mortality rates, while higher emissions to air were associated with higher mortality rates. Even with these extensive controls for other factors believed to be the mechanisms by which income inequality affects health and mortality, the gradient in mortality with income inequality remains significant. The gradient in mortality with increasing income inequality was not mediated as other variable groups were added. In the final model estimated, multicollinearity does not appear to be a problem (Belsley, Kuh, and Welsch 1980). The highest condition index was 24, with the only relatively large variance decompositions (close to .5) involving the measure of Putnam-type organizations and church membership and the two measures of physicians (physicians and physicians squared).

SPATIAL AUTOCORRELATION IN TOTAL AGE-SEX-RACE ADJUSTED MORTALITY RATES

Moran's I, a measure of spatial autocorrelation in variables, for age-sex-race adjusted total mortality rates had a value of 0.54, significantly higher than the expected value of Moran's I given the sample size (-0.003). Thus, there is substantial spatial autocorrelation in age-sex-race adjusted total mortality among counties, as observed in figure 6.1. Using a simple nearest-neighbor matrix we estimated a spatial linear model using a conditional autoregressive model containing the full set of variables. Generally, one strategy used to deal with spatial autocorrelation is to include additional independent variables that could help explain the spatial patterns in the model. In fact, the spatial distribution of several of our independent variables (e.g., environmental emissions and income inequality) echoes that of the mortality rates.

Residuals from the full-weighted least squares regression model (model 3) were examined. These residuals still display localized clusters of counties for which our model was least accurate in predicting actual mortality rates. Counties with predicted mortality lower than the actual values tend to be found in Wyoming, Washington, Nevada, and parts of Oklahoma and Texas. This suggests that these counties rates had other risk factors not included in our models or had combinations of risk factors that greatly increased their mortality rates. Counties with predicted mortality higher than the actual values tend to cluster in Florida, Minnesota, Arizona, and New Mexico and parts of Idaho, Colorado, and Nebraska. These counties seem to have conditions or combinations of conditions especially protective of their populations. Specialized study of these spatially clustered counties with mortality rates higher or lower than those predicted in our models may aid in identifying factors, or combinations of factors, related to health that may increase our understanding of how local social systems, services, and environmental conditions combine to influence mortality.

Adjusting statistically for the remaining spatial autocorrelation resulted in several coefficients statistically significant in the weighted least squares model changing sign or becoming statistically insignificant (see the spatial linear model in table 6.1). Particularly noteworthy in the spatial linear model is the decline (to 37 deaths per 100,000 population) in the mortality gradient with increasing income inequality, as the coefficient for the SES factor also became more negative. Church membership and percentage of the population who moved to new housing recently both became insignificant in the spatial model, as did the difference in hospital beds and the chemicals released to air. Coefficients losing significance in a spatial model is consistent with the assertion that spatial autocorrelation in a regression model results in underestimates of standard errors. Once spatial autocorrelation is considered, the corrected standard errors are larger. Despite including a relatively full set of independent variables, Rho, the spatial correlation coefficient in the spatial model, was 0.147 and was statistically significant. These results suggest that the spatial patterning of mortality is highly associated with the spatial patterning of environmental risks, social conditions (such as church membership), and shifts in hospital beds. The effects on mortality of income inequality, socioeconomic status, urbanicity, and some indicators of health care remain strong or became stronger in the spatial linear model.

DISCUSSION AND CONCLUSIONS

Despite vast improvements in socioeconomic status, physical health, availability of medical care, and sanitation, variations in mortality rates across counties in the United States remain substantial, even when adjusted for differences in the age, sex, and race composition of the local population. Explanations for these variations include income inequality and socioeconomic status, social conditions and safety, health services availability, and environmental risks. Equally important is the spatial patterning of mortality rates, with clear spatial clusters of counties with high and low mortality.

Our analysis documents the importance of income inequality as a correlate of county-level mortality rates. We also show, however, that the influence of income inequality on mortality is mediated when measures of socioeconomic status and rurality are included in weighted least squares regression models. While social conditions and safety, health care availability, and environmental risks are believed to be mechanisms through which income inequality influences mortality rates, adding these variables to the model did not substantially mediate the relationship of income inequality and mortality. These factors did influence mortality rates directly, however. This analysis has identified two pathways by which income inequality indirectly affects mortality rates and has documented other factors with direct effects on mortality that are important for understanding local variations in mortality rates. While the influence of income inequality remains significant when adjustments for spatial clustering are made, the gradient becomes smaller.

Equally interesting are the shifts occurring among all variable groups in the spatial linear model. Once an adjustment is made for the spatial clustering of counties with similar mortality rates, income inequality becomes less important, as does special interest organizations. Church membership, recent resident mobility, hospital beds, and environmental risks all become insignificant. One explanation already posed for this is the adjustment in standard errors occurring with the spatial modeling. An alternative explanation is that factors associated with high and low mortality are clustered together in places and controlling for their spatial proximity may reduce their influence in the model. This clustering of characteristics (e.g., high inequality, low SES, environmental risks, and higher church membership) may interact to put some places at particularly high risk of mortality. The combination of characteristics found in places might be most important for understanding mortality rates.

While alternative measures of some of the independent variables may modify these findings slightly, more attention needs to be paid to the relationships between local income inequality and local social conditions, health care availability, and environmental risks. Do all places with higher income inequality invest less in physical, educational, health, and social infrastructure? Does inequality, as measured by income inequality, prevent the establishment of social networks and ties in a community, thus preventing local action? Does inequality ensure exposure to man-made environmental risks? Are combinations of these conditions especially problematic or protective of human health? What are the local, regional, and national social systems and institutions that influence the allocation of resources and risks? What are the remedies to the very high levels of mortality found in specific places and spatial clusters? Are they local, regional, or national?

These questions make ecological analyses examining the spatial relationships across places essential. Without a clear understanding of local conditions associated with high (and low) mortality rates and without identification of actual places (counties) with risk factors for high mortality, policy solutions can be misdirected or targeted to localities that may not be most in need of policy intervention. The recognition that local places may have quite different characteristics or combinations of characteristics placing them at risk of higher mortality rates enables design and implementation of local as well as state or federal programs. Recognition of similar risks shared by neighboring counties could lead to regional and collaborative responses allowing for a stronger voice and better targeting of resources to focus on locally important risk factors, whether those are man-made environmental hazards or high levels of inequality within a county or cluster of counties. Focused recommendations to remedy local risks require analysis and interpretation that consider the influence of local inequality and the distribution or clustering of inequalities across space.[1]

NOTE

1. Support for this research was provided by Population Research Center Core Grant (P30 HD28263) from the National Institute of Child Health and Human Development to the Population Research Institute, and by Experiment Station Project 3692, College of Agricultural Sciences, The Pennsylvania State University. The analyses, interpretations, and conclusions in this chapter are those of the authors and not NCHS. NCHS is responsible only for the initial data.

REFERENCES

Allison, Paul D. 1978. "Measures of Inequality." *American Sociological Review* 43:865–880.

Anderton, Douglas L., Andy B. Anderson, John M. Oakes, and Michael Fraser. 1994. "Environmental Equity: The Demographics of Dumping." *Demography* 31:221–248.

Anselin, Luc and Anil K. Bera. 1998. "Spatial Dependence in Linear Regression Models With an Introduction to Spatial Econometrics." Pp. 237–289 in *Handbook of Applied Economic Statistics*, edited by Aman Ullah and David E. A. Giles. New York: Marcel Dekker.

Bates, David Vincent. 2000. "Lines that Connect: Assessing the Causality Inference in the Case of Particulate Pollution." *Environmental Health Perspectives* 108:91–92.

Belsley, David A., Edwin Kuh, and Roy E. Welsch. 1980. *Regression Diagnostics: Identifying Influential Data and Sources of Collinearity*. New York: John Wiley and Sons.

Berk, Marc L., Amy B. Bernstein, and Amy K. Taylor. 1983. "The Use and Availability of Medical Care in Health Manpower Shortage Areas." *Inquiry* 20:369–380.

Brown, David L. and Marlene A. Lee. 1999. "Persisting Inequality between Metropolitan and Nonmetropolitan America: Implications for Theory and Policy." Pp. 151–167 in *A Nation Divided: Diversity, Inequality, and Community in American*

Society, edited by Phyllis Moen, Donna Dempster-McClain, and Henry A. Walker. Ithaca, NY: Cornell University Press.

Brown, Kate. 1990. "Connected Independence: A Paradox of Rural Health?" *Journal of Rural Community Psychology* 11:51–64.

Bryant, Bunyan and Paul Mohai, eds. 1992. *Race and the Incidence of Environmental Hazards: A Time for Discourse*. Boulder, CO: Westview Press.

Daly, Mary C., Greg J. Duncan, George A. Kaplan, and John W. Lynch. 1998. "Macro-to-Micro Links in the Relation Between Income Inequality and Mortality." *The Milbank Quarterly* 76:315–339.

Deaton, Angus and Darren Lubotsky. 2003. "Mortality, Inequality, and Race in American Cities and States." *Social Science and Medicine* 56:1139–1153.

Duncan, Cynthia M. 1996. "Understanding Persistent Poverty: Social Class Context in Rural Communities." *Rural Sociology* 61:103–124.

Farmer, Frank L., C. Shannon Stokes, Robert H. Fiser, and Dennis P. Papini. 1991. "Poverty, Primary Care and Age-Specific Mortality." *Journal of Rural Health* 7:153–169.

Federal Bureau of Investigation. 1993. *Uniform Crime Reports for the United States*. Washington, DC: Bureau of Investigation, U.S. Department of Justice.

Feinstein, James S. 1993. "The Relationship Between Socioeconomic Status and Health: A Review of the Literature." *The Milbank Quarterly* 71:279–322.

Finch, Brian K. 2003. "Early Origins of the Gradient: The Relationship Between Socioeconomic Status and Infant Mortality in the United States." *Demography* 40:675–699.

Glenmary Research Center. 1992. *Church and Church Membership in the United States*. Atlanta: Glenmary Research Center.

Haan, Mary N., George A. Kaplan, and Terry Camacho. 1987. "Poverty and Health: Prospective Evidence From the Alameda County Study." *American Journal of Epidemiology* 125:989–998.

Hummer, Robert A., Richard G. Rogers, Charles B. Nam, and Christopher G. Ellison. 1999. "Religious Involvement and U.S. Adult Mortality." *Demography* 36:273–285.

Kalazny, S. P., S. C. Vega, T. P. Cardoso, and A. A. Shelly. 1998. *S+ Spatial Stats: User's Manual for Windows and UNIX*. New York: Springer.

Kamrin, Michael A., Lawrence J. Fischer, William A. Suk, James R. Fouts, Edo Pellizzari, and Keht Thornton. 1994. "Assessment of Human Exposure to Chemicals from Superfund Sites." *Environmental Health Perspectives Supplements* 102:221–228.

Kawachi, Ichiro and Bruce P. Kennedy. 1997. "The Relationship of Income Inequality to Mortality: Does the Choice of Indicator Matter?" *Social Science and Medicine* 45:1121–1127.

Kawachi, Ichiro, Bruce P. Kennedy, Kimberly Lochner, and Deborah Prothrow-Stith. 1997. "Social Capital, Income Inequality, and Mortality." *American Journal of Public Health* 87:1491–1498.

Kitagawa, Evelyn M. and Philip M. Hauser. 1973. *Differential Mortality in the United States: A Study in Socioeconomic Epidemiology.* Cambridge, MA: Harvard University Press.

LaVeist, Thomas A. 1993. "Segregation, Poverty, and Empowerment: Health Consequences for African Americans." *The Milbank Quarterly* 71:41–64.

Lobao, Linda M. 1990. *Locality and Inequality: Farm and Industry Structure and Socioeconomic Conditions.* Albany, NY: State University of New York Press.

———. 1996. "A Sociology of the Periphery Versus a Peripheral Sociology: Rural Sociology and the Dimensions of Space." *Rural Sociology* 61:77–102.

Lobao, Linda M. and Gregory Hooks. 2003. "Public Employment, Welfare Transfers, and Economic Well-being Across Local Populations: Does a Lean and Mean Government Benefit the Masses?" *Social Forces* 82:519–556.

Lynch, John W., George A. Kaplan, Elsie R. Pamuk, Richard D. Cohen, Katherine E. Heck, Jennifer L. Barbour, and Irene H. Yen. 1998. "Income Inequality and Mortality in Metropolitan Areas of the United States." *American Journal of Public Health* 88:1074–1080.

Lynch, John, George D. Smith, Sam Harper, Marianne Hillemeier, Nancy Ross, George A. Kaplan, and Michael Wolfson. 2004a. "Is Income Inequality a Determinant of Population Health? Part I. A Systematic Review." *The Milbank Quarterly* 82:5–99.

Lynch, John, George D. Smith, Sam Harper, and Marianne Hillemeier. 2004b. "Is Income Inequality a Determinant of Population Health? Part 2. U.S. National and Regional Trends in Income Inequality and Age- and Cause-Specific Mortality." *The Milbank Quarterly* 82:355–400.

McLaughlin, Diane K. and C. Shannon Stokes. 2002. "Income Inequality and Mortality in U.S. Counties: Does Minority Racial Concentration Matter?" *American Journal of Public Health* 92:99–104.

Miller, Michael K. and C. Shannon Stokes. 1978. "Health Status, Health Resources, and Consolidated Structural Parameters: Implications for Public Health Care Policy." *Journal of Health and Social Behavior* 19:263–279.

Morton, Lois Wright. 2003. "Rural Health Policy." Pp. 290–302 in *Challenges for Rural America in the Twenty-First Century,* edited by David L. Brown and Louis E. Swanson. University Park, PA: Pennsylvania State University Press.

Murray, Christopher J. L., Juilu Frenk, and Emmanuela E. Gakidou. 2001. "Measuring Health Inequality: Challenges and New Directions." Pp. 194–216 in *Poverty, Inequality, and Health,* edited by D. Leon and G. Walt. New York: Oxford University Press.

National Center for Health Statistics. 2003a. Compressed Mortality File, 1989–98 (machine readable data file and documentation, CD-ROM Series 20, No. E), National Center for Health Statistics, Hyattsville, Maryland.

———. 2003b. Compressed Mortality File, 1999–2000 (machine readable data file and documentation, CD-ROM Series 20, No. 2F), National Center for Health Statistics, Hyattsville, Maryland.

Neter, John, William Wasserman, and Michael H. Kutner. 1985. *Applied Linear Statistical Models.* Homewood, IL: Irwin.

Odland, John. 1988. *Spatial Autocorrelation.* Newbury Park: Sage Publications.

Office of Health Professions Analysis and Research. 1993. Area Resource File. Washington, DC.

Office of Technology Assessment. 1990. *Health Care in Rural America.* Washington, DC: U.S. Government Printing Office.

Pickle, Linda, Michael Mungiole, Gretchen K. Jones, and Andrew A. White. 1996. *Atlas of United States Mortality.* Hyattsville, MD: National Center for Health Statistics.

Putnam, Robert D. 1993. "The Prosperous Community: Social Capital and Public Life." *American Prospect* 13:35–42.

Rowland, Diane and Barbara Lyons. 1989. "Triple Jeopardy: Rural, Poor, and Uninsured." *Health Services Research* 23:975–1004.

Rupasingha, Anil, Stephan J. Goetz, and David Freshwater. 2000. "Social Capital and Economic Growth: A County-Level Analysis." *Journal of Agricultural and Applied Economics* 32:565–572.

Soobader, Mah-Jabeen and Felicia B. LeClere. 1999. "Aggregation and the Measurement of Income Inequality: Effects on Morbidity." *Social Science and Medicine* 48:733–744.

Stokes, C. Shannon and Kathy D. Brace. 1988. "Agricultural Chemical Use and Cancer Mortality in Selected Rural Counties in the USA." *Journal of Rural Studies* 4:239–247.

U.S. Bureau of the Census. 1993. *1990 Census of Population and Housing. Summary Tape File 3C* [MRDF]. Washington, DC: U.S. Bureau of the Census.

U.S. Department of Commerce, Bureau of the Census. *County Business Patterns, 1990 [United States]: U.S. Summary, State and County Data* [computer file]. Washington, DC: U.S. Department of Commerce, Bureau of the Census [producer], 1992. Ann Arbor, MI: Inter-university Consortium for Political and Social Research [distributor], 1993.

Wilkinson, Kenneth P. 1991. *The Community in Rural America.* Boulder: Westview Press.

Wilkinson, Richard G. 1996. *Unhealthy Societies: The Afflictions of Inequality.* New York: Routledge.

Williams, David R. and Chiquita Collins. 1995. "U.S. Socioeconomic and Racial Differences in Health: Patterns and Explanations." *Annual Review of Sociology* 21:349–86.

Woods, Robert. 2003. "Urban-Rural Mortality Differentials: An Unresolved Debate." *Population and Development Review* 29:29–46.

Young, Frank W. and Thomas A. Lyson. 2001. "Structural Pluralism and All-Cause Mortality." *American Journal of Public Health* 91:136–141.

Zanobetti, Antonella and Joel Schwartz. 2000. "Race, Gender, and Social Status as Modifiers of the Effects of PM_{10} on Mortality." *Journal of Occupational and Environmental Medicine* 42:469–474.

Zimmerman, Mary K., Rodney McAdams, and Burton P. Halpert. 2004. "Funding Health Services in the Rural United States: Federal Policies and Local Solutions." Pp. 211–224 in *Critical Issues in Rural Health*, edited by Nina Glasgow, Lois W. Morton, and Nan E. Johnson. Ames, IA: Blackwell Publishing.

SEVEN

Placing Family Poverty in Area Contexts

The Use of Multilevel Models in Spatial Research

DAVID A. COTTER
JOAN M. HERMSEN
REEVE VANNEMAN

POVERTY HAPPENS TO individual families, but it happens in contexts that shape the size and nature of each family's risk. We know many of the factors that put families at higher risk of poverty: loss of work, low wages, a lack of education that predisposes one to joblessness and low wages, single parenthood, and minority status, which raises the risk of all these factors. But these factors also vary across space and time in macro-level patterns affecting the life chances for all families. A multilevel design can show how individual family characteristics interact with broader spatial patterns to jointly determine poverty rates. In this paper, we use a hierarchical model to simultaneously investigate the effects of family and local labor markets on poverty chances.[1]

Joint analysis of family and area-level determinants of poverty answers three types of questions not easily addressed in other designs:

1. How much of each area-level effect is a consequence of compositional differences in the types of families in an area, and how much is a contextual effect that lowers poverty risks among all families?
2. How do area-level factors differentially affect the poverty risks of different types of families?
3. How much of each family effect gets translated into area-level differences in poverty rates, and how much is only a selection or queuing effect that determines *who* becomes poor but not the poverty rate?

Past work at either the family or area level only suggests answers to these questions that are best addressed within an explicit multilevel framework.

THE IMPORTANCE OF CONTEXT:
SPATIAL VARIATION AND THE RISK OF POVERTY

Social scientific analysis of poverty often begins and ends with an examination of how characteristics of individuals or families lead to higher or lower risks of being poor. These individual-level explanations are found in most accounts of poverty. Less often, attention is given to how contexts—whether spatial or temporal—may affect poverty risks. Temporal effects such as recessions, public policy, and other fluctuations are given some attention in the literature and sometimes treated as major theoretical subjects (see Gundersen and Ziliak 2004). The "territorial lumpiness" of economic life, however, has less often been addressed, despite recognition in both scholarly and policy discourse. However, attention to spatial variation is especially warranted because of the substantial variation in economic structure and poverty policy across places—differences that may be widening over time (Tickamyer 2000).

Structural theories seek to explain spatial variation in poverty by variation in the "opportunity structures" across areas—whether neighborhoods, communities, or labor markets. In such theories, economic activities, such as unemployment rates, industrial or occupational composition, and income distributions, determine the amount of poverty in a given locale. Understanding which contextual factors contribute to higher poverty rates is not only an inherently sociological enterprise but also an important issue for those interested in developing strategies at the local and national level to reduce poverty. Studies have identified numerous factors associated with variation in poverty rates over time and across places. Some of these include economic prosperity, earnings inequality, family structure, government transfers (Moffitt 1992), race and gender inequality (Haynie and Gorman 1999; Lichter and McLaughlin 1995; Massey and Eggers 1990), education levels, and industrial structure (Lobao and Schulman 1991; Tomaskovic-Devey 1991).

PROSPERITY, INEQUALITY, AND POVERTY

In keeping with a structural analysis, we argue that a more complete understanding of family poverty should account for the location's opportunity structure. We focus on the two most direct economic factors, prosperity and earnings inequality. Both have been cited repeatedly in explanations of poverty rates over the last half century (e.g., Danziger and Gottschalk 1995; Levy and Murnane 1992).

Economic prosperity has two complementary aspects—unemployment rates and average earnings—both of which warrant analysis (Okun 1973).

Plentiful, well-paying jobs reduce poverty. Both aspects of prosperity can be seen in the national poverty trends. The cyclical fluctuations of unemployment are reflected in the cyclical fluctuations in poverty, especially in the last quarter of the century. The secular rise then stagnation of average earnings has driven much of the long run change in poverty rates.

Few time-series or area-level studies have said much explicitly about how national or local prosperity affects individual families and the risk of poverty though important exceptions can be found primarily in the literature on rural poverty (e.g., Brown and Hirschl 1995; Lobao 1990). Perhaps it seems too straightforward: prosperity implies that individual families are more prosperous and thus more likely to escape poverty. For example, a lower unemployment rate means that parents have a greater likelihood of being employed and are then a lower risk of poverty. None of this is incorrect; it is just incomplete. As we outlined at the beginning, at least three interesting questions can be asked of how area-level and family-level factors interact in reducing poverty.

First, prosperity is likely to have both contextual and compositional influences on a family's poverty chances. For example, times and places with high unemployment rates have high poverty rates because they have more unemployed people who run a greater risk of being poor (a compositional effect). However, high unemployment rates also bring down wages, reduce public revenues, and disrupt marriages. These contextual effects impact the employed as well as the unemployed and amplify the macro-level effect beyond the direct effect of unemployed family members.

Second, prosperity has, in general, disproportionately affected the most disadvantaged (e.g., the least skilled and minorities). Prosperity pulls all types of families out of poverty, but the least skilled have benefited the most. Given that minorities tend to be "the last hired, first fired" and that working-class jobs have been the most vulnerable during recessions, the business cycle has had its greatest impact at the bottom of the stratification system. However, poverty among two-parent families has fluctuated more with the business cycle than has poverty among single-mother families (Bane and Ellwood 1989).

The third general issue is whether family-level effects translate into true area-level consequences (that is, have social effects) or whether the family-level effects include selection or queuing effects that do not imply area-level differences. Briefly, selection effects in this situation refer to differences in migration—families more likely to be poor may move to or stay in some places, thus raising the overall poverty rate. On the other hand, queuing effects represent the existence of a relative ranking of risks of being poor based on characteristics of the family (employment, education, etc.)—people higher in the queue have higher risks, and thus a family with similar characteristics may be more likely to be poor in one place than another simply because of a greater number of families with higher risks in the second area. This question is less relevant for family economic levels: providing more parents with employment or raising everyone's wages will directly reduce local or national poverty rates. However, other family-level determinants of poverty, such as race, do include selection and queuing effects so more minorities in an area will not necessarily produce higher poverty rates (but see Danziger and Gottschalk 1995).

Since our focus is on family economic levels and area prosperity, we concentrate on the first two issues in this analysis. The principal questions are to what extent the area-level prosperity effect is contextual and which families are differentially affected by prosperity. We offer three hypotheses to summarize these questions:

> Hypothesis 1: Higher levels of prosperity (lower unemployment, higher average wages, lower wage inequality) are associated with a greater chance of escaping poverty.

> Hypothesis 2: Some, but not all, of the prosperity effect on poverty chances is explained by the employment and earnings of parents. Less poverty-prone family structures (i.e., two-parent families), greater earnings by other household members, and higher public and private transfers account for some of the benefits of being in more prosperous areas.

> Hypothesis 3: Prosperity reduces the relationships between status and educational disadvantages (minority status, low skills of family heads) and the risk of family poverty although the risk of poverty for two-parent families is affected more than that of single-mother families.

METROPOLITAN AREAS AS SPATIAL UNITS

The publication of *The Truly Disadvantaged* (Wilson 1987) provoked a renewed interest in urban poverty, especially in the area-level effects of economic segregation and concentrated poverty. Much of this research has relied on neighborhoods as the unit of analysis with the assumption that neighborhoods are the context in which opportunities are structured (e.g., Danzinger and Lin 2000; Rankin and Quane 2002).

While our research contributes to this broader literature on urban poverty, it differs from much past work in two substantive ways. First, we focus directly on poverty as the outcome of interest rather than correlates of poverty such as delinquency or educational attainment. Second, we shift the unit of analysis from neighborhoods to metropolitan areas (MAs). The larger spatial unit is appropriate because the contextual factors we are interested in, namely those associated with economic prosperity, extend beyond neighborhood boundaries into regional labor markets (see Beggs and Villemez 2001 for a discussion of regional labor markets). People seek jobs outside of their immediate neighborhood, and the wages employers pay are conditioned on current rates in the larger labor market. Indeed, many of the factors determining poverty are based on regional labor markets (e.g., unemployment, wages), local marriage and housing markets (e.g., family structure, doubling

up), or networks and local institutions (e.g., transfers from friends or charities) that transcend immediate neighborhoods. Thus, the MA is an especially
appropriate spatial unit for studying the contextual conditions shaping the
risk of poverty.

Spatial analyses of poverty provide a unique opportunity to investigate
the interaction between family and labor market characteristics in determining poverty risks. Compared to annual time-series research, area-based
research provides many more macro-level units to study. This allows us to fit
more complex models at the macro-level. Moreover, regional areas are more
independent units of analysis than are years—at least in the sense that spatial autocorrelations appear to be lower than serial autocorrelations (Malhotra, Vanneman, and Kishor 1995; Vanneman 1998).

The cross-sectional range of poverty outcomes across metropolitan areas
(MAs) is also greater than the variation in poverty rates over time. In 1999
family poverty rates were especially high in places like McAllen-Edinburg-
Mission, Texas where the rate was 31.3 percent and much lower in places like
Rochester, Minnesota, where the rate was 3.8 percent. For comparison, estimates of the family poverty rate since 1959 range from a high of 18.5 percent
in 1959 to a low of 8.8 percent in 1973 (U.S. Census 1999)—a range only
one third that observed across MAs.

Finally, a practical advantage of MAs is that they are the smallest recog-
nizable geographic unit for which microdata are readily available from the
1990 Census (except for Public Use Microdata Areas, PUMAs, rarely used for
analyses). This enables us to construct area-level indicators that would not be
available for smaller geographic units and to incorporate PUMS (Public Use
Microdata Samples) data into a multilevel analysis. The MAs defined in the
1990 PUMS were constructed by the Census Bureau following definitions
from the Office of Management and Budget (U.S. Bureau of the Census
1992). Each MA contains a population center or central city with a population of at least 50,000 and the county or counties in which that population
center is located. Then additional counties are included in the metropolitan
area based on their social and economic ties, primarily commuting patterns,
with the population center.

RESEARCH DESIGN

SAMPLE

The family-level data are from the 1990 Census 1 percent and 5 percent PUMS.
All metropolitan area households with children under 18 are included. Households are assigned to metropolitan areas based on their residential "Public Use
Microdata Area" (PUMA). These are areas created by the census of at least
100,000 residents. Some PUMAs overlap MA boundaries. These are assigned to

the largest MA in that PUMA. The number of families in our sample is 1,565,344.

The primary results reported below are for 1990 Census data. However, we also present results using the 2000 Census data later in the chapter.

MEASURES

MA-level variables. We concentrate on three measures of the economic prosperity of the metropolitan area: unemployment rates, average earnings, and earnings inequality. Unemployment rates are taken from the Census STF3C files for all persons 16 years and over. The average unemployment rate in 1990 MAs was 6.4 percent; it ranged from 2.8 percent in Sioux Falls, South Dakota, to 14.3 percent in McAllen-Edinburgh-Mission, Texas. This variation across MAs, like the variation in poverty rates, is substantially greater than the variation over time in national unemployment rates.

Mean annual earnings are calculated from the PUMS for full-time, year-round male workers, ages 25 to 54. Individual male earnings are a more appropriate measure of the economic prosperity of a region than family income since average family income is determined by decisions about family formation and fertility as well as about who in the family will work. Average earnings in 1989 for metropolitan areas were $27,801. This ranged from $20,577 in Brownsville, Texas, to almost twice that level, $39,469, in New York. Average earnings in a metropolitan area are almost unrelated to the unemployment rate. The correlation across MAs (weighted by population size) is –0.056. Since we hypothesize that poverty is eliminated by good jobs that pay well, we expect both these factors to have independent effects on poverty rates.

Earnings inequality was also calculated from the PUMS sample of full-time, year-round male workers, ages 25 to 54. Gini coefficients were calculated for each MA; these coefficients range from 0.00 to 1.00 with scores closer to 1.00 indicating greater inequality in the distribution of earnings in the MA. The mean Gini coefficient was 0.346 and they ranged from 0.293 in Duluth-Superior, Minnesota, to 0.437 in Laredo, Texas. Bivariate correlations (not shown here) indicate that earnings are more unequal in areas with high average earnings but also in areas with more unemployment.

Poverty status. The dependent variable in this analysis is official poverty status. If the family is *poor*, the variable is coded 0; if the family is *not poor*, the variable is coded 1.

MA control variables. Several MA-level variables that might also be associated with poverty rates are used as controls. These include population size, region, racial/ethnic composition, religious composition, durable manufacturing, percent immigrant, age of the MA, and percent military. We expect families living in the following types of MAs to be less likely to escape poverty: those with a larger population, those incorporated longer ago, and those located in the south. Conversely, we expect families living in MAs with industrial structures favoring manufacturing and military activities to have a greater chance of avoiding poverty. Some of the MA controls reflect the racial, religious, and immigrant composition of the MA. We expect families in MAs with higher proportions of minorities, immigrants, and religious conservatives to have a greater risk of poverty. (For more information on these measures, see Cotter et al. 1998.)

Family-level variables. We include several measures in the family-level model typically included in analyses of family poverty. We group these measures into four broad categories representing common explanations for poverty. The first group represents demographic and human capital explanations as measured by mother's race, age, and education. The second set focuses on family structure as indicated by whether a father is present and the number and age of children. The third group includes labor supply variables measuring parental work effort, namely parent(s)' work status, number of hours worked, and wages. Finally, we include income from other household members and unearned family income, including public assistance, to account for the role of other sources of income in avoiding poverty.

MULTILEVEL MODELING

Multilevel models are often expressed as a series of equations. At the micro-level where $\log(p_{ia} / (1-p_{ia}))$ is the log odds of family i in area a being in poverty,

$$\ln \frac{p_{ia}}{(1 - p_{ia})} = \beta_{0a} + \sum_{j=1}^{N_j} \beta_{ja} * (X_{jia} - \overline{X_{jia}}) + r_{ia}$$

X_{jia} is a vector of j family-level variables (e.g., mother's race) describing family i in area a. The micro-level β_{ja} (including the intercepts β_{0a}) are then modeled at the macro-level as

$$\beta_{ja} = \gamma_{j0} + \sum_{j=1}^{N_j} \gamma_{jm} * (Z_{ma} - \overline{Z_{ma}}) + u_{ja}$$

where and Z_{ma} is a vector of m area-level variables (e.g., unemployment rate) describing area a. Both micro- and macro-variables are centered to facilitate interpretation of the intercepts, β_{0a} and γ_{j0}. (This is essential for the β_{0a}, merely convenient for the γ_{j0}.)

We compute these models by adding additional family-level variables to each subsequent model. By doing so we are able to sort out the compositional and contextual components of the MA-level effects. The ways in which macro-level prosperity reduce poverty chances can be identified by the steps at which the macro-level coefficient is reduced. For example, we expect the unemployment rate effect to be significantly reduced when we control for the employment and hours worked of family members. More interesting will be the changes in the unemployment rate coefficient when controls for family structure or wage rates are added. If high unemployment creates poverty in part through creating more single-parent families (either through separation and divorce or through the scarcity of marriage partners) then we should expect the unemployment rate coefficient to diminish when we control for family structure. Similarly, if part of the unemployment effect is to reduce wages even among the employed, then we should expect the MA-level unemployment coefficient to be reduced when family members' wages are controlled.

As with any spatial research, the possibility of selection bias should not be forgotten when drawing conclusions from the findings. In this case, the potential bias centers on the issue of inter-MA mobility. It is always possible that areas differ in the rate of family poverty because poverty-prone families move to (or fail to move out of) some areas; while we control explicitly for the measurable factors that may increase the risk of poverty for families, numerous unmeasured characteristics of those families may be associated with location. The kinds of people and families remaining in poor or violent neighborhoods may be different in many unmeasured ways from the people and families living in better neighborhoods. The problem of mobility exists for neighborhood research—only it is far worse there because of the greater rates of neighborhood mobility. In analyses of the 1990 PUMS we found that 1985 to 1990 *intra*-MA mobility rates ranged from a low of 35 percent for nonpoor married mothers to a high of 53 percent for poor unmarried mothers. These rates are substantially higher than the *inter*-MA mobility rates, ranging from a low of 13 percent for nonpoor unmarried mothers to a high of 21 percent for poor married mothers. As shown, mobility across MAs is lower, so the problem is not as severe, but nevertheless our conclusions would be stronger if we could sort out these area selection effects.

RESULTS

The Effect of Prosperity on Poverty Status

Table 7.1 presents the analyses of the MA-level prosperity variables predicting the poverty status of individual families. Our primary interest is the first three lines of the table that show how prosperity is translated into chances of

TABLE 7.1

MA-Level and Family-Level Effects on the Logged Odds of Not Being Poor

	MA-level only (1)	+ mother's characteristics (2)	+ family structure (3)	+ labor supply (4)	+parents' wages (5)	+ others' work and other income (6)
Variance of MA residual:	0.0230	0.0286	0.0338	0.0285	0.0058	0.0151
Overall intercept	1.838***	1.281***	1.732***	2.013***	2.815***	4.153***
MA effects on intercept						
Unemployment rate	-12.944***	-13.049***	-13.055***	-4.019***	-2.804*	-1.526
Average wage	0.094***	0.084***	0.109***	0.167***	0.084***	0.076**
Wage inequality	-3.856***	-3.319***	-3.898***	-2.124*	-1.226	0.215
Population size (log)	-0.042	-0.075*	-0.106**	-0.161***	-0.149***	-0.159***
Squared log population size	-0.004	-0.014+	-0.023**	-0.022**	-0.008	-0.009
South	0.006	0.093*	-0.019	-0.002	-0.046	-0.008
Percent African American	-0.932***	1.286***	1.192***	0.473**	0.281	0.150
Percent Hispanic	-0.293*	0.951***	0.892***	0.411*	0.606**	0.701**
Percent conservative religion	-0.107	-0.114	-0.102	-0.086	0.168	0.181
Missing religion data	0.032	0.033	0.049	0.058	0.150**	0.166**
Percent durable manufacturing	0.308	0.774**	0.534+	0.789**	0.396	0.377
Percent immigrant	-0.754	4.135*	4.386*	2.688	-3.703+	-6.273**
Age of MA	-0.001*	-0.001**	-0.001*	-0.000	0.000	-0.000
Percent military	0.894***	0.933***	0.777***	0.573***	0.833***	0.652**

(continued on next page)

TABLE 7.1 (continued)

	MA-level only (1)	+ mother's characteristics (2)	+ family structure (3)	+ labor supply (4)	+ parents' wages (5)	+ others' work and other income (6)
Family-level effects on intercept						
Mother present		0.141+	1.033***	1.847***	1.557***	2.272***
Mother African American		-1.748***	-0.852***	-0.729***	-0.625***	-0.465***
Mother Native American		-1.200***	-0.839***	-0.619***	-0.497***	-0.381***
Mother Asian American		-0.410***	-0.639***	-0.609***	-0.469***	-0.437**
Mother Latina		-0.818***	-0.650***	-0.597***	-0.498***	-0.523***
Mother's age		0.041***	0.044***	0.060***	0.064***	0.026***
Mother's education		0.228***	0.215***	0.108***	0.058***	0.061***
Father present			2.544***	3.435***	4.162***	5.179***
Father's age			-0.014***	0.035***	0.024***	0.011***
N children under 3			-0.661***	-0.467***	-0.506***	-0.762***
N children 3–5			-0.509***	-0.400***	-0.521***	-0.679***
N children 6–11			-0.414***	-0.434***	-0.588***	-0.658***
N children 12–17			-0.307***	-0.438***	-0.571***	-0.733***
Father's education				0.103***	0.048***	0.052***
Mother worked				2.108***	3.493***	4.070***
Father worked				3.633***	3.167***	3.941***
Mother's hours worked (log)				0.988***	1.196***	1.422***

(continued on next page)

TABLE 7.1 (continued)

	MA-level only (1)	+ mother's characteristics (2)	+ family structure (3)	+ labor supply (4)	+parents' wages (5)	+ others' work and other income (6)
Father's hours worked (log)				1.552***	2.215***	2.613***
Mother's wage (log)					1.823***	2.111***
Father's wage (log)					3.137***	3.598***
Other family women worked						2.175***
Other family men worked						2.276***
Other family women wage (log)						1.456***
Other family men wage (log)						1.634***
Other nonearned income						1.518***
Public assistance						0.122*

+ p < 0.10   * p < 0.05   ** p < 0.01   *** p < 0.001

avoiding poverty. Column 1 presents the MA-level associations of the prosperity measures with poverty chances before controlling for any characteristics of the family. As expected, a family's chances of escaping poverty are higher in MAs with higher average earnings and lower in MAs with greater earnings inequality and higher unemployment. This model accounts for 87 percent of the variance in poverty chances across MAs. Prosperity levels are the important factors and by themselves account for 81 percent of the total MA-level variance in poverty. Unemployment levels are especially predictive although the earnings levels also matter.

Some of these MA-level prosperity effects are a result of the different types of families who live in high prosperity areas versus those living in low prosperity areas. A rough idea of those compositional differences can be found in the results of column 2 where controls for the mother's race, age, and education are added. The MA-level earnings effects are somewhat reduced in this model although the unemployment effect is virtually unchanged. More educated women tend to live in MAs with high earnings, so part of the reason for less poverty in those MAs is because the families are less prone to poverty. But even comparing families in which the mothers have the same education, the families in higher earnings labor markets are much more likely to escape poverty. For example, a family with a mother who is a high school dropout is less likely to be poor in an MA with high average earnings (such as Duluth, Minnesota) than in an MA with lower earnings (such as Laredo, Texas).

Column 2 presents the addition of controls for the demographic and human capital factors mothers bring to the labor and marriage markets. It is striking how little the prosperity coefficients change after controls for the mother's characteristics are entered, though the census PUMS allows us to control for only a few of these. From these results it appears that area unemployment rates especially, but earnings levels too, have major impacts on *all* families' chances of escaping poverty.

At least some poverty among families results from the rise of nonnormative family structures, especially the spread of single-mother families (e.g., Cancian and Reed 2001; Gottschalk and Danziger 1993; Murray 1995). However, another dimension of family structure, the decline in average family size, has offset the risk of poverty for some families (Gottschalk and Danziger 1993). To account for these differences in family structure, the third column adds controls for family structure, measured by presence of the father and the number of children by ages. At the family level, these have the expected influences. The presence of a father greatly increases the family's chance of escaping poverty while more children, especially younger ones, reduce that chance. Our interest here is in whether these family structure differences explain much of the area prosperity effect. Since unemployment and low earnings can provoke more family disruptions and provide fewer marriageable partners for women, some of the prosperity effect might be explained by more intact family structures in the more prosperous areas. The results in column 3 do not support this interpretation. The unemployment and earnings coefficients are not reduced by controls for family structure. Higher poverty rates in less prosperous MAs are not a consequence of more single mothers or more children per family in those MAs.

Conventional thought suggests that the most obvious way for a family to avoid poverty is through employment. Welfare reforms of the mid-1990s were to some extent predicated on this assumption. Thus, we expect the prosperity effects on the logged odds of being nonpoor to be reduced when controls for family labor supply are included. Controls for the extent of work by the mother and, if present, the father are added to the model in column 4. As expected, these family-level labor supply controls account for most of the association between high unemployment rates in a local labor market and higher poverty. MAs with high unemployment have higher poverty rates primarily because mothers and fathers work less often in those MAs and, when they do work, work fewer hours. Although the coefficient for the MA unemployment rate is substantially reduced in this model, it is still negative and statistically significant. The poverty-inducing effects of unemployment are not solely a consequence of the lack of work for parents. In other words, even families in which parents have jobs are more likely to be classified among the poor in MAs with higher unemployment rates than in MAs with lower unemployment rates.

There has been some discussion in policy circles that part of the explanation for higher poverty rates is a quasi-discouraged worker effect. Some speculate that the declining wages for less educated male workers has led to more men withdrawing from the labor market entirely. If part of the reason families are poor is because low average wages in an MA drive potential workers out of the labor market, then we would expect the coefficient for average earnings to decrease in size in column 4. However, in this model, the coefficient for average earnings *increases* once the parents' labor supply is held constant. That is, if parents across the country were all to work the same hours, the average wage rate of their local labor market would be even more important in determining their chances of avoiding poverty. This also implies that in areas with low wage rates parents in fact work *more*, not fewer, hours. At least across MAs, we find no support for the argument that families are more likely to be poor in areas with lower average wages because of quasi-discouraged work effort.

Unlike that for average earnings, the coefficient for earnings inequality does decline substantially (from −3.898 to −2.124, about 46 percent) when parents' labor supply is held constant. In MAs with high wage *inequality*, parents work less, and this leads to higher rates of poverty. Thus the rising earnings inequality in the last quarter of the 20th century may have had a double impact on creating higher poverty rates: inequality reduces earnings for the lowest earnings groups when they do work and also reduces labor supply by not offering sufficient incentives to work.

Controls for the parents' actual wage rates are added in the fifth column. As expected, parents' wages explain much of the effect of MA average wage rates and wage inequality on poverty. The MA coefficient for average wage rates declines from 0.167 to 0.084, almost by half. Nevertheless, the MA coefficient is still statistically significant: average wage rates in a labor market increase a family's chances of escaping poverty even after controlling for the parents' wages. However, the association between *wage inequality* and poverty chances is no longer significant once parents' wages are controlled. Considering the decline in the size and statistical significance of the inequality coefficient from model 3 to model 5, we conclude that the impact of inequality on poverty is primarily explained by parents working less and by their working for lower wages in more unequal labor markets. If families averaged the same amount of work effort and earned comparable wages for that effort across all MAs, then inequality would have less of an impact on families' risks of poverty. However, we know that families do not average the same work effort or earn comparable incomes for that effort across MAs. Families in areas with greater inequality in fact work less and, when employed, earn less for that work, both of which contribute to a greater risk of poverty.

Similarly, the now small effect of unemployment rates is further reduced (from −4.019 to −2.804) when parents' wage rates are held constant. This documents the double impact of high unemployment on poverty rates. Mostly, high unemployment means parents are employed less (compare the unemployment rate coefficients in columns 3 and 4), but it also means that when employed, many parents earn less in high unemployment areas, sending more families into poverty. Parents may earn less in these high unemployment areas in part because the competition for jobs is greater, allowing employers set lower wages for those who do find jobs. Nevertheless even these two effects to do not explain all the negative impacts of unemployment: the MA coefficient for the area unemployment rate is still statistically significant in column 5.

Families may be able to avoid poverty (or at least the worst experiences of poverty) by turning to others in their immediate and extended network for assistance, including family and friends, other household members, and charities and welfare offices (Edin and Lein 1997; Nelson and Smith 1999; Cotter, Hermsen, and Vanneman 2001). To account for this, the final column adds additional controls for the wages and labor supply of other household members and for the receipt of public assistance and other unearned income (e.g., rental income and dividends). These controls reduce all three MA-level prosperity coefficients. The MA unemployment rate is no longer significantly associated with a family's poverty chances. High unemployment not only hurts parents' labor market outcomes (as noted above), but it also hurts the labor market outcomes of other family members, increasing poverty risks. In MAs with high unemployment, members of a family's extended network also have difficulty finding jobs and when they do find work, these jobs pay less. Hence, extended family members and friends have fewer economic resources themselves, limiting their capacity to help others avoid poverty. Unemployment is also related to other income generation strategies. Residing in an MA with high unemployment would not necessarily translate into a higher risk of poverty if the families in that MA had greater access to public assistance and other forms of unearned income.

Higher wage areas offer families a greater chance of escaping poverty even when all the family level controls are included. More complex family-level models would be needed to fully explain these advantages of high-wage areas (e.g., possible interactions among family-level characteristics or alternative functional forms of the family-level effects).

THE DIFFERENTIAL EFFECTS OF PROSPERITY

The second part of our analysis looks at how area-level prosperity may affect families differentially. For example, are minorities or the less educated especially hurt by high unemployment or low wages in the local labor market? And are local economic conditions especially important for the poverty chances of two-parent families while single-mother poverty is less determined by the economy?

These questions are easily addressed in multilevel analyses by allowing the family-level coefficients to vary across MAs. In the previous analyses, only the family-level intercept was allowed to vary with economic conditions. By dropping the assumption that, for example, the effect of a father's absence is the same in all labor market areas, we can test whether some types of families are especially vulnerable to economic misfortune.

We use the model in column 3 in table 7.1 to test these questions. That model includes family-level coefficients for the mother's race, age, and education, the presence of the father, and the number and ages of the children. The variation of these coefficients across MAs is reported in table 7.2.

Differential effects of prosperity by race and class. Columns 2 through 5 report how the disadvantages due to race and ethnicity vary across MAs. Our hypotheses lead us to believe that minorities, being the last hired and first fired, are the most vulnerable to economic downturns. The results do not support that hypothesis. In fact, the reverse is more nearly the case. While the intercepts for each race coefficient are negative (reflecting minorities' greater poverty chances on average), a higher MA unemployment rate makes all these coefficients *less* negative (i.e., the effect of the MA unemployment rate on the mother's race coefficient is positive). None of these coefficients are so large that they would cancel the minority disadvantages entirely under usual conditions. For example, it would take an unemployment rate of 15.3 percent

TABLE 7.2

The Differential Effects of MA-Level Characteristics on the Logged Odds of Not Being Poor, by Family Characteristics

	Intercept (average effect)	Racial/ethnic group of mother					
		African American	Latina	Asian American	Native American	Mother's education	Mother's age
MA-level effects							
Intercept (average effect)	1.719***	-0.772***	-0.537***	-0.996***	-0.825***	0.238***	0.046***
Unemployment rate	-14.591***	5.260***	5.412**	9.748***	5.979*	0.774***	0.166***
Average wage	0.100***	-0.012	-0.034	-0.094**	0.021	-0.009**	0.002**
Wage inequality	-4.301***	-7.386***	6.136***	5.123*	-1.306	-0.263	-0.022
Population size (log)	-0.089*	0.089*	0.014	0.167**	-0.013	0.009	-0.006***
Square log population	-0.015	0.028**	0.001	0.023	-0.013	0.003+	-0.001*
South	0.030	0.125*	0.011	0.225*	0.280**	0.025**	-0.008***
Percent African American	1.766***	-1.350***	-0.829*	-1.617**	-0.849	-0.059	-0.017*
Percent Hispanic	0.892***	-0.373	-1.009***	0.014	-0.030	-0.088*	0.002
Percent conservative religion	-0.396**	-0.089	0.721***	0.340	0.088	0.029	0.008+
Religion data missing	0.029	-0.030	0.034	-0.009	-0.095	0.001	0.000
Percent durable manufacturing	0.473	-1.299**	0.180	1.195	0.752	0.012	0.038**
Percent immigrants	4.682*	-0.497	-4.796*	-11.420**	0.941	-2.030***	-0.192**
Age of MA	-0.001**	-0.001	0.000	-0.001	-0.001	0.000***	0.000***
Percent in military	0.637***	0.654***	-0.090	1.026+	-0.245	-0.089*	0.008

(continued on next page)

TABLE 7.2 (continued)

| | Father present | Father's age | Number of children | | | | Mother present |
			Under 3	3–5	6–11	12–17	
MA-level effects							
Intercept (average effect)	2.557	-0.018***	-0.682***	-0.489***	-0.399***	-0.296***	0.861
Unemployment rate	1.540	0.022	2.003***	0.499	0.404	0.230	-5.624***
Average wage	0.020*	-0.002*	0.032***	0.021*	0.021**	0.025***	-0.041***
Wage inequality	-3.157***	0.096*	0.102	0.781+	0.714*	0.121	0.141
Population size (log)	-0.089***	0.004**	-0.013	-0.038**	-0.027**	-0.018+	0.050*
Square log population	-0.006***	0.000	0.007+	-0.005	-0.002	-0.001	-0.004***
South	-0.207***	-0.006**	-0.021	-0.040*	-0.042**	-0.005	-0.110***
Percent African American	0.417	-0.031***	-0.005	0.017	-0.023	-0.134	1.611
Percent Hispanic	-0.871***	0.000	0.223**	0.042	-0.006	-0.023	0.994
Percent conservative religion	-0.444***	0.013**	0.138*	0.113+	0.119*	0.066	-0.340***
Religion data missing	-0.014***	0.001	-0.005	0.047*	0.002	-0.004	0.009**
Percent durable manufacturing	0.504	-0.012	-0.086	0.333*	0.072	0.123	-1.056***
Percent immigrants	-3.686***	0.036	0.838	1.811**	0.931+	0.272	4.503
Age of MA	0.001**	0.000	0.000	0.000	0.000	0.000+	-0.001***
% in military	0.541	0.006	0.028	0.177*	-0.040	0.044	-0.529***

+ p < 0.10   * p < 0.05   ** p < 0.01   *** p < 0.001

above the average (6.1 percent) before African Americans' predicted poverty was the same as whites' (the intercept, −0.772, minus 0.153 times the unemployment rate coefficient, −5.260, equals 0.0). Nevertheless, all the signs of the unemployment rate coefficients are positive, and all are statistically significant. Gunderson and Ziliak (2004) observed a similar effect of state-level changes in unemployment on changes in black pretax poverty rates. Thus, white families' chances of poverty increase the most when the local labor market has higher unemployment.

Lower average wage rates do not affect racial groups quite so differently. White, African American, Latina, and Native American women all have greater chances of being poor in areas where average wage rates are lower. Or, looked at alternatively, the disadvantages of these women are fairly constant across low-wage and high-wage MAs. The poverty of Asian American mothers, on the other hand, is less affected by MA wage rates than is the poverty of other groups.

Area inequality has contrasting effects on different minority groups. Greater inequality increases the risk of poverty for families headed by African American women more than for families headed by white women. This is the only example of economic disadvantage increasing the poverty chances for African American families more than for white families. In contrast, for families with Latina and Asian American women, greater inequality has less effect on their poverty chances than it does for families headed by white women. Of course, these minority families begin with a greater risk of poverty in the average MA, but with increasing inequality, white families' chances of poverty rise to meet Latina and Asian American rates. Native American women are affected by inequality similarly to white women. But African American families are hurt most by living in a labor market with high inequality. Their poverty rates are high in low inequality areas, and those rates rise faster with inequality than do rates of other racial-ethnic groups.

The effects of prosperity on families with less educated and more educated mothers are closer to the expected results of prosperity helping especially the most disadvantaged. High unemployment rates increase the risk of poverty among families headed by less educated mothers more than among families with well-educated mothers. Similarly, low average wages increase poverty especially among less educated families. Thus, our hypothesis of greater prosperity effects on families disadvantaged by class or race is supported for class disadvantages but not for racial/ethnic disadvantages.

Differential effects of prosperity by family structure. Finally, we look at how the local economy affects poverty rates differently for single-mother families versus two-parent families and for large and small families. Our hypothesis leads us to expect that two-parent families' economic well-being is more related to economic conditions. The results only partially support that hypothesis.

Unemployment rates affect single-mother families about the same as two-parent families. There is no significant difference in the father-present coefficient between high unemployment areas and low unemployment areas; indeed, the sign is in the wrong direction for our hypothesis. Average earnings levels and especially earnings inequality do affect two-parent families more than single-parent families. But this is still somewhat different from Bane and Ellwood's (1989) conclusion that more short-term fluctuations of unemployment rates differentially impact intact families while long-term increases have dominated the poverty trends for single mothers. Our cross-area patterns suggest that low earnings and high inequality—economic conditions that change more gradually than unemployment rates—affect the poverty risk of two-parent families.

Comparing families with more children and fewer children, the most consistent result is that low area-wage rates contribute to greater poverty among large families more than among small families. The impact of unemployment rates varies less across family sizes (although poverty in families with young children is less responsive to unemployment rates). Perhaps parents in larger families already have maximized their total feasible labor supply so that unemployment rates have little impact on their labor supply and thus poverty chances. But if the wages are low for the available jobs, then larger families have a greater risk of becoming the working poor.

CENSUS 2000 RESULTS

As noted earlier, we replicated the analyses presented above using data from the 2000 Census PUMS. However, due to the use of more extensive strategies to protect confidentiality, we were able to identify only 80 MAs that appear in both the 1 percent and 5 percent 2000 PUMS (U.S. Bureau of the Census 2004). This is far less than the 261 MAs available in the 1990 PUMS. The 2000 results are substantively similar to the results from 1990, although they do not reach conventional levels of statistical significance due, we believe, to the reduced sample size at the MA level.

In table 7.3 we present a general comparison of results from the 1990 PUMS (shown in table 7.1) and 2000 PUMS. The table indicates the change in the size of the coefficients for unemployment rate, average wages, and wage inequality as additional controls are added to the model. For example, the first column shows that in both the 1990 and 2000 analyses, the coefficient for the unemployment rate increases as the controls for mother's characteristics are added to the model. In addition, the coefficient for wage inequality declines in both analyses as these same characteristics are held constant. Fifteen pairs of coefficients are presented in table 7.3, yet only four show different patterns comparing the 1990 and 2000 analyses, and three of these reflect the fact that the average wage measure changed very little with the addition

TABLE 7.3

Comparison of Results from the 1990 and 2000 PUMS Analyses

	Change in size of coefficient from col. 1 to col. 2		Change in size of coefficient from col. 2 to col. 3		Change in size of coefficient from col. 3 to col. 4		Change in size of coefficient from col. 4 to col. 5		Change in size of coefficient from col. 5 to col. 6	
	1990	2000	1990	2000	1990	2000	1990	2000	1900	2000
Unemployment Rate	+	+	+	−	−	−	−	−	−	−
Average wage	−	none	+	none	+	none	−	−	−	−
Wage inequality	−	−	+	+	−	−	−	−	−	−

of controls to the first three models. We interpret the similarities between coefficients for the 1990 and 2000 PUMS analyses as further evidence in support of the results we report above.

Although not shown in table 7.3, the largest declines in coefficient size for the wage inequality measure in both the 1990 and 2000 analyses occur with the addition of controls for parental labor supply (table 7.1, column 4) and parental wage rates (table 7.1, column 5). Similarly, the coefficient for average wage rates changes the most in both years with the addition of controls for parental wage rates. This confirms one of our central findings: greater inequality and lower average wage rates contribute to a higher poverty risk because of the suppression of parental labor supply and the reduction of earnings among those who work. The 2000 results for the effect of unemployment rate on poverty chances are slightly less supportive of the 1990 results. In the 1990 analyses, the largest decline in the coefficient for the unemployment rate occurred with the addition of labor supply measures to the model (table 7.1, columns 3 and 4). However, in the 2000 analyses, the effect of unemployment was reduced equally (15 percent) between columns 2 and 3 as between columns 3 and 4, that is, with the addition of family structure and labor supply controls. Nonetheless, we find the broad support in the PUMS 2000 analyses for the extensive results we reported above.

Because the MA sample size is restricted in the 2000 PUMS, researchers may want to find solutions for identifying more areas in the 2000 data. It may be possible to increase sample size by combining together as an area those households in "unidentified MAs" in each state, for example, by taking all the records in Missouri identified as in an unnamed MA and treating that as an MA. This would obviously be a less than perfect solution. Another alternative is to use one of the secure Research Data Centers operated by the Bureau of the Census (Tolbert et al. 2002) to access restricted geographic information.

DISCUSSION

This analysis began with the unremarkable fact that poverty is higher in areas of higher unemployment, lower wages, and greater earnings inequality. Analysts and policymakers have long identified these macro-economic conditions as crucial to determining poverty rates. Our multilevel analyses sought to ask two additional types of questions. First, *how* do economic conditions affect family poverty risks? Second, do economic conditions *differentially* affect the poverty risks of different families? Our answers to these questions sometimes confirm our hypotheses and sometimes yield unexpected results.

High unemployment areas do have higher poverty rates primarily because parents are less likely to be working, and when they do work, they work fewer hours. But families who are working the same hours still fare worse in high unemployment areas, primarily because their wage rates are lower. On the other hand, there was no evidence that a father's absence is a link between high unemployment areas and more poverty. While a father's absence sub-stantially raises the risk of poverty, it does not appear to be related to area unemployment rates. Moreover, unemployment rates appear to affect the poverty chances of single-mother and two-parent families almost equally. Nor do unemployment rates especially hurt the chances of minority families; in fact, unemployment rates appear to increase the risk of poverty more for white families. The poverty rates of families with less educated parents are especially sensitive to unemployment rates.

Low average wages in an area substantially raise the risk of poverty for all families. The most obvious way in which low wage rates increase poverty is that equivalent parents earn less money in low wage areas. There is also a small effect mediated by the earnings of other household members and through unearned income (lower likelihoods of both public assistance and other types of income in low wage areas). Low area wages do not reduce labor supply. In fact, it appears that low wages have counterbalancing impacts on poverty chances through labor supply: while their main effect is to increase poverty through lower earnings, low wages also have a slight negative effect on poverty chances through increasing labor supply. Where wages are low, both parents are more likely to work and to work more hours. Nor is there any evidence in these data that low wages increase poverty by raising the pro-portions of single-mother families. Having eliminated the family structure and labor supply explanations for the low wage effect, it is still important to note that the multilevel analysis fails to explain all the poverty differences between high wage and low wage areas.

Area wage rates are especially important for explaining poverty among the less educated. However, low area wages appear to increase the risk of poverty among white families as much as among minority families. The poverty chances of two-parent families are somewhat more dependent on area wage rates than are the poverty chances of single-mother families. And larger families are especially sensitive to the local average wage rates.

Wage inequality also increases families' poverty risks. The main mecha-nisms appear to be lower parental earnings and less other household income, but labor supply also declines when wage inequality is high. This may reflect a relative judgment among families. Since low average earnings do not by themselves reduce family labor supply, it must be low earnings relative to the average that discourages family members from working more. A surprising proportion of the effect of inequality on poverty is mediated through this lack of incentive that results from greater inequality. Wage inequality is especially important for the poverty chances of two-parent families and of African Americans. On the other hand, the poverty chances of Latino and Asian American families are less responsive to wage inequality than are the poverty chances of white families. Why might this be? Latino and Asian families are disproportionately located among newer immigrant families. Perhaps immigrant families are less deterred by large income gaps than are African American and other native-born families who understandably feel more entitled to an equitable division of rewards for work (Waldinger and Lichter 2003).

What do our findings mean for families today? The economic conditions of the 1990s and early 2000s present a mixed bag. Although average earnings increased in the 1990s, wage inequality continued to increase. In addition, the unemployment rate has fluctuated in concert with short-term economic cycles, although there is concern that a growing segment of adults are discouraged and have left the labor force altogether. These facts do not bode well for American families and their chances of escaping poverty. Particularly disconcerting is the continuing rise in wage inequality. It is a key mechanism in increasing family poverty as it not only lowers parental earnings and the earnings of others in the household (earnings obviously important in escaping poverty) but also serves as a disincentive to work. That is, family members are less likely to seek work when their relative rewards for that work will be lower. If wage inequality continues unabated, we should expect to see no substantial decline in family poverty in coming years.

What do our findings mean for the study of poverty? Although research on poverty had been a long-standing intellectual project for many scholars in the social sciences, the publication of *The Truly Disadvantaged* (Wilson 1987) and the subsequent *When Work Disappears* (Wilson 1996) generated new interest in the study of poverty, especially urban poverty. A central claim of this work is that limited opportunities for employment and good wages contribute to the spread of single-mother families in an area, which in turn contribute to a greater risk of family poverty. Our results lend little support to this argument. We find that families in areas with limited economic prosperity do have greater risks of poverty, but much of this is accounted for by the negative impacts on high unemployment, low wages, and high inequality on the labor supply of parents (both mothers and fathers) as well as on wages these parents can earn. Differences in family structure, however, are unable to account for much the impact of poor economic conditions on the risk of poverty. These results affirm the importance of testing spatial theories with spatially variable data using appropriate methods such as multilevel analyses.

In conclusion, we believe multilevel analyses can strengthen the emphasis of this volume that spatially oriented research is necessary to test adequately our social science theories and to develop more complex and nuanced understandings of social life. Sorting out compositional and contextual effects and investigating cross-level interactions are greatly facilitated by these models. However, rethinking contextual dimensions is difficult when, even as researchers, we are embedded in a larger culture that sees the world primarily in individualistic and reductionist terms. Spatially-oriented multilevel modeling provides an opportunity to overcome these difficulties and to advance many areas of social science inquiry, including but by no means limited to poverty.

NOTE

1. Authors are listed alphabetically to reflect the equal sharing of work. Support for this research was provided by grants from the National Science Foundation (SBR-9422546, SBR-9870949, SBR-9870980, and SBR-9871204).

REFERENCES

Bane, Mary Jo and David T. Ellwood. 1989. "One Fifth of the Nation's Children: Why Are They Poor?" *Science* 245:1047–1053.

Beggs, John J. and Wayne J. Villemez. 2001. "Regional Labor Markets." Pp. 503–530 in *Sourcebook of Labor Markets: Evolving Structures and Processes*, edited by I. Berg and A. L. Kalleberg. New York: Kluwer Academic/Plenum Publishers.

Brown, David L., and Thomas A. Hirschl. 1995. "Household Poverty in Rural and Metropolitan-Core Areas of the United States." *Rural Sociology* 60:1:44–66.

Cancian, Maria and Deborah Reed. 2001. "Changes in Family Structure: Implications for Poverty and Related Policy." Pp. 69–96 in *Understanding Poverty*, edited by S. Danziger and R. Haveman. Cambridge, MA: Harvard University Press.

Cotter, David A., JoAnn DeFiore, Joan M. Hermsen, Brenda Marsteller Kowalewski, and Reeve Vanneman. 1998. "The Demand for Female Labor." *American Journal of Sociology* 103:1673–1712.

Cotter, David A., Joan M. Hermsen, and Reeve Vanneman. 2001. "Where the Ends Don't Meet: Spatial Variation in Economic Hardships." Presented at the Annual Meetings of the Society for the Study of Social Problems, Anaheim, CA, August.

Danziger, Sheldon, and Peter Gottschalk. 1995. *America Unequal*. Cambridge, MA: Harvard University Press. New York: Russell Sage Foundation.

Danziger, Sheldon and Ann Chih Lin, eds. 2000. *Coping with Poverty: The Social Context of Neighborhood, Work, and Family in the African American Community*. Ann Arbor, MI: University of Michigan Press.

Edin, Kathryn, and Laura Lein. 1997. *Making Ends Meet: How Single Mothers Survive Welfare and Low-Wage Work*. New York: Russell Sage Foundation.

Gottschalk, Peter and Sheldon Danziger. 1993. "Family Structure, Family Size, and Family Income." Pp. 167–193 in *Uneven Tides*, edited by S. Danziger and P. Gottschalk. New York: Russell Sage Foundation.

Gundersen, Craig and James P. Ziliak. 2004. "Poverty and Macroeconomic Performance across Space, Race, and Family Structure." *Demography* 41:61–86.

Haynie, Dana L. and Bridget K. Gorman. 1999. "A Gendered Context of Opportunity: Determinants of Poverty Across Urban and Rural Labor Markets." *Sociological Quarterly* 40:177–197.

Levy, Frank and Richard J. Murnane. 1992. "U.S. Earnings Levels and Earnings Inequality: A Review of Recent Trends and Proposed Explanations." *Journal of Economic Literature* 30:1333–1381.

Lichter, Daniel T. and Diane K. McLaughlin. 1995. "Changing Economic Opportunities, Family Structure, and Poverty in Rural Areas." *Rural Sociology* 60:688–706.

Lobao, Linda. 1990. *Locality and Inequality: Farm and Industry Structure and Socioeconomic Conditions.* Albany, NY: State University of New York Press.

Lobao, Linda M. and Michael D. Schulman. 1991. "Farming Patterns, Rural Restructuring, and Poverty: A Comparative Regional Analysis." *Rural Sociology* 56:565–602.

Malhotra, Anju, Reeve Vanneman, and Sunita Kishor. 1995. "Fertility, Dimensions of Patriarchy, and Development in India." *Population and Development Review* 21:281–305.

Massey, Douglas S. and Mitchell L. Eggers. 1990. "The Ecology of Inequality: Minorities and the Concentration of Poverty." *American Journal of Sociology* 95:1153–1188.

Moffit, Robert. 1992. "Incentive Effects of the U.S Welfare System: A Review." *Journal of Economic Literature* 30:1–61.

Murray, Charles. 1995. *Losing Ground: American Social Policy 1950–1980.* 10th Anniversary Edition. New York: Basic Books.

Nelson, Margaret K. and Joan Smith. 1999. *Working Hard and Making Do: Surviving in Small Town America.* Berkeley: University of California Press.

Okun, Arthur M. 1973. "Upward Mobility in a High-Pressure Economy." *Brookings Papers on Economic Activity* 207–252.

Rankin, Bruce H. and James M. Quane. 2002. "Social Contexts and Urban Adolescent Outcomes: The Interrelated Effects of Neighborhoods, Families, and Peers on African-American Youth." *Social Problems* 49:79–100.

Tickamyer, Ann. 2000. "Space Matters: Spatial Inequality in Future Sociology." *Contemporary Sociology* 29:805–813.

Tolbert, Charles, Michael Irwin, Thomas Lyson, and Alfred Nucci. 2002. "Civic Community in Small-Town America: How Civic Welfare is Influenced by Local Capitalism and Civic Engagement." *Rural Sociology* 67:90–114.

Tomaskovic-Devey, Donald. 1991. "A Structural Model of Poverty Creation and Change: Political Economy, Local Opportunity, and U.S. Poverty, 1959–1979." *Research in Social Stratification and Mobility* 10:289–322.

U.S. Bureau of the Census. 1992. Census of Population and Housing, 1990: Public Use Microdata Sample U.S. Technical Documentation. Washington, DC: Bureau of the Census.

———. 1999. "Historical Poverty Tables—Families." Retrieved August 18, 2006 (http://www.census.gov/hhes/poverty/histpov/hstpov13.html).

———. 2004. Census of Population and Housing, 2000: Public Use Microdata Sample: 5–percent Sample. Washington, DC: Bureau of the Census.

Vanneman, Reeve. 1998. "Whose Age at Marriage Matters for Gender Inequality? Hers, His, or the Difference Between Them?" Presented at the Conference on Unequal Partnerships: Gender and Initiation of Sexual Activity, June 25–26, Bethesda, Maryland.

Waldinger, Roger and Michael I. Lichter. 2003. *How the Other Half Work: Immigration and the Social Organization of Labor*. Berkeley: University of California Press.

Wilson, William J. 1987. *The Truly Disadvantaged*. Chicago: University of Chicago Press.

———. 1996. *When Work Disappears*. Chicago: University of Chicago Press.

EIGHT

Adios Aztlan

Mexican American Out-Migration from the Southwest

ROGELIO SAENZ
CYNTHIA M. CREADY
MARIA CRISTINA MORALES

THIS CHAPTER EXAMINES the migration patterns of Mexican Americans, the nation's second largest minority group and the principal Latino population, out of the Southwest region where the group has historically been concentrated. This region is a "homeland" of Mexican Americans due to ancestral roots of the Aztecs in the area prior to migrating south into the Valley of Mexico and to the region's continued hold on Mexican Americans. Nevertheless, there has been significant migration activity and the establishment of settlements outside the Southwest beginning in the early 20th century. As in the case of African Americans (Burr et al. 1992; Fligstein 1981), the movement of Mexican Americans out of the Southwest has been stimulated by relatively high levels of inequality and discrimination in the region (Saenz 1993, 1999). The earliest farm labor migration streams initiated in the early 1900s began in response to better wages and working conditions outside of the Southwest (Montejano 1987).

While sociologists and demographers recognize the links between inequality and out-migration among minority groups, researchers commonly resort to broad conceptualizations of the regions external to where such groups are concentrated. For example, in the case of African Americans, we tend to see research examining the South-North movement or the movement across census-designated regions (e.g., South, Northeast, Midwest, and West). The underlying assumption of such an approach is that the areas comprising the region(s) outside the traditional homeland are relatively similar along a broad array of dimensions (e.g., distance, cultural barriers, potential for integration, etc.). Such an approach also hides the historical processes through which minority group members venture into new destinations and establish settlements that eventually facilitate the continued movement of co-ethnics to these localities. As such, minority group members in the group's homeland may find it easier to migrate to some places where co-ethnics have established migration routes but more difficult to move to other areas. We suggest it takes varying levels of resources (i.e., human capital and social capital) for minority group members to venture into these two distinct areas. We introduce the concepts of "periphery" and "frontier" areas relative to the "core" (or "homeland") area for Mexican Americans to better account for the diverse nature of locations outside the Southwest (see also Saenz 1991). These concepts reflect variations in the contemporary and historical presence of Mexican Americans in the three regions. We suggest that this approach is a more nuanced attempt to capture the extent to which space varies in its potential attractiveness as destination areas for potential migrants and in the resources necessary for migration.

The persistent hold of the Southwest, characterized as "Aztlan," on the Mexican-origin population is demonstrated by its overwhelming representation there compared to other parts of the country throughout the 20th century. In 1910, for example, 95 percent of the Mexican origin population lived in the Southwest. In 1990, and in 2000, the region's share of the population was still quite large at 83 percent and 74 percent, respectively (Guzman 2001; U.S. Bureau of the Census 1991).

Because of the ongoing, large-scale concentration of Mexican Americans in the Southwest, they are often portrayed as a "regional minority." This view, however, masks their historical and contemporary presence in other regions. As early as the first decades of the 20th century, some began to venture out of the Southwest to midwestern and western "frontier" areas where relatively few of them lived. The presence of Mexican American enclaves in certain parts of the country today reflects the establishment and solidification of social ties linking the Southwest to these regions. Yet many parts of the United States represent new frontiers for Mexican Americans. Indeed, their movement to areas with few Mexican Americans suggests continual exploration of frontier areas.

The late 1980s, the time frame of this analysis, represents an important stage in the migration patterns of Mexicans Americans. Two important events arose during the period which signaled potential changes in the distribution patterns of Mexican Americans. First, in 1986, the U.S.

Congress enacted the Immigration Reform and Control Act (IRCA), which allowed selected groups of undocumented immigrants to eventually become U.S. citizens, thus enhancing the opportunity structure outside the traditional Southwest region, which is marked by high levels of inequality among persons of Mexican origin (Murdock, Zhai, and Saenz 1999; Saenz 1993, 1999). Second, at the same time, the meat and poultry processing industry experienced significant restructuring, which resulted in the movement of low-wage jobs to rural areas of the Midwest and South (Saenz and Torres 2003). These two events represented the harbingers of the important shifts in the geographic distribution of Mexicans American in the following decade. The 1985 to 1990 period represents an under-studied segment preceding the significant change in the distribution patterns of this population.

This paper uses data from the 1990 Public Use Microdata Sample (PUMS) to examine the migration patterns of Mexican Americans to areas outside the Southwest between 1985 and 1990 (U.S. Bureau of the Census 1993a). We categorize the 50 states and the District of Columbia into three regions on the basis of the presence of Mexican Americans in the area: the "homeland" or core, the periphery, and the frontier. The homeland is made up of the five southwestern states (Arizona, California, Colorado, New Mexico, and Texas), where the vast majority live. The periphery consists of about one-half of the nonsouthwestern states with much smaller Mexican-origin populations than the five southwestern states but relatively large Mexican-origin populations compared to other nonsouthwestern states. With relatively few Mexican Americans, the remaining nonsouthwestern states and the District of Columbia are included in the frontier. The analysis draws on migration theory to examine the selectivity of Mexican American migrants moving from the Southwest to the other two regions between 1985 and 1990 and also identifies the roles of human capital and social capital resources in facilitating this movement. The paper concludes with a descriptive comparison of the geographic distribution of Mexican Americans across the core, periphery, and frontier in 2000 relative to the context of the observed migration patterns from 1985 to 1990.

THEORETICAL FRAMEWORK

We draw on several theoretical perspectives from the migration literature to guide our analysis. First, we view the migration of ethnic groups as occurring in stages (Massey 1990; Saenz 1991). The process is initiated when a select group of ethnic members ventures out to frontier areas, which may eventually become peripheral areas of the homeland given the establishment of further migration flows. Second, we use the neoclassical economics and social capital perspectives of migration to identify factors helping ethnic migrants overcome obstacles to their movement away from their homeland. Accordingly, we highlight the importance of human capital and social capital resources in this type of migration.

SPACE, FRONTIERS, AND PERIPHERIES

As noted earlier, in attempts to understand the movement of minority groups, research has tended to focus on broad regions, for example, South-North (in the case of African Americans) or the census-designated regions, South, Northeast, Midwest, and West. One of the problems with this approach is that space is viewed in a homogeneous fashion, suggesting that the various areas comprising, for example, the North represent similar potential relocation areas for African Americans. However, regions are far from uniform and they vary in their attractiveness to minority group members and in their ability to provide the necessary resources needed to undertake migration.

Migration is a highly selective phenomenon (Shaw 1975). Migration selectivity is especially apparent in movements to "frontiers" (Saenz 1991) due to the larger presence of "intervening obstacles" hindering mobility (see Lee 1966). Such obstacles include distance, an inhospitable environment, physical barriers, laws prohibiting movement, and an absence of ethnic culture and co-ethnics. Thus, individuals with particular attributes (e.g., the younger or the more educated) are most likely to overcome these barriers. The highly selective nature of frontier migration is evident in the Mexican American experience. Historically, Mexican immigrants coming to the United States, especially those coming either on a contractual or an undocumented basis, have been predominantly male (Davila and Saenz 1990; Donato 1993). Moreover, younger male laborers disproportionately comprised the earliest flows of Mexican migrants venturing out of the Southwest early in the 20th century (Saenz 1991).

These pioneers are crucial in the establishment of social networks linking the homeland and the frontier (Gurak and Caces 1992; Massey et al. 1987; Saenz 1991; Tilly 1990). The pioneers and their social networks communicate information about social and economic opportunities in the frontier to their co-ethnics in the homeland. Furthermore, the early migrants may also form a social support system through which they provide general assistance, food, shelter, and help in locating employment to co-ethnics from the homeland who arrive in the frontier (Gurak and Caces 1992; Portes and Bach 1985; Tilly 1990).

As more co-ethnics move to the frontier, the social network system matures, thus facilitating further movement. At this point, then, migration becomes less selective. The decreasingly selective nature of migration is related to the development of ethnic communities in the frontier, especially when families, rather than only individual members, move there (Hondagneu-Sotelo 1994). Once individuals establish roots, it becomes more difficult to return to the homeland on a permanent basis (Massey 1987). This condition serves to enhance migration, a phenomenon referred to as "cumulative causation of migration" (Massey 1990) or "migrant syndrome" (Reichert 1981). Over time, as ethnic group members become firmly established in their new homes, the frontier may be more appropriately described as a "periphery area" of the homeland (Saenz 1991).

THE PERIPHERY AND FRONTIER OF MEXICAN AMERICANS

The designation of space outside the Southwest as "periphery" and "frontier" areas for Mexican Americans helps highlight variations related to their relative presence. Because of their relatively larger presence in periphery areas, Mexican Americans in the Southwest have faced relatively few obstacles as well as low economic and psychic costs in movements to these areas. In contrast, greater barriers and steeper economic and psychic costs have been associated with movement to frontier areas.

At the beginning of the 20th century, Mexican Americans were almost exclusively located in the Southwest, where 95 percent resided in 1910. At this time, places outside the Southwest were frontier areas for them. Ethnic group members initially ventured out to the Midwest and West (Saenz 1991; Tienda 1982), where they were attracted by opportunities in agriculture and mining (Arreola 1985; Baker 1995; Campa 1990; Gamboa 1990; Nostrand 1992; Oppenheimer 1985; Valdes 1991).

The early Mexican American migrants to the Midwest and West served as trailblazers for their co-ethnics remaining in the Southwest (Saenz 1991). These migrants were the first to confront obstacles (Lee 1966) separating the frontier from the Southwest. As the early migrants overcame these barriers and developed communication lines back to the home region, co-ethnics from the Southwest and Mexico followed. Agriculture continues, even today, to influence the movement of southwestern Mexican American farm workers to places located in the Midwest and Pacific Northwest (Cook 1986), but also increasingly to areas in the South and Northeast. In addition, Mexican Americans are continually lured to the Midwest by other types of jobs, most recently in its meatpacking plants. In fact, in the last decade, the growth of the Mexican-origin population in many midwestern communities with meatpacking plants has exploded (Gouveia and Saenz 2000; Stull, Broadway, and Griffith 1995), as has been the case increasingly in the South (Saenz et al. 2003). Thus, portions of areas outside the Southwest, especially in the Midwest and West, can now be thought of as "periphery" areas rather than "frontiers." In 1990, the Midwest and West (excluding Arizona, California, Colorado, and New Mexico) had the second and third largest Mexican American populations in the country (Saenz and

Greenlees 1996), although in 2000 it was the Midwest and South (excluding Texas) with this distinction (Saenz 2004).

While the development and strengthening of social linkages between these periphery areas and the Southwest have facilitated the movement of Mexican Americans to these areas, they are still relatively absent (in absolute and relative terms) in other parts of the country, primarily in the Northeast and South, although this changed somewhat after 1990, especially with respect to the South. At least from 1985 to 1990, these areas can be considered the frontier for Mexican Americans exploring them in the absence of co-ethnics. For Mexican Americans from the Southwest, frontier areas represent greater challenges because, in the absence of a critical mass of co-ethnics, greater obstacles and greater economic and psychic costs are associated with migration.

Our perspective shows the great variation in spatial settings outside the Southwest for Mexican Americans. All else equal, periphery areas tend to be relatively more attractive to Mexican Americans from the Southwest given the relatively large presence of co-ethnics. However, a larger question not addressed here is whether the inequality and discrimination found in the Southwest is replicated in periphery areas as the size of the Mexican American population increases. As Blalock (1967) observes, there is a positive association between the relative group size of a minority group and the level of inequality and discrimination it experiences (see also Saenz 1997). Hence, it may be that the most favorable economic payoffs await Mexican Americans in frontier areas. The prevailing approach in the migration literature characterized by broad notions of regions and the homogeneous treatment of space suggests that resources needed to migrate outside the group's homeland do not vary much on the basis of destination. Our more nuanced treatment of regions outside the Southwest on the basis of the historical and contemporary presence of Mexican Americans, however, allows us to assess how the role of resources varies by periphery and frontier regions. We turn our attention to theoretical perspectives identifying factors facilitating the movement of Mexican Americans out of the Southwest.

HUMAN AND SOCIAL CAPITAL AS FACILITATORS
OF MEXICAN AMERICAN MIGRATION

According to the human capital perspective, individuals migrate when they decide that the benefits of moving—including maximizing returns on their human capital investments, such as education, skills, and experience—outweigh the costs of moving (Becker 1964; Sjaastad 1962). Indeed, studies have consistently found human capital in general and education in particular to be one of the strongest predictors of migration (Greenwood 1985; Shaw 1975; see also Voth, Sizer, and Farmer 1996). Individuals with higher levels of education are more likely than their less educated peers to make a move across interstate lines (Foulkes and Newbold 2000; Giordono 2000; Kritz and Nogel 1994) as well as across international boundaries (Poot 1996).

The propensity of those with more human capital resources to migrate is associated with their generally greater participation in regional and national labor markets, as opposed to more restricted local labor markets, and their usually greater knowledge of labor market alternatives (Ehrenberg and Smith 1985). In the case of international migration, Poot (1996) suggests that the deterrent effect of distance on migration is weaker at higher levels of education. Potential immigrants with higher levels of education are more likely to be bilingual and more efficient processors of information regarding opportunities. Furthermore, placed within the human capital approach, the assimilationist perspective (Gordon 1964) also provides a framework to explain migration (see Foulkes and Newbold 2000). Ethnics with higher levels of education are more likely to have contact with nonethnics, thus decreasing the potential for culture shock outside the homeland. Hence, we expect that Mexican Americans with greater human capital resources were more likely to leave the Southwest between 1985 and 1990. In addition, based on our earlier discussion of the selectivity associated with frontier migration, we expect that the human capital effect on geographic mobility is especially strong in the case of migration to the frontier. In particular, we suggest that the relatively minimal obstacles and low psychic and economic costs associated with the presence of co-ethnics in the periphery results in a broad array of individuals migrating there regardless of human capital resources. In contrast, the relatively significant obstacles and high psychic and economic costs associated with the absence of co-ethnics in the frontier results in a greater probability of migration to the frontier among those with greater levels of human capital.

On the whole, the Mexican-origin population is, however, relatively limited on the human capital dimension. Consequently, the human capital investments of individual Mexican Americans, or, for that matter, of individual members of any other minority group, may play a lesser role than group- or network-based resources, such as social capital, in the propensity to leave the home region (Gurak and Kritz 2000:1019; Kritz and Nogle 1994). The term "social capital" refers to the advantages that people or groups may receive through their relationships with others (Coleman 1988; Massey and Espinosa 1997) and reflects Granovetter's (1973, 1985) insight that the experiences and behavior of actors, whether they be individuals or groups, are embedded in their social ties. Bourdieu and Wacquant (1992:119) define social capital as "the sum of the resources, actual or virtual, that accrue to an individual or a group by virtue of possessing a durable network of more or less institutionalized relationships of mutual acquaintance and recognition." It has been used extensively in past attempts to understand internal migration (e.g., Marks 1983; Saenz 1991; Stack 1996) and in more recent attempts to understand international migration (Gurak and Caces 1992; Hagan 1994; Hondagneu-Sotelo 1994; Massey 1987, 1990; Massey and Espinosa 1997; Massey et al. 1987).

Significantly, though, as Portes notes (1998), social capital is a multifaceted construct. Thus, it is not surprising that its effects on migration are mixed. On the one hand, the sense of community, solidarity, and mutual obligation often emanating from a preponderance of co-ethnics in the home region may discourage individuals from leaving (e.g., Gurak and Kritz 2000; Kritz and Nogle 1994). On the other hand, as Massey and his associates observe (Massey 1987; Massey and Espinosa 1997; Massey et al. 1987, 1993), communities tend to accumulate migration experience and solidify ties with areas of destination through the continual movement of people between the two places. In the case of Mexican Americans in the Southwest, potential migrants learn of areas outside the Southwest from co-ethnics in the region who have recent experience living in them. The greater the availability of such information is, the greater the chance that a member will be able to tap into it, lowering the economic and psychic costs of his or her migration (Massey and Espinosa 1997; Tilly 1990). Thus, controlling for the relative size of the Mexican-origin population in their southwestern communities in 1985, we hypothesize that Mexican Americans living in communities receiving relatively large numbers of co-ethnics from states outside the Southwest during 1985 to 1990 are more likely to leave the region between 1985 and 1990 compared to their counterparts residing in areas receiving smaller numbers.

Following insights from Massey and his colleagues (Massey et al. 1987; Massey and Espinosa 1997) on the use of social capital by Mexican immigrants, we distinguish between "community" social capital and "household" social capital (see also Liang 1994). Household social capital refers to direct linkages potential migrants have with a particular destination. Potential migrants living in households with at least one person born outside the Southwest have direct knowledge about areas outside the home region. Like community ties, household ties are expected to facilitate migration from the home region to these areas by decreasing its costs. Accordingly, we predict that Mexican Americans living in the Southwest in 1985 and having a household tie to periphery or frontier regions are more likely to migrate out of the Southwest between 1985 and 1990 than those not having a household tie. This is consistent with Ravenstein's observation (1885) over a century ago that migration flows between two areas generate counterflows.

METHODS

Data from the 1990 Census PUMS are used to conduct the analysis. The PUMS is the most extensive data source available to study the migration patterns of racial and ethnic groups. The analysis is based on 104,991 Mexican American householders 25 to 64 years of age who lived in one of the five southwestern states (Arizona, California, Colorado, New Mexico, and Texas) in 1985. The age band of 25 to 64 is used in order to reduce the number of college students and military personnel whose movements are distinct in nature from those of the general population. The PUMS contains person weights that are a function of both the "full census sample weight and the PUMS sample design" (U.S. Bureau of the Census 1993a:4–1). Since our goal is not to produce population estimates, we remove the effect of the full census sample weight from the person weights by dividing each person weight by the average sample weight (i.e., 19.84695) for the entire PUMS. These revised weights are used throughout our analysis to account for differential sampling probabilities. The weighted sample size is 107,293.

Migration information contained in the PUMS is based on the five-year migration question asking respondents to report their place of residence in 1985 and 1990. Our analysis is based on Mexican American householders living in the Southwest in 1985. Out-migrants are those individuals who lived outside the Southwest in 1990, while nonmigrants are those persons who continued living there in 1990. We further categorize out-migrants into "periphery" migrants and "frontier" migrants. States outside the Southwest are divided into "periphery" states and "frontier" states based on the relative and absolute presence of Mexican Americans. States with more than 49,100 Mexican Americans (the average size of the Mexican American population for the 46 nonsouthwestern states) or populations in which Mexican Americans accounted for more than 1.27 percent (the average percentage for the nonsouthwestern states) of the state's population in 1990 are defined as "periphery" states. Nineteen states are classified as "periphery" states: Alaska, Florida, Georgia, Hawaii, Idaho, Illinois, Indiana, Kansas, Michigan, Nebraska, Nevada, New York, Ohio, Oklahoma, Oregon, Utah, Washington, Wisconsin, and Wyoming. As figure 8.1 shows, the periphery states are predominantly located in the Midwest and West. The remaining states and the District of Columbia are treated as "frontier" states. With these distinctions, then, Mexican Americans living in the Southwest in 1985 are classified into one of three migration categories based on their 1990 state of residence: (1) nonmigrants (lived in the Southwest in 1990); (2) periphery migrants (lived in a periphery state in 1990); and (3) frontier migrants (lived in a frontier state in 1990).

We realize that the procedure used to categorize states into the three regions is somewhat simplistic. Still, we believe it represents an improvement over the more common approach in which space for minority groups is treated more broadly and in a more homogeneous fashion. Furthermore, Saenz (1991) has shown that a similar categorization of states into regions using 1980 census data on the absolute and relative presence of Mexican

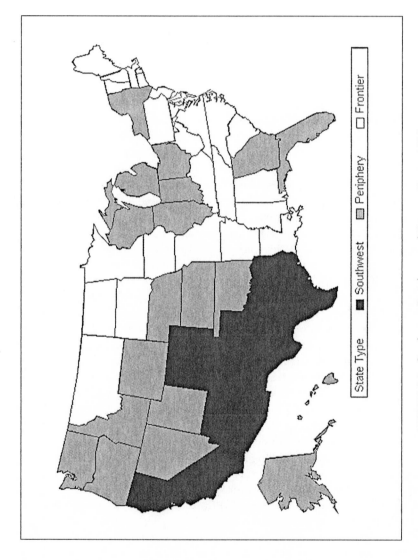

FIGURE 8.1. Southwest, Periphery, and Frontier States, 1990.

Americans is consistent with interregional differences on a variety of related indicators: the number of Mexican Americans per square mile; the presence of Spanish-language radio stations; Mexican American organizations; and the distribution of Mexican Americans relative to Anglos across counties in the states comprising a region. Additional information based on the 1980 and 1990 Censuses suggests that our categories are valid. For example, while the Southwest or core contained 83.3 percent of the Mexican-origin population in the country, the periphery had 14 percent and the frontier only 2.7 percent. Hence, only one out of 37 Mexican Americans in the United States was located in the frontier in 1990. In addition, while the Southwest (55.5 percent) and the periphery (59.3 percent) regions each experienced impressive growth rates of upwards of 55 percent in the Mexican American population between 1980 and 1990, the frontier managed only a modest gain of 13.2 percent. Therefore, of the national gain of 4,755,499 Mexican Americans during the 1980s, the frontier region accounted for a mere 0.9 percent of the increase.

Since our dependent variable, migration status in 1990, has three categories (i.e., nonmigrant, periphery migrant, and frontier migrant), we use multinomial logistic regression to estimate our model. We estimated it for two contrasts of migration status in 1990: the log-likelihood of leaving the U.S. Southwest for a periphery state versus remaining in the region and the log-likelihood of leaving the U.S. Southwest for a frontier state versus remaining in the region. This strategy allows us to compare each of the two types of migration with nonmigration.

Key independent variables include measures of human capital and both types of social capital. The person's level of education represents the human capital dimension. Educational level is measured with four dummy variables: (1) some high school (completed between nine and eleven years of schooling); (2) high school graduate; (3) some college; and (4) college graduate. Persons with eight or fewer years of education represent the reference category. Similar to Massey and Espinosa (1997:945), potential migrants' household social capital is measured by two dummy variables: (1) household with at least one member born in a periphery state; and (2) household with at least one member born in a frontier state. For each of these dummy variables, individuals who lived in households not containing persons born in the specified region are the reference group. Note that the PUMS data do not allow us to reconstruct households back to 1985, the beginning of the migration period. As a proxy, we base our household social capital measure on the birthplace of the respondents' household members five years of age or older in 1990, insuring that children born after the beginning of the migration period are not included.

Massey and Espinosa (1997:945) operationalize the community form of social capital as the percentage of persons 15 and older in the Mexican place of origin who had immigrated to the United States. Our measure of "community" ties is similar, specifically, the percentage of the Mexican-origin population in a prospective migrant's southwestern community of origin (actually 1985 PUMS area) that moved into it from a periphery or a frontier state between 1985 and 1990.

We control for the effects of seven other variables. Age is measured by three dummy variables: (1) 25 to 34; (2) 35 to 44; and (3) 45 to 54. Persons 55 to 64 years old serve as the reference group. Gender and marital status are measured by a single dummy variable, with females and people not currently married as reference groups. Nativity/immigration period status is determined by three dummy variables indicating immigrants' period of entry into the United States: (1) entered between 1975 and 1984; (2) entered between 1965 and 1974; and (3) entered prior to 1965. We include this series of dummy variables in the model to take into account any variation in the probability of migrating out of the Southwest due to length of residence in the United States. The reference group is the native-born category. Household size simply refers to the number of people living in one's household. As mentioned earlier, we also control for the effects of the relative size of the Mexican-origin population in the southwestern community of origin (or 1985 PUMS area) on the propensity of members to out-migrate. Finally, we introduce the 1985 state of residence to control for structural influences such as the economic setting at the beginning of the period, the location of the state relative to periphery and frontier states, and variations in migration propensities across states.

RESULTS

Mexican American Out-Migration from the Southwest, 1985 to 1990

In both our descriptive analysis (not shown) and our multinominal logistic regression analysis, nonmigrants serve as the baseline group for comparisons. The bulk of our sample of Mexican American householders aged 25 to 64 fall into this group; 98.2 percent who lived in the Southwest in 1985 remained in the region in 1990. In contrast, only 1.3 percent and 0.5 percent left the region for a periphery or frontier state, respectively. Of the group of migrants leaving the Southwest between 1985 and 1990, nearly three-fourths (73.4 percent) moved to the periphery region, illustrating the greater popularity of places with a critical mass of Mexican Americans as destinations.

As expected, both periphery and frontier migrants possess greater human capital resources and, in general, more household and community social capital than nonmigrants. For example, 12.1 percent of periphery migrants were college graduates compared to only 7.3 percent of nonmigrants. The education gap between frontier migrants and nonmigrants was even larger. Slightly over one-fourth (25.1 percent) of frontier migrants had college degrees, suggesting that migration to the frontier is more selective on the basis of human capital than is migration to the periphery. In addition, Mexican Americans who moved from the Southwest to a periphery state were more likely to have a household tie to a periphery state than those who remained in the region (32.6 percent versus 6.6 percent). Likewise, Mexican Americans who left the Southwest for a frontier state were more likely to have a household tie to a frontier state than those who did not leave the region (27.8 percent versus 3.3 percent). Furthermore, migrants tend to dif-fer from nonmigrants on the prevalence of recent in-migrants from the periphery and frontier regions among the Mexican-origin populations in their 1985 southwestern communities of residence. On average, these recent community ties to places outside the home region were slightly more preva-lent in the migrants' home communities.

Both types of migrants also differ from nonmigrants on a number of the control variables. Mexican American migrants were more likely than non-migrants to be young males from Texas. Moreover, consistent with our expectations about the selective nature of migration, frontier migrants were more likely than periphery migrants to be native-born males from smaller households, from southwestern communities with fewer co-ethnics, and from Texas.

Table 8.1 presents the results of the multinomial logistic regression ana-lyzing the relationship between the independent variables (human capital, household social capital, and community social capital indicators) and migra-tion status. The model shows general support for the predicted effects of human capital and household and community social capital on geographic mobility. Indeed, global chi-square tests (not shown) for the effects of each independent and control variable on the dependent variable indicate that all but two (i.e., marital status and relative size of the Mexican-origin population in the 1985 home community) have statistically significant effects on migra-tion status in 1990.

The first column in table 8.1 reports the odds ratio of being a periphery migrant as opposed to staying in the Southwest. The odds ratio can be inter-preted as the change in odds of migrating to the periphery relative to not migrating given a unit change in an independent variable. Among the human capital indicators, those with a college degree were one and one-fourth (1.256) times as likely to migrate to the periphery relative to not migrating as were their peers with only a grade school education.

The second column reports the change in the odds of being a frontier migrant as opposed to not migrating. As expected, the human capital indica-tors significantly influence the odds of being a frontier migrant as opposed to not migrating. Specifically, high school graduates, those with some college,

TABLE 8.1
Multinomial Logistic Regression (Odds Ratios) of Migration Status in
1990 on Selected Characteristics for 107,293 Mexican American Householders
Aged 25–64 Who Lived in the Southwest United States in 1985

Independent and Control Variables	Periphery Migrant versus Nonmigrant	Frontier Migrant versus Nonmigrant
Human Capital:		
Education:		
Some High School	0.915	1.183
High School Graduate	0.861	1.522**
Some College	0.969	1.772**
College Graduate	1.256*	3.827**
Household Social Capital:		
At Least One Member Born in Periphery	7.050**	2.293**
At Least One Member Born in Frontier	2.286**	9.152**
Community Social Capital:		
Percent of Mexican-Origin Population in 1985 Community of Residence that Migrated between 1985 and 1990 from:		
Periphery	1.127**	1.099
Frontier	0.796*	1.244
Control Variables:		
Age:		
25–34	4.604**	12.441**
35–44	3.001**	8.134**
45–54	1.846**	5.546**
Male	1.168*	1.501**
Married	0.983	1.010
Nativity/Immigration Status:		
Immigrated in 1975–1984	1.935**	1.539**
Immigrated in 1965–1974	1.145	1.166
Immigrated Before 1965	0.996	0.864
Household Size	0.894**	0.854**
Percent Mexican-Origin Population in 1985 Community of Residence	1.001	0.995*

(continued on next page)

TABLE 8.1 *(continued)*

Independent and Control Variables	Periphery Migrant versus Nonmigrant	Frontier Migrant versus Nonmigrant
State in 1985:		
Arizona	0.547**	0.367**
California	0.598**	0.340**
Colorado	0.908	0.717
New Mexico	1.091	0.886
Model Chi-Square	2,293.7	
Degrees of Freedom	44	

Note: Reported sample size (N) is the weighted N. The reference groups for education, age, nativity/ immigration status, and state in 1985 are grade school education only, aged 55 to 64, native-born, and Texas, respectively. The reference group for each of the household social capital dummy variables is persons who lived in households with no members born in the specified region.

*p < .05   **p < .01   (two-tailed tests)

and college graduates were approximately one and one-half (1.522), two (1.772), and nearly four (3.827) times, respectively, as likely as their grade school counterparts to leave the Southwest between 1985 and 1990 for a frontier state. Furthermore, as hypothesized, the human capital effect appears to be stronger in the case of migration to the frontier. Indeed, comparing columns one and two, migrants with a college degree were about three times (3.047 = 3.827 / 1.256) as likely as those with only a grade school education to move from the Southwest between 1985 and 1990 to a frontier state instead of a periphery state. This suggests greater obstacles and psychic and economic costs associated with movement to the frontier compared to movement to the periphery, resulting in migrants with higher levels of human capital as most likely to migrate to the frontier.

Table 8.1 also shows support for our hypotheses on the influence of household social capital on migrating to the periphery and frontier regions. Beginning with column one, as predicted, Mexican Americans who have a household tie to a periphery state were seven (7.050) times as likely as their peers without such a tie to leave the Southwest between 1985 and 1990 for a periphery state. The corresponding odds ratio in the second column (2.293) indicates that a household tie to a periphery state also significantly increased the odds of leaving the region between 1985 and 1990 for a frontier state. Nonetheless, comparing the figures in the two columns, we see that migrants with a household tie to a periphery state were three times (3.075 = 7.050 / 2.293) as likely as migrants without such a tie to leave for a periphery state rather than a frontier state.

The pattern is similar for the second indicator of household social capital. As the odds ratios for this indicator in columns one and two of table 8.1 show, having a household tie to a frontier state significantly increased the chances of moving out of the Southwest between 1985 and 1990 to a state in either the periphery or the frontier. Again, however, migration tends to favor the region with ties. That is, if we compare the two odds ratios, we see that migrants with a household tie to a frontier state were four times (4.003 = 9.152 / 2.286) as likely as migrants without such a tie to move to a state in the frontier rather than the periphery.

The results suggest that community as well as household ties to destinations facilitate migration. In line with our community social capital hypothesis, in column one we see that Mexican Americans living in home communities where relatively large shares of their co-ethnics are recent in-migrants from the periphery region were more likely to move out of the Southwest between 1985 and 1990 to a periphery state. The predicted odds of a Mexican American making such a move increase about 12.7 percent with each one-point increase in the percentage of recent in-migrants from the periphery region in the Mexican-origin population of his/her home community.

This same effect is not observed for our second indicator of community social capital. As the statistically insignificant odds ratio in column two suggests, Mexican Americans living in home communities where relatively large shares of their co-ethnics are recent in-migrants from the frontier region were about as likely to stay in the Southwest as to leave it between 1985 and 1990 for a frontier state. Interestingly, however, in column one we find that living in these communities tends to discourage Mexican American migration to the periphery. Specifically, each one-point increase in the percentage of recent in-migrants from a frontier state in the Mexican-origin population of a southwestern home community decreases the predicted odds of leaving it between 1985 and 1990 for a periphery state by 20.4 percent.

The effects of human and social capital are particularly evident in differences in the predicted probability of migrating out of the Southwest between 1985 and 1990 to a state in one of the other regions. For example, for Mexican Americans who possess very little human and social capital (i.e., have only a grade school education, live in a household without ties to a state outside the Southwest, and are from a home community with no co-ethnic ties to the periphery or frontier regions), the predicted probability of migrating to a frontier state is only 0.001. It increases to 0.294 for those who possess ample amounts of both types of capital (i.e., have a college degree, live in a household with ties to the periphery and frontier regions, and are from a home community with a relatively large number of co-ethnic ties to these regions).

Effects of the control variables are consistent with other studies. For instance, the young were more likely than the old to leave the Southwest between 1985 and 1990. Those aged 25 to 34 were about 4.6 times as likely as those aged 55 to 64 to out-migrate to a periphery state versus remaining in the Southwest. The young were even more likely than their older peers to out-migrate to a frontier state. Other factors associated with a greater likelihood of a Mexican American leaving the Southwest include being male and immigrating between 1975 and 1984. Having a large household, living in a southwestern community with a relatively large Mexican-origin population, and residing in Arizona or California rather than Texas lower the odds of leaving the Southwest.

RECENT CHANGES IN THE REGIONAL DISTRIBUTION
OF MEXICAN AMERICANS, 1990 TO 2000

Preliminary analyses of data from the 2000 Census confirm the designation of the years 1985 to 1990 analyzed above as a watershed stage for Mexican Americans. For example, while about 83 percent of persons of Mexican-origin in the United States lived in the Southwest in 1990, the percentage dropped significantly to 74 percent in 2000 (Guzman 2001; U.S. Bureau of the Census 1991). Furthermore, while native- and foreign-born Mexicans did not differ appreciably in their geographic distribution across the United States in 1990, they should be expected to differ substantially in 2000. The geographic distributions of the two nativity groups are compared across the two years in table 8.2. Based on data from the 1990 Census Summary Tape File 4B and the 2000 Census Summary File 4B (U.S. Bureau of the Census, 1993b; U.S. Census Bureau, 2004), table 8.2 presents region by nativity/period of entry into the United States for the Mexican-origin population for both 1990 and 2000. As described earlier, states included in the periphery region in 1990 were located primarily in the West and Midwest. In 2000, there were some changes. Applying the "relative/absolute size of the Mexican-origin population" criteria used in 1990 but with 2000 data to classify nonsouthwestern states into periphery and frontier areas, the number of states in the periphery dropped from 19 in 1990 to 16 in 2000. Specifically, four of the periphery states (Alaska, Hawaii, Ohio, and Wyoming) in 1990 were reclassified as frontier in 2000 and a southern frontier state (North Carolina) joined two other southern states (Georgia and Florida) in the periphery.

As the 1990 panel of table 8.2 shows, as expected, large and nearly equal majorities of both native- and foreign-born Mexicans (83.4 percent and 84.1 percent, respectively) lived in the Southwest in 1990. By 2000, however, while majorities of both native- and foreign-born Mexicans made their home in the region, these majorities had decreased, most noticeably for the foreign-born. In 2000, about 78 percent of native-born Mexicans resided in the Southwest compared to only about 70.7 percent of their foreign-born peers. The opposite is observed for the periphery. That is, in 1990, a small and nearly equal minority of each nativity group (13.5 percent and 14.1 percent,

TABLE 8.2

Region by Nativity/Period of Entry into the Country for the
Mexican-Origin Population in the United States, 1990 and 2000

1990

Nativity/Period of Entry	Southwest	Periphery	Frontier	Total (N)
Native-born	83.4%	13.5%	3.1%	100.0% (8,933,371)
Foreign-born	84.1%	14.1%	1.8%	100.0% (4,459,837)
Before 1965	86.9%	11.4%	1.7%	100.0% (546,929)
1965 to 1974	86.1%	12.7%	1.2%	100.0% (869,045)
1975 to 1984	84.1%	14.3%	1.5%	100.0% (1,702,700)
1985 to March 1990	81.6%	15.9%	2.5%	100.0% (1,341,163)

2000

Nativity/Period of Entry	Southwest	Periphery	Frontier	Total (N)
Native-born	78.0%	17.1%	4.9%	100.0% (12,222,799)
Foreign-born	70.7%	24.0%	5.3%	100.0% (8,677,303)
Before 1965	85.3%	12.4%	2.3%	100.0% (419,768)
1965 to 1974	82.8%	15.1%	2.1%	100.0% (819,442)
1975 to 1984	78.9%	18.2%	2.8%	100.0% (1,708,709)
1985 to 1994	70.3%	24.7%	5.0%	100.0% (3,219,602)
1995 to March 2000	59.3%	32.0%	8.8%	100.0% (2,509,782)

Note: Authors' estimates using Census 1990 Summary Tape File 4B (STF4B) and
Census 2000 Summary File 4B (SF4B). Periphery and frontier classifications vary
slightly across the two time periods. See the text for the states included in the two
regions for each time period.

respectively) lived in a state located in the periphery, but a decade later, in
2000, nearly one-fourth (24.0 percent) of foreign-born Mexicans compared
to less than one-fifth (17.1 percent) of native-born Mexicans lived in a state
located in this region. Interestingly, among both nativity groups in both time
periods, only a small percentage live in states designated as frontier areas (i.e.,
about 2 to 3 percent in each nativity group in 1990 and roughly 5 percent in
each nativity group in 2000).

Even more striking than the development of differences in the regional
distribution of Mexicans by nativity group in 2000 is the variation by period
of entry into the United States among the foreign-born. Comparing the two
panels in table 8.2, we see that recent immigrants in both time periods were
more likely than earlier immigrants to reside in a nonsouthwestern state. For

instance, in 1990, approximately 15.9 percent of immigrants who had entered the United States in the last five years lived in a periphery state compared to only about 11.4 percent of their peers who had entered the country over 25 years ago (i.e., before 1965), a difference of about 4.5 percentage points. However, the corresponding difference in 2000 is much larger. In 2000, nearly one-third of immigrants who had entered the United States in the last five years lived in a periphery state compared to only about 14.2 percent of those who had entered the country over 25 years ago (i.e., before 1975). Indeed, in 2000, recent immigrants also were more likely than earliest of immigrants to reside in a frontier state (8.8 percent versus 2.2 percent).

CONCLUSIONS

Given Mexican Americans' historical and cultural attachment to the Southwest, this region has been viewed as the homeland of the Mexican American population. Even as recently as 2000, three of every four persons of Mexican origin living in the United States made their home in the region. This paper sought to assess the extent to which Mexican Americans have made inroads to other regions of the country and factors promoting such movement. The results indicate that a very small proportion (roughly 2 percent) of Mexican American householders aged 25 to 64 living in the Southwest in 1985 migrated out of the region between 1985 and 1990. When migration did occur, it was much more likely to be directed to the periphery region comprised of 19 states that contain a substantial presence of Mexican Americans, with three-fourths of migrants relocating to this region. Drawing on the human capital and social capital perspectives of migration, we examined several hypotheses suggesting that human and social capital resources facilitate the migration of Mexican Americans out of the Southwest. The findings support the hypotheses. Mexican Americans endowed with more advantageous human capital resources were more likely to leave the Southwest, with a particularly strong association in the case of frontier migration. In addition, people with household ties to the periphery and frontier were more likely to migrate. Finally, those from home communities with recent co-ethnic ties to the periphery were more likely to move there.

The results of the preliminary analyses from the 2000 census indicate that the years 1985 to 1990 were, indeed, a turning point in the spatial distribution of Mexicans across the United States. First, from 1990 to 2000, the percentage of the Mexican-origin population in the United States living in the Southwest dropped dramatically from 83 percent to 74 percent, nearly ten percent. Second, while the regional distribution of the Mexican-origin population in the United States did not differ by nativity in 1990, it differed significantly in 2000. In 2000, foreign-born Mexicans were quite a bit more likely than native-born Mexicans to live outside the Southwest. Third, while

recent immigrants in both time periods were more likely than earlier immigrants to reside in a periphery state, they were considerably much more likely
to do so in 2000. These findings are consistent with research suggesting that
traditional Mexican-receiving states, especially California and Texas, continue to be gateway sites attracting immigrants directly from abroad but have
experienced internal net losses to other states during later years, including
between 1995 and 2000 (e.g., Saenz 2004). The findings are also consistent
with our expectation that these other states, especially those located in midwestern and southern portions of the country, became especially attractive to
Mexicans, particularly recent immigrants, in the 1990s for the opportunities
the states represented to them in the wake of IRCA and the restructuring of
the meat and poultry processing industries.

The major contribution of this study is that it helps expand our notions
of space related to the migration of racial and ethnic groups. Much existing
research on the migration of minority groups assumes that space beyond the
confines of the regions where minority groups are clustered is relatively
homogeneous. Such approaches fail to take into account the historical
processes linking some areas to the homeland of minority groups while others remain frontier areas. They also assume that resources needed to navigate
migration out of the homeland do not vary much. We provide a more
nuanced examination of space by introducing the concepts of "core," (or
"homeland"), "periphery," and "frontier" in the study of Mexican American
migration (see also Saenz 1991). Our results indicate that relatively few Mexican Americans left the Southwest between 1985 and 1990. However, when
migration occurred, the majority of out-migrants (approximately three-
fourths) relocated to a periphery that has a migration history linking the
regions and a critical mass of Mexican Americans. Furthermore, our conceptualization of space outside of the Southwest allowed us to assess the extent
to which the effect of human capital varies across destination regions.
Because of the absence of co-ethnics in the frontier, there are greater obstacles as well as higher psychic and economic costs associated with migration
to the frontier compared to the periphery. Our results clearly indicate that
more educated Mexican Americans in the Southwest are the most likely to
migrate to the frontier, resulting in a selective population moving there.

Our study also illustrates the usefulness of PUMS data for developing
social capital measures. Few studies of the role of social capital resources on
migration have used secondary census data. In addition, the classification
scheme used here to designate periphery and frontier regions was useful in
monitoring emerging Mexican American enclaves outside the Southwest.
For instance, compared to Saenz's (1991) designation of periphery and frontier states based on the 1980 Census, in which all were in the Midwest or
West, we found that five states (Alaska, Florida, Georgia, Hawaii, and New
York) and two in the South became periphery states in 1990. There were

more changes when we applied the classification scheme in 2000. Another southern state (North Carolina) became a periphery state. We also observed some periphery-to-frontier movements. Two of the states new to the periphery in 1990 (Alaska and Hawaii) and two states that had been in the periphery since 1980 (Ohio and Wyoming) rejoined the frontier region in 2000.

While this study fills a gap in the literature on the geographic mobility of Mexican Americans, a series of important questions remain. First, given the positive association between relative group size and inequality and discrimination (Blalock 1967; Saenz 1997), the looming question is whether the high levels of inequality and discrimination more commonly found in the Southwest (Saenz 1993, 1999) will be replicated in the periphery regions as the Mexican American population increases. If so, Mexican Americans from the Southwest—and those from the periphery as well—may have to seek opportunities in frontier areas. Second, our findings suggest that a small "brain drain" migration of Mexican Americans is taking place, with the most educated segment of the Mexican American population being the most likely to leave the Southwest. Mexicans from Texas were more likely to leave the Southwest between 1985 and 1990 compared to those living in other southwestern states. Third, given the anti-immigrant sentiment in certain parts of the country, especially in California, the question arises whether states such as California will experience net outflows of immigrants to other parts of the country. Preliminary analyses based on the 2000 U.S. Census indicate that Texas and California continued to be net exporters of persons of Mexican origin in the late 1990s (Saenz 2004). Fourth, further research is needed to determine the extent to which the out-migration of Mexican Americans from the Southwest represents long-term versus short-term migration. Saenz and Davila (1992), using data from the 1980 Census, identified a significant flow of Mexican American *return* migrants from areas of the country with relatively small Mexican American populations. Fifth, future research should explore the extent to which Mexican American migrants become socially and economically integrated into their new communities and the degree to which social capital resources assist migrants in their integration. As Portes (1998) notes, social capital needs to be explored not only as a source of access to resources but also as restricting freedom from access to the same resources.[1]

NOTE

1. Direct correspondence to Rogelio Saenz, Department of Sociology, Texas A&M University, College Station, TX 77843–4351 (rsaenz@tamu.edu). The authors thank David Brown, Douglas Gurak, Sean-Shong Hwang, and Helen Potts for their comments on an earlier draft. They also express their gratitude to Gregory Hooks, Linda Lobao, and Ann Tickamyer for their useful comments, guidance, and encouragement.

REFERENCES

Arreola, Daniel D. 1985. "Mexican Americans." Pp. 77–94 in *Ethnicity in Contemporary America: A Geographical Appraisal*, edited by J. O. Mckee. Dubuque, IA: Kendall/Hunt.

Baker, Richard. 1995. *Los Dos Mundos: Rural Mexican Americans, Another America*. Logan: Utah State University Press.

Becker, Gary S. 1964. *Human Capital: A Theoretical and Empirical Analysis, With Special Reference to Education*. New York: National Bureau of Economic Research, distributed by Columbia University Press.

Blalock, Hubert M. 1967. *Toward a Theory of Minority-Group Relations*. New York: Wiley.

Bourdieu, Pierre and Loic Wacquant. 1992. *An Invitation to Reflexive Sociology*. Chicago: University of Chicago Press.

Burr, Jeffrey A., Lloyd B. Potter, Omer R. Galle, and Mark A. Fossett. 1992. "Migration and Metropolitan Opportunity Structures: A Demographic Response to Racial Inequality." *Social Science Research* 21:380–405.

Campa, Arthur. 1990. "Immigrant Latinos and Resident Mexican Americans in Garden City, Kansas: Ethnicity and Ethnic Relations." *Urban Anthropology* 19:345–60.

Coleman, James S. 1988. "Social Capital in the Creation of Human Capital." *American Journal of Sociology* 94:S95–S120.

Cook, Annabel Kirschner. 1986. "Diversity among Northwest Hispanics." *Social Science Journal* 23:205–216.

Davila, Alberto and Rogelio Saenz. 1990. "The Effect of Maquiladora Employment on the Monthly Flow of Mexican Undocumented Immigration to the U.S., 1978–1982." *International Migration Review* 24:96–107.

Donato, Katharine M. 1993. "Current Trends and Patterns of Female Migration: Evidence from Mexico." *International Migration Review* 27:748–771.

Ehrenberg, Ronald G. and Robert S. Smith. 1985. *Modern Labor Economics: Theory and Public Policy*. 2nd ed. Dallas: Scott, Foresman, and Company.

Fligstein, Neil. 1981. *Going North: Migration of Blacks and Whites from the South, 1900–1950*. New York: Academic Press.

Foulkes, Matt and K. Bruce Newbold. 2000. "Migration Propensities, Patterns, and the Role of Human Capital: Comparing Mexican, Cuban, and Puerto Rican Interstate Migration, 1985–1990." *The Professional Geographer* 52:133–145.

Gamboa, Erasmus. 1990. *Mexican Labor and World War Two*. Austin: University of Texas Press.

Giordono, Leanne Schroeder. 2000. "Out-of-State vs. In-State Migration in the United States." *Journal of Public and International Affairs* 11:157–184.

Gordon, Milton. 1964. *Assimilation in American Life: The Role of Race, Religion, and National Origins*. New York: Oxford University Press.

Gouveia, Lourdes and Rogelio Saenz. 2000. "Global Forces and Latino Population Growth in the Midwest: A Regional and Subregional Analysis." *Great Plains Research* 10:305–328.

Greenwood, Michael J. 1985. "Human Migration: Theory, Models, and Empirical Studies." *Journal of Regional Science* 25:521–544.

Granovetter, Mark. 1973. "The Strength of Weak Ties." *American Journal of Sociology* 78:1360–1380.

———. 1985. "Economic Action and Social Structure: The Problem of Embeddedness." *American Journal of Sociology* 91:481–510.

Gurak, Douglas T. and Fe Caces. 1992. "Migration Networks and the Shaping of Migration Systems." Pp. 150–177 in *International Migration Systems: A Global Approach*, edited by M. M. Kritz, L. L. Lim, and H. Zlotnik. New York: Oxford University Press.

Gurak, Douglas T. and Mary M. Kritz. 2000. "The Interstate Migration of U.S. Immigrants: Individual and Contextual Determinants." *Social Forces* 78: 1017–1039.

Guzman, Betsy. 2001. *The Hispanic Population*. Census 2000 Brief. C2KBR/01–3. Washington, DC: U.S. Census Bureau.

Hagan, Jacqueline Maria. 1994. *Deciding to be Legal: A Maya Community in Houston*. Philadelphia: Temple University Press.

Hondagneu-Sotelo, Pierrette. 1994. *Gendered Transition: Mexican Experiences of Immigration*. Berkeley: University of California Press.

Kritz, Mary M. and June Marie Nogle. 1994. "Nativity Concentration and Internal Migration among the Foreign-Born." *Demography* 31:509–524.

Lee, Everett S. 1966. "A Theory of Migration." *Demography* 3:47–57.

Liang, Zai. 1994. "Social Contact, Social Capital, and the Naturalization Process: Evidence from Six Immigrant Groups." *Social Science Research* 23:407–437.

Marks, Carole. 1983. "Lines of Communication, Recruitment Mechanisms, and the Great Migration of 1916–1918." *Social Problems* 31:73–83.

Massey, Douglas S. 1987. "Understanding Mexican Migration to the United States." *American Journal of Sociology* 92:1372–1403.

Massey, Douglas S. 1990. "Social Structure, Household Strategies, and the Cumulative Causation of Migration." *Population Index* 56:3–26.

Massey, Douglas S., Rafael Alarcon, Jorge Durand, and Humberto Gonzalez. 1987. *Return to Aztlan: The Social Process of International Migration from Western Mexico*. Berkeley: University of California Press.

Massey, Douglas S. and Kristin E. Espinosa. 1997. "What's Driving Mexico-U.S. Migration? A Theoretical, Empirical, and Policy Analysis." *American Journal of Sociology* 102:939–999.

Massey, Douglas S., Joaquin Arango, Graeme Hugo, Ali Kouaouci, Adela Pellegrino, and J. Edward Taylor. 1993. "Theories of International Migration: A Review and Appraisal." *Population and Development Review* 19:431–466.

Montejano, David. 1987. *Anglos and Mexicans in the Making of Texas, 1836–1986.* Austin: University of Texas Press.

Murdock, Steve H., Nanbin Zhai, and Rogelio Saenz. 1999. "The Effect of Immigration on 1980 to 1990 Change in Poverty in the Southwestern United States." *Social Science Quarterly* 80:310–324.

Nostrand, Richard L. 1992. *The Hispano Homeland.* Norman: University of Oklahoma Press.

Oppenheimer, Robert. 1985. "Acculturation or Assimilation: Mexican Immigrants in Kansas, 1900 to World War II." *Western Historical Quarterly* 16:429–448.

Poot, Jacques. 1996. "Information, Communication, and Networks in International Migration Systems." *The Annals of Regional Science* 30:55–73.

Portes, Alejandro. 1998. "Social Capital: Its Origin and Applications in Modern Sociology." *Annual Review of Sociology* 24:1–24.

Portes, Alejandro and Robert L. Bach. 1985. *The Latin Journey: Cuban and Mexican Immigrants in the United States.* Berkeley: University of California Press.

Ravenstein, E. G. 1885. "The Laws of Migration." *Journal of the Royal Statistical Society* 48:167–235.

Reichert, Joshua S. 1981. "The Migrant Syndrome: Seasonal U.S. Wage Labor and Rural Development in Central Mexico." *Human Organization* 40:56–66.

Saenz, Rogelio. 1991. "Interregional Migration Patterns of Chicanos: The Core, Periphery, and Frontier." *Social Science Quarterly* 72:135–148.

Saenz, Rogelio. 1993. "Exploring the Regional Diversity of Chicanos." Pp. 117–129 in *American Mosaic: Selected Readings on America's Multicultural Heritage,* edited by Y. I. Song and E. C. Kim. Englewood Cliffs, NJ: Prentice-Hall.

Saenz, Rogelio. 1997. "Ethnic Concentration and Chicano Poverty: A Comparative Approach." *Social Science Research* 26:205–228.

Saenz, Rogelio. 1999. "Mexican Americans." Pp. 209–229 in *The Minority Report: An Introduction to Racial, Ethnic, and Gender Relations,* 3rd edition, edited by A. G. Dworkin and R. J. Dworkin. Fort Worth, TX: Holt, Rinehart, and Winston.

Saenz, Rogelio. 2004. *Latinos and the Changing Face of America.* New York and Washington, DC: Russell Sage Foundation and Population Reference Bureau.

Saenz, Rogelio and Alberto Davila. 1992. "Chicano Return Migration to the Southwest: An Integrated Human Capital Approach." *International Migration Review* 26:1248–1266.

Saenz, Rogelio, Katharine M. Donato, Lourdes Gouveia, and Cruz Torres. 2003. "Latinos in the South: A Glimpse of Ongoing Trends and Research." *Southern Rural Sociology* 19:1–19.

Saenz, Rogelio and Clyde S. Greenlees. 1996. "The Demography of Chicanos." Pp. 9–23 in *Chicanas and Chicanos in Contemporary Society,* edited by R. M. De Anda. Boston: Allyn and Bacon.

Saenz, Rogelio and Cruz Torres. 2003. "Latinos in Rural America." Pp. 57–70 in *Challenges for Rural America in the Twenty-First Century*, edited by David L. Brown and Louis E. Swanson. University Park, PA: Pennsylvania State University Press, Rural Studies Series.

Shaw, R. Paul. 1975. *Migration Theory and Fact*. Philadelphia: Regional Science Research Institute.

Sjaastad, Larry A. 1962. "The Costs and Returns of Human Migration." *Journal of Political Economy* 70:S80–S93.

Stack, Carol. 1996. *Call to Home: African Americans Reclaim the Rural South*. New York: Basic Books.

Stull, Donald D., Michael J. Broadway, and David Griffith. 1995. *Any Way You Cut It: Meat Processing and Small-Town America*. Lawrence: University Press of Kansas.

Tienda, Marta. 1982. *Residential Distribution and Internal Migration Patterns of Chicanos: A Critical Assessment*. Center for Demography and Ecology Working Paper 82–26. Madison: University of Wisconsin, Center for Demography and Ecology.

Tilly, Charles. 1990. "Transplanted Networks." Pp. 79–95 in *Immigration Reconsidered: History, Sociology, and Politics*, edited by V. Yans-McLaughlin. New York: Oxford University Press.

U.S. Bureau of the Census. 1991. *1990 Census of Population and Housing: Summary Tape File 1 Technical Documentation*. Washington, DC: U.S. Government Printing Office.

———. 1993a. *1990 Census of Population and Housing: Public Use Microdata Sample U.S. Technical Documentation*. Washington, DC: U.S. Government Printing Office.

———. 1993b. *1990 Census of Population and Housing: Summary Tape File 4 Technical Documentation*. Washington, DC: U.S. Government Printing Office.

———. 2004. *2000 Census of Population and Housing: Summary File 4 Technical Documentation*. Washington, DC: U.S. Government Printing Office.

Valdes, Dennis Nodin. 1991. *Al Norte: Agricultural Workers in the Great Lakes Region, 1917–1970*. Austin: University of Texas Press.

Voth, Donald E., Molly Sizer, and Frank L. Farmer. 1996. "Patterns of In-Migration and Out-Migration: Human Capital Movements in the Lower Mississippi Delta Region." *Southern Rural Sociology* 12:61–91.

NINE

A Spatial Analysis
of the Urban Landscape

What Accounts for Differences
across Neighborhoods?

DEIRDRE A. OAKLEY
JOHN R. LOGAN

NEIGHBORHOODS VARY FROM one another in many ways that make a difference in residents' lives. Among these is the range and type of urban services nearby. As a dimension of spatial inequality, urban services are not neatly arranged on a hierarchy of better to worse. Residents of some exclusive zones resolutely oppose the establishment of more public and private services; more typically, issues arise in terms of the types of services provided. It is common knowledge that some community services are perceived as desirable (e.g., schools, churches, and fire stations), while others are considered out of place in a good neighborhood (e.g., homeless shelters and group homes). It is widely suspected that poor neighborhoods get inadequate community services while being over-provided with social services and unwanted facilities serving the entire city. Results on this issue are mixed. Some observers argue that the narrow scope of extant research has not disproved the connection between race, class, and uneven distribution of services but rather overlooked it (Cingranelli 1981). The purpose of this chapter is to reexamine this issue. Using spatial analytic techniques to identify affluent and poor neighborhoods in New York City, we focus our analysis the following questions: (1) are urban services similarly distributed across neighborhoods with differing socioeconomic composition? and (2) is the mix of types of services consistent across these neighborhoods?

INTERPRETING SERVICE INEQUALITIES

It is well understood that the spatial distribution of residents across neighborhoods varies by socioeconomic status and race (Massey and Denton 1993). The same holds true concerning the location of needed services. Some areas have more schools, churches, libraries, and other public facilities while others have more homeless shelters and group homes. The question is how to account for the clustering of various types of services, and particularly whether the outcomes reflect discriminatory processes that lead to disadvantages for poor and minority neighborhoods.

A number of scholars (e.g., see Dear and Wolch, 1987; Rich, 1982; Smith, 1988; Wolch, 1982) have argued that various social services, unwanted in more affluent neighborhoods, become concentrated in disadvantaged places due to the inability of poorer residents to protect their neighborhood from unwanted facilities. In addition, these neighborhoods will not have the same quality of other needed services as more affluent neighborhoods. The assumption here is that poor neighborhoods cannot effectively demand help from external providers, nor do they have the internal social resources to generate civic institutions. Thus, a spatial mismatch will exist between service availability and service needs. This spatial mismatch reflects the hierarchy of political and social capital within the city.

An alternative interpretation of service location (and any spatial mismatches that may emerge) emphasizes bureaucratic decision rules and routines coupled with idiosyncratic historical events that result in "unpatterned inequality." In other words, government services are allocated according to bureaucratic decision rules that are nondiscriminatory and apolitical in nature. Although the rules are apolitical, over time inequalities can develop in the spatial distribution of services due to changing administrations, demographic shifts within neighborhoods, and changes in the overall urban infrastructure, but these are likely to have a random or unpatterned character.

Using information on urban service provision in New York City and neighborhood data from Census 2000, this chapter takes another look at issues concerning how various types of services are distributed across census tracts using spatial analytic techniques. As noted above, we attempt to answer the questions: (1) are urban services similarly distributed across neighborhoods with differing socioeconomic composition? and (2) do different neighborhoods have a different mix of types of services? What is novel in our approach is an explicit consideration of spatial relationships. The typical study of urban service distribution is a quantitative cross-sectional comparison of a geographic unit (e.g., census tract, district, or ward) without consideration of spatial clustering. We measure service provision not within each single tract in isolation but taking into account the social characteristics of other tracts in nearby areas. This is a useful step forward in the urban services literature. Single census tracts within a large city like New York comprise relatively small areas compared to zones within which public services are delivered. By combining clusters of tracts with similar socioeconomic characteristics into "neighborhoods," we deal with geographic units much closer to natural service areas.

PRIOR RESEARCH ON SERVICE INEQUALITIES

We review the urban services literature in terms of the two aspects of services we study here: who gets more or less service, and who gets better or worse types of services.

More or Less Services

Much of the urban services research has focused on equity in delivery of key services, such as libraries, schools, police, fire protection, and sanitation. Questions about equity arose in part because of two important federal court cases. In the first case, *Hobson v. Hansen* (1967), the U.S. District Court found an inequitable distribution of school expenditures within a single district located in Washington, DC. In the second case, *Hawkins v. Shaw* (1971), the U.S. Court of Appeals determined that the municipal government of Shaw, Mississippi, had engaged in racial discrimination in its provision of city services (Sharp 1990). These cases spurred the widespread belief that neighborhoods that are poorer, have larger shares of minority residents, or are politically weak receive less services for their tax dollars (Feiock 1986). Thus, the urban services research literature grew out of subsequent attempts to confirm or deny the generalizability of this assertion (Boyle and Jacobs 1982).

Three hypotheses have been examined concerning the distribution of urban services. The first, the "underclass" hypothesis, posits that poor, minority neighborhoods get fewer services than more advantaged neighborhoods. The second, the "contributory/compensatory" hypothesis, states that distributions are not systematically biased based on the socioeconomic characteristics of neighborhoods, but rather situationally biased (Boyle and Jacobs, 1982). In other words, compensatory services such as welfare, health, and elementary and secondary education are unequally distributed but favor the poor neighborhoods. On the other hand, contributory services like fire protection, police, and sanitation are also not distributed equally, but unlike compensatory services, these favor neighborhoods contributing more taxes (Koehler and Wrightson 1987). The third, the "bureaucratic decision rules" hypothesis, holds that government services are allocated according to decision rules formulated by the bureaucracy (Meirer et al. 1991). According to Meirer et al., although these rules have impacts that may result in uneven distribution of specific services, they are nondiscriminatory and apolitical in nature, or unpatterned.

Although the underclass hypothesis was the genesis for much of the initial urban services research, it received little support (Meier et al. 1991). Instead the bureaucratic decision hypothesis has been favored. Koehler and Wrightson (1987) state that by the late 1980s, research over more than a decade had produced the following conclusions:

1. Services are often equitably distributed; however, types of services are not the same within municipalities over time.
2. When distributions are inequitable, there is no systematic underclass bias. Instead, distributions are best characterized as unpatterned inequality.
3. Unpatterned inequality is the result of bureaucratic decision rules and routines coupled with idiosyncratic historical events.

However, support has also been found for the contributory/compensatory hypothesis. In their study of urban services in New York City, Boyle and Jacobs (1982) found that when property services were at issue, public resources went to areas contributing the most revenue to the city budget. In contrast, when social services were at stake, resources went to those areas needing them the most. Similarly, in his review of the urban services literature, Lee (1994) concluded that need and conditions were the most important determinants. He argues that because of the association between need, conditions, and distribution, poor neighborhoods are likely to receive a greater share of those services most needed (Kelly and Swindell 2002). Wolch (1980) also contends that the distribution of facilities providing social services is linked to the location of service-dependent households.

Good Services and Bad Services

In addition to issues concerning the level of service, questions about what kinds of services go where have been debated widely in the literature. Taken as a whole, urban services are considered essential for city livability (Lineberry 1977) According to Janowitz and Suttles (1978), both private and public community services—such as libraries, schools, police and fire departments, and churches—are considered vital to the development and maintenance of cohesive communities because they are "a natural repository of sacred involvement" (p. 89). At the same time, however, a range of health and social services—such as mental health and substance abuse treatment facilities, group homes, homeless shelters, and other social services—are acknowledged as necessary for specific populations but are not wanted by residents in both poor and more wealthy neighborhoods (Dear and Wolch 1987). Therefore there is the perception that services fall into "good" and "bad" categories so the planning involved at the bureaucratic level concerning location decisions has the potential to ignite community opposition.

This type of opposition is commonly known as NIMBY-ism or "Not In My Backyard." As it relates to social services, NIMBY is a label most commonly applied to people who oppose service facilities, subsidized dwelling, group homes, and housing for homeless and low-income individuals (Pendall 1999). According to the National Law Center on Homelessness and Poverty (1997), this opposition is frequently motivated by community resident fears that such facilities will lead to a decline in neighborhood quality. According to Wolch (1982), local opposition is strongest and most successful in nonpoor neighborhoods and suburban jurisdictions, and weakest in low-income zones, thus providing additional rationale (aside from service need) for local planning decisions to locate these facilities where poor people live. This results in the tendency for social service facilities to be unevenly distributed across the urban landscape and overrepresented in poor neighborhoods (Dear and Wolch 1987). Dear and Wolch (1987) argue that social service ghetto-ization plays a crucial role in the dynamics of urban deterioration. From this point of view it is generally assumed that the presence of so many social services exacerbates the social problems of poor neighborhoods. Therefore such places are unable to sustain the institutions necessary for community cohesion like churches and neighborhood associations, and at the same time, local planning decisions neglect them in distributing other essential ("good") community services like libraries, schools, and police and fire departments (Rich 1982; Smith 1988).

Other interpretations of urban service distribution have also surfaced. For example, Miranda and Tunyavong (1994) argue that given the narrow range of services examined in previous studies, it may be premature to conclude that all municipal resource-allocation decisions are made solely on the basis of bureaucratic decision rules. In their examination of the distribution of Community Development Block Grants (CDBG) in Chicago, they concluded that politics did indeed play a significant role—and, in fact, the scope of distributive politics was far greater than past urban services research had indicated. Likewise, in his reexamination of the distribution of recreational resources and services in Chicago, Mladenka (1989) argues that the altered demographic and economic structure of the city over the last four decades has forced public officials to use urban services—particularly recreational services—as a weapon in the struggle to combat the deterioration of the social fabric. Thus, while bureaucratic decision rules remains the dominant theory concerning the distribution of urban services, several studies have produced alternative explanations.

A SPATIAL APPROACH TO SERVICE INEQUALITY

We take a new look at issues of service equitability—including how community ("good") and social ("bad") services are distributed across neighborhoods of varying socioeconomic status—using recently developed spatial analytic tools to assess the spatial distribution and patterning of services systematically. Concerns about spatial autocorrelation prompted geographers to develop several indicators of the extent to which the spatial distribution of place characteristics departs from a random pattern. Spatial autocorrelation exists when the value of a variable is associated with the values in neighboring geographic areas (Kamber et al. 1999). This phenomenon follows Tobler's "First Law of Geography": Everything is related to everything else, but near places are more related than far places (Tobler 1970). Anselin (1995) has extended this work to a class of "local indicators of spatial association" (LISA), which offer a measure for each place of the extent of *significant spatial clustering* of similar values around it. In brief, LISA indicators identify "hot spots" that take into account not only unusually high or low values in a single place (such as a census tract) but also the values in nearby places. Our approach to identifying service patterns is based mainly on this kind of spatial clustering. Because the main question in the literature has been inequalities based on the class composition of neighborhoods, we identify "rich" and "poor" neighborhoods by searching for clusters of census tracts that have similarly high or low wealth. This is the same approach that some authors (Logan, Alba, and Zhang 2002) have used to identify boundaries of ethnic neighborhoods.

We match service information supplied by the City of New York's Department of City Planning with small area population data from Census 2000. Like previous studies (see Miranda and Tunyavong 1994), we conduct a cross-sectional comparison of service levels for a specific geographic unit (in this case, a census tract). We identify clusters of high-income and low-income census tracts through the analysis of spatial autocorrelation in their median household income using a LISA statistics called Local Moran's I. In other words, first we define neighborhoods as clusters of census tracts with similar class characteristics and then evaluate the availability of services within the entire neighborhood. Hence, unlike previous research, the areas of analysis are not predetermined but rather identified more systematically as statistically significant spatial clusters of high- and low-income levels.

DATA AND METHODS

In addition to Census 2000 data, we use information on urban services from the City of New York, Department of City Planning's *Selected Facilities and Program Sites in New York City 1998* database to examine the spatial distribution of urban services across census tracts in New York City. The *Selected Facilities* database contains geo-referenced data matched to 1990 Census tract boundaries for the following services: public and private schools, public libraries, police and fire stations, hospitals, senior centers, substance abuse and mental health treatment and residential facilities, day care, and homeless services and shelters. Geo-referenced data provide an X Y coordinate (latitude/longitude) for each facility location from which a point theme is generated. This theme is then aggregated to the census tract level for subsequent spatial analysis. Thus a count of each type of service per census tract is created. Similar information for churches is also included. Churches are included in our analysis to assess the assumption that poorer neighborhoods have a diminished capacity to sustain community institutions. The street addresses of churches in the five boroughs of New York City were entered into a database from the *National Directory of Churches, Synagogues, and Other Houses of Worship, 1994*. These data were then geo-coded, matched to the Census and facilities data, and aggregated to the tract level.

In addition to examining the distribution of the individual services mentioned above, our analysis also includes a classification of services types. Our classification scheme includes four categories: (1) total services; (2) social and health services; (3) community services; and (4) community institutions. The total services category includes the sum of all services. The social and health services category includes substance abuse, mental health, homeless shelters and services, hospitals, and senior centers. The community services category includes public schools, libraries, police and fire stations, and day care. Lastly, the community institutions category includes churches and private schools.

Tract-level data from Census 2000 Summary Files 1 and 3 are used for socioeconomic and racial indicators. Variables representing total households, population size, median household income, percent non-Hispanic white, percent non-Hispanic black, percent Hispanic, percent Asian, percent homeowner, percent poverty, percent unemployment, percent professional, percent college graduates, and percent recent immigrant have been computed from these files. There are 2216 census tracts across the five boroughs that comprise New York City.

Using these data, spatial analysis is undertaken to determine the spatial clustering of income levels. More specifically, we use SpaceStat exploratory spatial analysis software in conjunction with ArcView mapping software to identify clusters of census tracts with statistically significant values of local Moran's I (I_i). Statically significant Local Moran values indicate unusually high or low median household income values. According to Logan et al. (2002), as measured this way, a "cluster" is made up of a single focal census tract along with all tracts that surround and share a boundary with it. In fact, most such clusters are not isolated but extend continuously over areas containing many tracts.

Statistically significant values of the Local Moran's I statistic have four categories: (1) high-high—indicating a concentration of high incomes in contiguous census tracts compared to other areas in the city; (2) low-low—

indicating clusters of very low income levels; (3) high-low—indicating that a tract with high median household income is surrounded by low income tracts; and (4) low-high—indicating that adjoining tracts with high income surround a tract with low income. This analysis will focus on clusters of tracts with high-high and low-low values. By concentrating on these values, we are identifying the extreme cases of spatially concentrated affluence (i.e., not only is a single tract relatively affluent but it is surrounded by other affluent tracts) and spatially concentrated poverty. If there is a pattern of service provision inequity, we would expect to see the most concrete evidence of this by comparing these polar opposites.

COMPARISON OF AFFLUENT AND
LOW-INCOME NEIGHORHOODS

Figure 9.1 shows the location of the income clusters based on the Local Moran's I statistic. Table 9.1 shows the total number, range, and average number of each service type across the 17 income clusters. There are 11 affluent clusters and six low-income clusters. Affluent neighborhoods are found in Staten Island; Upper East and West Sides; Lower and Midtown Manhattan; Carroll Gardens, Prospect Park and Howard Beach in Brooklyn; Jamaica and Flushing in Queens; and Riverdale in the Bronx. Taken together the affluent clusters comprise 699,883 households with a total population of 1,147,188. Their average median household income is just over $75,000. Staten Island has the highest median household income ($90,392), and Riverdale the lowest ($55,353). In terms of population size, the affluent clusters range from large places like Staten Island, Flushing, and the Upper East Side (where the zones all have more than 200,000 residents) to smaller areas like Prospect Park (32,270), Carroll Gardens (35,721), Riverdale (40,846), and Howard Beach (46,587). Midtown, the Upper Westside, Lower Manhattan, and Jamaica are in the middle, with populations over 100,000.

Low-income clusters include East New York, Bay Ridge, and Coney Island in Brooklyn; the Lower East Side; Harlem and the Bronx. Taken altogether these neighborhoods include 544,955 households with a total population of 1,608,445. Their average median household income is under $22,000. The income gap between the affluent and low-income clusters is substantial. Of the low-income clusters, Bay Ridge has the highest median income at $27,758 and the Bronx has the lowest ($19,678). Although there are only a few low-income clusters, three cover very extensive territories. The largest is the Bronx with 634,719 residents, followed by East New York (488,992), Harlem (276,297), the Lower East Side (73,578), Bay Ridge (72,170), and Coney Island (62,690).

Table 9.1 shows the overall socioeconomic, racial, and service characteristics of the affluent and low-income clusters. Not surprisingly, blacks and His-

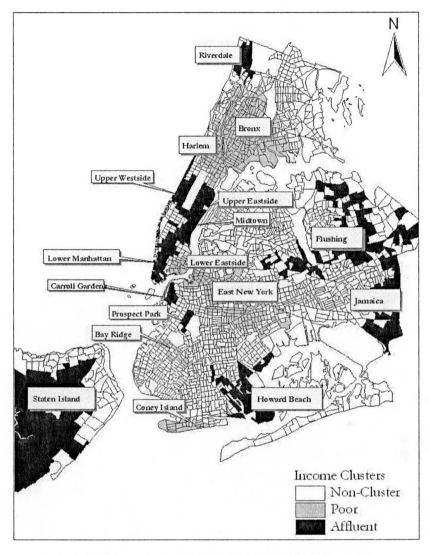

FIGURE 9.1. Location of Income Clusters, New York City, 2000

panics are overrepresented in the low-income clusters (38.3 percent and 45.9 percent, respectively, of the total populations of these areas) while whites comprise the majority in the affluent clusters (71.5 percent). However, one affluent neighborhood, Jamaica, is predominantly black. One of the poor neighborhoods, Lower East Side, has an Asian (mainly Chinese) majority, and two other poor neighborhoods, Bay Ridge and Coney Island, are white.

TABLE 9.1
Socioeconomic, Racial, and Service Characteristics by Type of Cluster

Socioeconomic and Racial	Low-Income Clusters	Affluent Clusters	Services*	Low-Income Clusters	Affluent Clusters
Total Population	1,608,445	1,147,188	Public Schools	22.6	11.0
Median HH Income	$21,463.2	$75,817.0	Private Schools	10.2	14.0
Percent Non-Hispanic White	9.4	71.5	Libraries	2.4	3.3
Percent Non-Hispanic Black	38.3	11.9	Police	2.1	1.5
Percent Hispanic	45.9	8.3	Fire	3.8	3.9
Percent Asian	5.3	7.4	Hospitals	0.9	1.4
Percent Homeowner	10.4	37.8	Senior Centers	6.0	2.7
Percent Poverty	38.6	7.7	Substance Abuse	8.8	8.7
Percent Unemployed	17.6	4.8	Mental Health	22.3	23.4
Percent Professional	17.9	55.9	Day Care	19.8	18.0
Percent College Educated	10.5	56.0	Homeless	29.2	11.4
Percent Recent Immigrants	15.4	7.8	Churches	61.4	47.1

* Indicates services per 100,000

Affluent neighborhoods have close to four times as many homeowners (37.8 percent compared to 10.4 percent), three times as many people in professional/managerial positions (55.9 percent compared to 17.9 percent) and five times as many over age 25 who have graduated from college (55.9 percent compared to 10.5 percent). In contrast, the low-income areas have five times more poverty (38.3 percent versus 7.7 percent), three and half times more unemployment (17.6 versus 4.8 percent), and twice as many recent immigrants (15.4 percent versus 7.8 percent). The only socioeconomic characteristic with overlap in the distribution between the two types of areas is homeownership. Both Lower and Midtown Manhattan have relatively low levels of homeownership (23.5 percent and 24.4 percent, respectively), about the same as low-income Bay Ridge (24.3 percent).

Despite the contrasts in socioeconomic and racial composition, however, we find surprisingly broad similarities in the distribution and level of services. This is evident in the third and fourth columns of table 9.1 where the level and type of service is shown by neighborhood type (standardized for population size by displaying rates per 100,000 residents). Low-income neighborhoods have significantly more public schools (22.6 versus 11.0) than high-income neighborhoods. They also have more churches (61.4 versus 47.1) as well as homeless shelters and services (29.2 versus 11.4). But there is little difference between low-income and affluent areas in the number of libraries, police and fire stations, hospitals, and day care per 100,000. There are also similar numbers of substance abuse and mental health services. Affluent neighborhoods have more private schools (14.0 per 100,000), but the low-income areas are not far behind at 10.2 per 100,000.

Therefore our key finding is that the spatial distribution of services does not fit the notion of "service ghetto" (as argued by Dear and Wolch) or the "underclass" model of deprived poor neighborhoods. Rich and poor neighborhoods are more alike than they are different, and to the extent that low-income neighborhoods have greater concentrations of services, these include both community institutions (of the sort that reinforce social life in the neighborhood) and social services.

SERVICE VARIATIONS IN INDIVIDUAL NEIGHBORHOODS

Variations are apparent in the distribution of services per 100,000 across individual clusters. In general, the trends in service distribution mirror the results shown in table 9.1. However, several neighborhoods diverge from these trends. For example, although Midtown Manhattan is an affluent cluster, it has significantly more homeless shelters and services per 100,000 than the other affluent clusters (23.9 versus an average of 11.4). Likewise, in contrast to the other low-income clusters, Bay Ridge, Brooklyn, has few homeless shelters and services per 100,000 (2.2 per 100,000 versus 29.1). In addition Bay Ridge has far more private schools per 100,000 (38.8) than both the other low-income and all the affluent clusters. Other variants include the affluent clusters of Carroll Gardens and Prospect Park in Brooklyn. Carroll Gardens has a disproportionate number of mental health services (72.8 per 100,000) compared to all the other affluent and low-income clusters. Prospect Park, on the other hand, has more churches (114.7 per 100,000) than all other clusters but no police services.

Table 9.2 shows the distribution of service by categories—total services, social services, community services, and community institutions—for each neighborhood. This table is also sorted from highest to lowest median household income. The total service category indicates that, overall, low-income clusters have more services. The three exceptions are Midtown, Carroll Gardens, and Prospect Park, all of which have just as many services as the low-income clusters. The same trend is apparent for social services: with the exception of the high-income Midtown and Carroll Gardens, other than Bay Ridge the low-income clusters have significantly more social services. But the trend in community services is not clearly demarcated between low-income and affluent clusters. While the affluent cluster of Prospect Park has

TABLE 9.2
Services by Categories Per 100,000 (sorted high to low Median HH Income)

Neighborhood	Median HH Income	Total Services	Social & Health	Community Services	Community Institutions
Staten Island	$90,391.9	142.9	35.5	28.7	78.7
Upper East Side	$84,247.0	106.6	32.1	34.6	40.0
Upper West Side	$74,584.7	146.8	51.6	30.1	65.2
Lower Manhattan	$73,122.9	151.2	65.1	49.5	36.7
Midtown	$68,923.3	196.3	86.5	42.1	67.8
Carroll Gardens	$67,430.9	221.2	98.0	67.2	56.0
Prospect Park	$65,179.8	210.7	34.1	40.3	136.4
Jamaica	$62,714.8	135.6	29.6	43.0	63.0
Howard Beach	$59,806.2	83.7	6.4	38.6	38.6
Flushing	$59,353.1	130.6	31.5	39.5	59.5
Riverdale	$55,359.7	127.3	39.2	46.5	41.6
Bay Ridge	$27,758.2	169.1	29.1	30.5	109.5
Lower East Side	$25,415.1	214.7	76.1	62.5	76.1
Harlem	$22,383.9	228.7	91.6	56.5	80.7
East New York	$21,884.6	206.6	58.1	53.6	94.9
Coney Island	$19,985.9	140.4	55.8	39.9	44.7
Bronx	$19,677.7	163.1	67.9	47.7	47.4

the most community services (67.2 per 100,000), the low-income clusters of the Lower East Side, Harlem, and East New York have more community services than the other affluent clusters except Prospect Park. However, the low-income cluster neighborhoods of Coney Island and the Bronx have about the same number of community services as the affluent clusters. The category of community institutions is more evenly distributed across all clusters with the exception of affluent clusters Staten Island and Prospect Park, as well as the low-income clusters of Bay Ridge, Harlem, and East New York. These neighborhoods have significantly more community institutions than the other clusters.

DISCUSSION

This chapter utilized a spatial analytic approach to examine urban services distribution in New York City. Unlike previous studies, this approach did not predetermine the neighborhoods for investigation. Instead the Local Moran test was used to assess the degree of spatial autocorrelation (or clustering) among various levels of median household income. This allowed us to identify areas of spatially concentrated affluence and poverty, precisely those parts of the city that might be expected to be particularly well treated or poorly served.

Results indicate that urban services are by and large similarly distributed across neighborhoods with differing socioeconomic and racial composition. With the exception of Bay Ridge, the low-income neighborhoods have more social services than the affluent neighborhoods. However, low-income neighborhoods also have just as many schools, libraries, police and fire stations, and day care facilities and churches as the affluent neighborhoods. Thus, these findings do not support the underclass contention that poor neighborhoods get less of the "good" services and a disproportionate share of the "bad." Nor do they support the political economy (contributory/compensatory) hypothesis. In their study of urban services in New York City, Boyle and Jacobs (1982) found that levels of social and health services were higher in low-income neighborhoods but levels of community services, with the exception of schools, were higher in the neighborhoods that contributed the most taxes. Although the present study confirms that more social services are located in low-income neighborhoods, the results do not support Boyle and Jacobs' previous findings concerning community services. Indeed, our findings indicate that community services are equitably distributed despite differing levels of income: poor neighborhoods get just as many of these services as affluent neighborhoods.

The equitability in service distribution is partially explained by New York City's zoning resolution of 1961. This was the first comprehensive update to the 1916 Zoning Resolution and coincided with the city's urban renewal program. Because all community services were viewed as advantageous to the communities they served at that time, the 1961 zoning revision was extremely permissive regarding these facilities (Kintish and Shapiro 1993). The revision permitted "community facilities" in any residential district and did not put any restriction on the number allowed. (These facilities were not permitted in either commercial or manufacturing districts without a use variance.) The revision defined community services broadly including the following types of facilities: colleges or universities, libraries, museums, schools, community centers, churches, hospitals, health clinics, nursing homes, welfare services, group residential care, public parks, recreational, and playgrounds (NYC Department of City Planning 2002). This meant that almost every residential area within the five boroughs of New York City was essentially zoned to include mixed land uses including public services.

Within this context, which may be unique to New York City, we found considerable variations in levels of specific services both between neighborhoods of differing socioeconomic and racial characteristics and among neighborhood of similar economic status. This result is consistent with the "unpatterned" prediction of the bureaucratic decision model. A more complete examination of the history of service establishment across neighborhoods would be needed in order to validate that interpretation. When were specific schools, churches, or public service centers established? What were the surrounding residential areas like at that time? Who participated in these investment decisions, and what was the rationale for the outcome? We are not able to assess such evidence here, but certainly the failure of the underclass and service ghetto hypotheses would encourage further research in this direction.

We noted above that results might be different in other cities. We should also emphasize that by examining variations within a single city, we have certainly missed an important dimension of spatial inequalities—the common disadvantage of cities compared to their outlying suburbs and growing disparities among suburban jurisdictions. The bureaucratic decision model posits a single bureaucracy spanning neighborhoods and potentially redistributing public goods among them. Jurisdictional fragmentation within the metropolis disrupts such coordination.

A dimension of private and nonprofit decision making underlies the provision of services to city residents. Among these, churches and private schools are the institutions least constrained by governmental decisions. Nonprofit service providers are indirectly steered toward certain areas by the availability of public funding, but at the same time they often have strong roots in the areas where they operate. Our results for these services undermine assumptions about the institutional weakness of the poorest neighborhoods based on their lack of social capital or weakness of connections to outside organizations. Just as some other researchers have rediscovered strong family and neighborhood support networks of the inner city poor, we find unexpected organizational vitality in the city's most vulnerable neighborhoods.

REFERENCES

Anselin, Luc. 1995. "Local Indicators of Spatial Association—LISA." *Geographical Analysis* 27:93–115.

Boyle, John and David Jacobs. 1982. "The Intracity Distribution of Services: A Multivariate Analysis." *The American Political Science Review* 76:371–379.

Cingranelli, David. 1981. "Race, Politics, and Elites: Testing Alternative Models of Municipal Service Distribution." *American Journal of Political Science* 25:664–692.

Dear, Michael and Jennifer Wolch. 1987. *Landscapes of Despair: From Deinstitutionalization to Homeless.* Princeton, NJ: Princeton University Press.

Feiock, Richard. 1986. "The Political Economy of Urban Service Distribution: A Test of the Underclass Hypothesis." *Journal of Urban Affairs* 8:31–42.

Janowitz, Morris and Gerald Suttles. 1978. "The Social Ecology of Citizenship." Pp. 80–104 in *The Management of Human Services*, edited by Rosemary Sarri, and Yeheskel Hasenfeld. New York: Columbia University Press.

Kamber, Thomas, John Mollenkopf, and Timothy Ross. 1999. "Crime, Space, and Place: An Analysis of Crime Patterns in Brooklyn." Pp. 107–152 in *Analyzing Crime Patterns: Frontiers of Practice*, edited by Victor Goldsmith, Philip McGuire, John Mollenkopf, and T. Ross. Thousand Oaks, CA: Sage Publications.

Kelly, Janet and David Swindell. 2002. "Service Quality Variation Across Urban Space: First Steps Toward a Model of Citizen Satisfaction." *Journal of Urban Affairs* 24:271–288.

Kintish, Brian and John Shapiro. 1993. "The Zoning of Today in the City of Tomorrow." Pp. 119–164 in *Planning and Zoning New York City: Yesterday, Today, and Tomorrow*, edited by Todd W. Bressi. New Brunswick, NJ: Center for Urban Policy Research, Rutgers University.

Koehler, David and Margaret Wrightson. 1987. "Inequality in the Delivery of Urban Services: A Reconsideration of the Chicago Parks." *The Journal of Politics* 49(1):80–99.

Lee, Seung Jong. 1994. "Policy Type, Bureaucracy, and Urban Policies: Integrating Models of Urban Service Distribution." *Policy Studies Journal* 22:87–108.

Lineberry, Robert. 1977. "Introduction: On the Politics and Economics of Urban Services." *Urban Affairs Quarterly* 12:267–271.

Logan, John, Richard Alba, and Wenquan Zhang. 2002. "Immigrant Enclaves and Ethnic Communities in New York and Los Angeles." *American Sociological Review* 67:299–322.

Massey, Douglas and Nancy Denton. 1993. *American Apartheid: Segregation and the Making of the Underclass.* Cambridge, MA: Harvard University Press.

Meier, Kenneth J., Joseph Stewart, and Robert England. 1991. "The Politics of Bureaucratic Discretion: Educational Access as an Urban Service." *American Journal of Political Science* 35:155–177.

Miranda, Rowan and Ittipone Tunyavong. 1994. "Patterned Inequality? Reexamining the Role of Distributive Politics in Urban Service Delivery." *Urban Affairs Quarterly* 29:509–534.

Mladenka, Kenneth. 1989. "The Distribution of An Urban Public Service: The Changing Role of Race and Politics." *Urban Affairs Quarterly* 24:556–583.

National Law Center on Homelessness and Poverty. 1997. *Access Delayed, Access Denied: Local Opposition to Housing and Services for Homeless People Across the United States.* Washington, DC: National Law Center on Homelessness and Poverty.

New York City Department of City Planning. 2002 Revision. *Zoning Resolution: The City of New York.* New York, NY: City Planning Commission.

Pendall, Rolf. 1999. "Opposition to Housing: NIMBY and Beyond." *Urban Affairs Review* 35:112–136.

Rich, Richard C. 1982. "The Political Economy of Urban-Service Distribution." Pp. 1–16 in *The Politics of Urban Public Services,* edited by Richard C. Rich. Lexington, MA: Lexington Books.

Sharp, Elaine. 1990. *Urban Politics and Administration: From Service Delivery to Economic Development.* New York: Longman.

Smith, Christopher, J. 1988. *Public Problems: The Management of Urban Distress.* New York: Guilford Press.

Tobler, Waldo. 1970. "A Computer Movie Simulating Urban Growth in the Detroit Region." *Economic Geography* 26:234–240.

Wolch, Jennifer. 1980. "Residential Location of the Service-Dependent Poor." *Annals of the Association of American Geographers* 70:330.

———. 1982. "Spatial Consequences of Social Policy: The Role of Service-Facility Location in Urban Development Patterns." Pp. 19–36 in *The Politics of Urban Public Services,* edited by Richard C. Rich. Lexington, MA: Lexington Books.

PART III

The Sociology of Spatial Inequality:
Toward a Common Vision

TEN

Space for Social Inequality Researchers

A View from Geography

VINCENT J. DEL CASINO JR.
JOHN PAUL JONES III

WE ARE WRITING as geographers attempting to engage a sociological audience on what we see to be two important domains of contemporary spatial theory. Our goal is to create bridges of understanding between disciplines that, as the editors note in their introduction, have for too long developed on nonintersecting paths. There are of course exceptions to this general rule. Over the 20th century, one can certainly point to the sharing of concepts and methodologies found in the Chicago School of urban sociology and to the postwar conversations in subfields such as human ecology, demography, and community studies. More recently, there has been productive theoretical traffic between the fields in the study of structure and agency, particularly in its Giddensian form. Yet we agree with the editors that there is room for much greater productive interchange.

Geographers have, of course, produced a rich literature on the theorization of space; after all, this is the discipline's core object, parallel to that of society for sociologists. In this paper, we offer a discussion of two distinct versions of spatial theory, both of which are relevant to the study of social inequality, broadly conceived. The first of these is the discrete understanding of space carried out within geography's dominant rubric of "spatial science," and in particular its more recent "socially relevant" offshoot. Discrete space is conceptualized as abstract and absolute, a backdrop to social relations that unfold unevenly across space and at a number of different scales, from the local and regional to the national and global. The method-ological focus in this tradition is to begin with spatial variations in social inequalities and to employ modeling strategies to gain insight into social processes underlying these variations. The studies by McLaughlin et al. and Cotter et al. in this volume, for example, employ modeling strategies often seen in this approach. The second approach is relational in character, focused on internal relations of space and society. As opposed to external relations that identify causes and effects operating between discrete spaces and social forces, internal relations require a dialectical approach that refuses separation between them. Tickamyer et al.'s article in this volume most closely reflects this approach, while Leicht and Jenkins also suggest that political sociology might usefully move in this direction. In this dialec-tical perspective, one that has found favor among critical realists in geog-raphy (e.g., Sayer 2000), researchers direct attention to the broader social processes that work themselves out, often in unique ways, in particular places, but see those places as simultaneously part-and-parcel of social rela-tions as they operate at a number of scales. Because this tradition requires attention to the dialectic within and between social *and* spatial processes, it stands as a relational counterpart to the more discrete view of space adopted in socially relevant spatial science. While the articles in this col-lection may be seen as falling closer to one or the other approach above, many also contain elements that straddle both approaches, a point dis-cussed further below.

Our larger goal in discussing the evolution of these two traditions, as well as their theoretical and methodological principles and selected applications, is to create a stronger bridge of understanding between sociologists and geo-graphers concerning different approaches to studying space and social rela-tions. With these two theoretical reference points in mind, the paper then turns to address one of the other primary goals of the volume—achieving a better understanding of scale in the analysis of social inequality. Scale emerges as a completely different object of analysis under the two theories of space: on the one hand, it is the level at which data is collected and theories and models developed and tested; on the other hand, it is the socially pro-duced outcome of both horizontal and vertical sociospatial relations—what Brenner has called scalar structuration (1998). In the following section, we present the broader historical and theoretical context for the development of both the spatial scientific and critical realist perspectives of space and spatial relations. Next, we offer a brief review of scale from the standpoint of these two theoretical positions, showing how they lead to quite different approaches to the question of the "missing middle" noted by the editors of this volume. We conclude the paper by arguing for the value of using both approaches in the study of social inequality.

THEORIZING GEOGRAPHY'S OBJECT OF ANALYSIS

In order to facilitate sociological comparisons with geography, we begin by referencing the larger epistemological and ontological categories that form the foundation for discrete and relational theorizations of space. Figure 10.1 lists some of the most important binaries to have influenced both theories of and methodological approaches to space. The account we provide below discusses how theorizations of discrete and relational space differentially crisscross the other binary relations shown in the figure. For example, in our discussion of discrete and relational space, spatial science is shown to be characterized, in the broadest terms, by generality and order, while critical realist geography is structured by particularity and chaos. Keeping this picture in mind, we can now move to some of the specifics behind the theorization of space as an object of study in geography.

Toward a Socially Relevant Spatial Science

Prior to the 1950s, a largely empiricist, "regional geography" (Hartshorne 1939) dominated the field. Ontologically speaking, this school was predicated on the understanding that geography's objects included both natural and cultural phenomena, and that they and their associated processes interacted in specific areal settings to give a unique character to places. Though regional geographers claimed objectivity (Hartshorne 1939) and ultimately sought to identify causal processes under the banner of explanation (James

Epistemology	Objectivity General Explanation	Subjectivity Particular Interpretation
Ontology	Order Society Discrete	Chaos Individual Relational

FIGURE 10.1. Major Epistemological and
Ontological Binaries Structuring Geographic Theory

1952), they were better known for providing in-depth but idiosyncratic descriptions of local settings. Methodologically, the interdependence of phenomena in space limited the extent to which regional geographers might generalize their findings, much less discern spatially or temporally invariant laws under a model of positivist science (Hart 1982). They were, in this view, particularlists rather than generalists, describers rather than explainers. Accordingly, in studies of this period, researchers were quick to ascribe causality to the particular qualities of a region, especially those of the natural environment and to the people who labored in them, rather to large-scale social forces that connected those regions in wider webs of resource or labor exploitation.

Schaeffer (1953) provided the first significant challenge to the regional school in what became known as "spatial science." He argued against the prevailing methodological provincialism of regional geography, suggesting that geography should adopt the explanatory objectives of other, more mature social sciences, such as economics. In strongly generalist terms, Schaeffer challenged geographers with the task of identifying spatial laws, an objective consistent with an orderly worldview in which spatial processes (e.g., distance-decay with respect to a node or location) played a role independent of other processes. The notion that space could have independent effects on other processes and was worthy of investigation in its own terms deepened in the succeeding years in the programmatic statements of Bunge (1962) and Nystuen (1968). Their geometric approach conceived of space through a Cartesian absolutism built on an isotropic plane filled with objects whose coordinates underwrote several "geographic primitives," including location, distance, direction, scale, and connectivity. Developed from these were higher-level concepts and models, including those dealing with cores and peripheries, inertias and mobilities, and the locations of production and consumption centers.

A slightly different approach was found in the delineation of spatial units under the directives of what Berry (1964) called a geographic matrix, a conceptual device that carved up absolute space enabling researchers to theorize variations across any conceivable spatial unit. Berry's conceptualization helped underwrite countless studies of spatial variation, wherein researchers measured, described, and (usually statistically) explained magnitudes or proportions of natural or social variables by reference to measures of other variables taken on the same spatial units. What Bunge's and Nystuen's deductive, geometric approach had in common with Berry's inductive, data-analysis approach was a common privileging of the left-hand side of each of the epistemological terms in figure 10.1. The paradigm was characterized, at least in its early phase, by a largely unquestioned faith in objectivity, and its practitioners also sought general determinations through the identification of presumptively orderly causal processes. Allied to these moments was an ontological view of space as an absolute rather than relational object, and this in turn underwrote spatial science's strict separation of spatiality from social relations.

Notwithstanding this separation, many spatial scientists were quick to engage the social upheavals of the late 1960s and early 1970s. An important development from the standpoint of social inequality research was the emergence of what has been called a "socially relevant spatial science"—an emphasis on the spatial side of social justice that continues today and is emblematic of some of the studies appearing in this volume. Socially relevant geographers loosened their earlier adherence to a model of objective science in order to focus normative attention to social problems (Morill 1969). This effort sanctioned interventionist policy statements under the assumption that spatial analytic tools (e.g., optimization routines, regression) were well suited for determining the best (from most efficient to most egalitarian) spatial arrangements for societies (e.g., King 1976; Smith 1974).

Spatial scientists also turned their attention to human cognition and action in space and time (see Golledge and Stimson 1997 for a review). In the initial flush of spatial science, the role of individuals in the construction of spatial variations was largely ignored, but in the late 1960s a move to behavioral approaches redressed this oversight (see Brown et al. 1972). Drawing on both the psychological literature and the influential work of Herbert Simon (1947), behavioral geographers argued that the neoclassical assumption of *homo economicus*, which provided one foundation for most deductive spatial theories (such as those governing the locations of firms), was unrealistic (Wolpert 1964). More relevant to understanding spatial patterns were the perceptions, decision-making processes, and actions of individuals, as well as the wider decision-making environments within which they operated. While both achievements advanced thinking in spatial science by introducing discussions of subjectivity and the active role of individuals, neither overthrew the dominant ontology that led, methodologically speaking, to geography's definition as the field that mapped and analyzed spatial variations.

Throughout the 1970s, 1980s, and 1990s, the ontological view of space as a planar dimension filled with objects underwrote the application of increasingly more sophisticated statistical, mathematical, and technological approaches to spatial measurement and analysis. Models were tested in the real world, often with large data sets analyzed through applications of the general linear model (Johnston 1978).

The development of geographic information systems (GIS) technology in the 1980s and 1990s extended the range of analytic approaches within spatial science (see Longley et al. 1998.). GIS has made it possible to combine overlay and statistical analyses using different types of spatially distributed data—collected for areas, points, lines, or surfaces—whether derived through a special survey, the census, satellite-based remote sensors, or some combination of these. During the mid-1990s, there developed powerful critiques of the power/knowledge implications of GIS (e.g., Pickles 1995), but within a few short years normative concerns came to play a central role in what is now variously known as critical, participatory, or community GIS (Elwood and Leitner 2003).

What, then, are some of the implications of a spatial scientific view of space for researchers interested in the class, gender, race, and other foundations of social inequality? It seems pertinent first to remark that while spatial science has traditionally been associated with the objective aims of science more generally, a distinction should be made between objectivity as the absence of bias, on the one hand, and the possibility or even responsibility of normative analysis, on the other. For as we have noted, spatial scientists have not been averse to drawing either policy (King 1976) or even radical conclusions (Peet 1977) from their analyses. Glasmeier's (2006) use of spatial analytic tools to investigate poverty at both the national and regional scales, identifies, in a U.S. context, regions "in distress" and is one such example of this ongoing tradition. Indeed, there are numerous other examples of research informed by Marxist and other critical theories that employ quantitative analyses to examine variations based on discrete spatial units for which social and other variables have been collected (Conway et al. 2001; Lobao et al. 1999; McHaffie 1998). Sociologists studying inequality from a critical perspective, as does the new generation of research on spatial inequality, clearly have at their disposal a wide range of research questions and associated methodologies, many of which can be informed from the perspective of spatial science. This combination is present and informs research questions in many of the empirical analyses assembled in this volume. An overview of these questions, written from the perspective of socially relevant spatial science might look as follows:

- How is social inequality manifested differently across geographic areas, and with what sort of dynamics?
- What are the factors—whether rooted in local, regional, or more general processes—that can be brought to bear on our explanation of inequality?
- How do these factors themselves vary in their explanatory power across different contexts?

In considering these sorts of questions for the study of one form of social inequality, that of poverty, we here point briefly to the work of Jones and Kodras, who in 1980s and 1990s produced a number of spatial analyses of poverty, with an emphasis on women's poverty (Jones 1987; Jones and Kodras 1986, 1990; Kodras 1986, 1997; Kodras and Jones 1991; Kodras et al. 1994). Their work was conducted at both the state and county scales, and consisted of analyses of rates of poverty and welfare program adoption. Independent variables selected in these analyses ranged from social-demographic and economic factors, such as minority populations and unemployment rates, to political ones, such as the administrative rules and payment levels of state-run welfare programs. In addition to assessing the nationwide significance of these factors in explaining variability in poverty, their research program concentrated on identifying both social and spatial instabilities in these models, a task that involved modeling parameter variation (Jones and Casetti 1992) as a result of unique spatial effects or of the copresence of interactive social, economic, and political factors (Jones 1987; Jones and Kodras 1986; Kodras 1986; Kodras et al. 1994). The major finding from these studies is that poverty and welfare participation models are highly sensitive to spatial and social contexts: there is no justification for a single, nationwide model of poverty or welfare. The factors that influence deprivation and use are actually regional or "subnational" in character, as Lobao and Hooks discuss in this volume, owing either to the unique characteristics of places or to particularities of copresent substantive determinants, such as the strength of the social safety net of welfare programs or the structure of the local economic mix. Accordingly, these works point to a paradigm of instability and particularity in modeling inequality, a task that is also well addressed by the theoretical framework of critical realism, to which we now turn.

CRITICAL REALISM AND RELATIONAL SPACES OF INEQUALITY

For several reasons, the mid-1980s was a propitious period for the entry of critical realism into geography (Sayer 1984). First, at the time geography was theoretically divided between what appeared to be an overly structural Marxism, on the one hand, and an overly volunteristic humanism, on the other. For some, structuration theory (e.g., Giddens 1984) was one solution to this opposition (see discussion by Peet 1998). Commensurate with structuration theory was critical realism's theorization of social systems as "open" (Sayer 2000). In both structuration theory and critical realism, "practical knowledge" is key to everyday and long-term reproduction, transformation, and mediation, and, potentially, elimination of a particular structure and its associated causal mechanisms.

Second, critical realism offers a hierarchical ontology of structures, mechanisms, and events, with social processes mediated and activated under conditions of "contingency." This leads to a both/and stance with respect to the general and particular binary. Critical realists distinguish between necessary relations (i.e., underlying causal structures and their mechanisms), without which an object/event could not be possible, and contingent relations, which determine the actual occurrence and specific qualitative and quantitative aspects of objects/events (Jones and Hanham 1995). Contingencies impart their own causal power on objects/events, but whether they do so or not is purely a contextual matter requiring empirical investigation, usually

through case studies of their actual, on-the-ground operation. Realists therefore assume that general processes exist (via necessary structures and mechanisms) and that the role of the social scientist is to explain their operation.
At the same time, they retain concepts of particularity and indeterminacy (at
least in the sense of "to-be-decided") by theorizing and investigating the
operation of contingencies in the realm of the empirical (Sayer 2000).

With this in mind, we can now turn to the question of space in critical
realism. In any early account of this issue, Sayer (1985) appeared to adopt the
"space-as-stage" perspective that was prevalent in spatial science at the time.
He argued that space can explain events only at the concrete, empirical level.
Aspects of the real world, such as local contextuality and the effects of different on-the-ground spatial arrangements (propinquity, juxtaposition, spatial effects from other areas, etc.), cannot be theorized at the necessary level
of abstraction; they exist at an entirely different level in realist ontology. This
argument, however, came during a period of robust theorizing by geographers
aimed at understanding the conjointed and mutually constitutive roles of
space and social relations (Harvey 1989; Massey 1984; Soja 1980). This theory, which came to be known as the "sociospatial dialectic" (Lefebvre 1991;
Soja 1989), was well suited for a merger with the causal language of critical
realism, such that today most critical realists in geography—as well as most
Marxist-feminist geographers—subscribe to a dialectical view of social and
spatial relations.

In this view, social structures and mechanisms, as well as contingencies,
need to be theorized alongside space, putting spatialization—to borrow from
E. P. Thompson—"at every bloody level" of the realist ontological hierarchy.
Thus, for example, the uneven incorporation of places into capitalism (Smith
1990) is intrinsic rather than extrinsic to capitalism's very nature (Harvey
1982) and must, therefore, be incorporated into the understanding of the
most abstract conceptualizations of necessary relations. Space-time compres-
sion (Harvey 1989), for example, refers to the capitalist compulsion, identified by Marx, to "annihilate space by time," speeding up accumulation by
compressing spatiality so as to overcome barriers to value realization, and
thereby bringing into close contact ever more distant spaces. Nor can we
understand social relations of patriarchy and racism without reference to the
role of built environments that alternatively embed and express these relations in material and symbolic forms—how else (on the head of a pin?) could
these relations be understood, much less practiced? At the same time, the
dialectical embeddedness of these structures and mechanisms within fields of
spatial relations greatly complicates their study, for together they undermine
the taken-for-granted delineations of social and spatial relations. Not only do
social processes and resultant inequalities operate in tandem with concrete
spatial contexts, but they can also be theorized as stretched relations connected to more distant structures, which are themselves spatialized.

In figure 10.2 we offer a hypothetical example illustrative of critical realism. It shows an approach to the study of poverty, as informed by a critical realist theorization of class, gender, and race relations. Here, gender- and race-based processes are shown to operate as contingent relations alongside class-based capitalist relations. The latter, a set of necessary relations, operate through the mechanism capital mobility, which leads in turn to uneven regional development and ultimately to pockets of locally manifested poverty, a process described by the editors in the introductory chapter to this volume. These pockets are differentially inflected by the contingencies of race and gender in specific contexts. At each level of the analysis, space (on the right-hand side) is shown to inform understandings of the social relations behind these structures, mechanisms, and events. Spatial relations infuse these social processes, from the uneven development of capitalism, which depends on the opening of new spaces of accumulation (Harvey 1989; Smith 1990), through the meso-level geographies of production and social reproduction (Marston 2000), which are tied to patriarchy and racism as they operate through the built environment and the particularities of local contexts and their interdependencies with other more remote contexts. Finally, poverty is lived in concrete places and shaped through the everyday microgeographies of livelihood and social action, demanding, perhaps, a sensitivity to the subjective practices of various social actors, as Tickamyer et al. in this volume indicate.

In this way, the figure sketches a critical realist research framework of social inequalities that can be investigated for the ways in which social and spatial relations work together to facilitate flows of capital across spaces and to create new social structures of difference in distinct locations and at particular scales. Social inequality studies informed by this dialectical view of spatiality must therefore grapple with the interconnected sociospatial relations that operate through space, stratified by scales that are global, regional, and local. Finally, it should be noted that critical realism, while lending itself better to qualitative research, does not inherently preclude the use of quantitative data analyses. Rather, it calls for such analyses not to be simple variable-based interpretations: research needs to be grounded in assumptions about space-society as mutually constituted, to take into consideration social-spatial processes, and to recognize that general relationships and outcomes expected from theory will be spatially contingent.

SCALING SOCIAL INEQUALITY

One of the goals of this volume is to promote research on social inequality at the spatial scale of the "missing middle," a level of analysis between the national and urban at which the geographic dimensions of social inequality show perhaps their greatest relief. This is because, on the one hand, national-

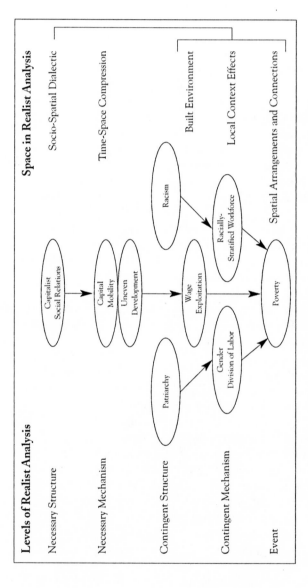

FIGURE 10.2. Hypothetical Case of Sociospatial Explanation in Critical Realism

or even state-level analyses will necessarily mask many internal variations, especially in the operation of social and economic forces that become averaged for such units. On the other hand, while urban and intra-urban analyses of social problems such as poverty or health and educational disparities can be finely tuned to reveal the micro-geographies of social and economic processes, these units of analysis are often covered by the same policy regimes, making it difficult to both discern the interaction between socioeconomic and policy factors and to assess the impact of variations in policy on social inequality. Given the tensions between the general analyses of spatial science—even when modulated by a concern for the particular in studies that explicitly examine the variability in model behavior across context—and the resolutely contextual character of critical realist studies—even when guided by theoretical understandings of general causal forces such as capitalist wage relations—the "missing middle" takes on a weight of importance that exceeds a mere filling of the gap. One could argue, in fact, that analyses attuned to the middle might help split the difference, both theoretically and methodologically, between the general explanatory aims of spatial science and the more contextual ones of critical realism.

It is important to realize, however, that any effort to construct such a ground—or even a conversation between adherents of both theoretical perspectives—will not be easy, for their underlying ontological differences over discrete versus relational understandings of space result in two rather different conceptualizations of scale itself. It will therefore not be enough to argue that meso-level scales hold not only empirical but also theoretical solutions to wider debates over theory and methodology in geographical or social inequality research. In the remainder of this section we address some of these fundamental differences over scale, noting how they direct researchers to theorize scale in different ways, with distinct implications for researching social inequality.

Scale, of course, has a long history within the discipline of geography (see Sheppard and McMaster 2004). From regional geography through contemporary spatial science, the existence of scales as independent empirical objects has been unquestioned. One can find occasional references in the early literature that tied commonly employed scales of analysis to our bodily size and field of vision (e.g., James 1952), but for the most part the hierarchy of local-to-global, intersected by a cascade of neighborhood, urban, metropolitan, regional, subnational, and national levels, was taken as an a priori truth. As Taylor (1982) put it, "the three scales—global, national, and urban—are as 'natural' as social science's division of activities into economic, social, and political. This spatial organization is simply given."

Such a perspective was thoroughly commensurate with the discrete ontology of spatial science, in which social processes were divorced from spatial ones and research designs followed suit accordingly (e.g., Haggett 1965).

Spatial scientists were therefore trained to ask themselves these sorts of questions: At what spatial scale can we best see this or that social process operating? How can we handle spillover effects when the spatial scales available to us in the form of secondary data are nonoverlapping with the processes we are interested in studying? And how do we handle situations in which the processes we are studying are working at multiple or even different scales? In response, they developed a series of analytic approaches. They were first careful not to commit the ecological fallacy, and so tied generalizations to the spatial unit of analysis rather than to, for example, individual behavior. Second, knowing that different processes were captured by different scalar units and that without a careful match of the two one might miss entirely the operation of important processes, they worked to redesign their data collection according to the nature of the problems of interest. Berry (1973), for example, proposed using an empirically derived, multicounty "daily urban system" as preferable to state, single-county, or urban data sources in the study of urban systems. Research devoted to constructing appropriate scalar units continues (Wheeler 2001). Work on spatial autocorrelation by Cliff and Ord (1981) contributed to geographers' ability to model spillover effects and to control for interdependencies in spatial units, a topic addressed by Irwin in this volume. And research using multilevel modeling (Jones and Duncan 1996; Subramanian et al. 2001) has led to a growth industry (Centre for Multilevel Modeling 2005) for assessing the joint and separate effects of variables operating at different scales in a single, multihierarchy model. What all these methodological developments have in common is their reliance on a discrete ontology of social forces operating across distinct (if interacting) spatial levels of varying degrees of extensiveness. This reflects the view of scale put forth in socially-relevant spatial science.

In the mid-1980s, paralleling the rise of critical realism, a number of geographic researchers began developing a different theory of scale—one based on the assumption that fixed scales do not exist and that, instead, scale is socially produced or even constructed (Brenner 1998; Cox and Mair 1988; Herod and Wright 2002; Jonas 1994; Jones 1998; Marston 2000; Smith 1990; Swyngedouq 2004). Swyngedouw (2004:132–133), for example, ties the production of scale to the operation of social power:

> I conceive scalar configurations as the outcome of sociospatial processes that regulate and organize power relations. . . . Scale configurations change as power shifts, both in terms of their nesting and interrelations and in terms of their spatial extent. In the process, new significant social and ecological scales become constructed, others disappear or become transformed.

While other writers differ in terms of their theoretical and substantive interests, they all share in common a relational approach that seeks, like the sociospatial dialectic, to theorize scale and social relations together. Given the messy geographies of social relations, scales are theorized to emerge in complex ways but always in tandem with the uneven unfolding of social relations, especially of capital (Smith 1990). Typical in this regard is the concept of "scalar structuration," developed by Brenner (2001:605–606), in which

> [s]cales evolve relationally within tangled hierarchies and dispersed interscalar networks. The meaning function, history and dynamics of any one geographical scale can only be grasped relationally, in terms of upwards, downwards, and sidewards links to other geographical scales situated within tangled scalar hierarchies and dispersed interscalar networks. . . . Each geographical scale is constituted through its historically evolving positionality within a larger relations grid of vertically 'stretched' and horizontally 'dispersed' sociospatial processes, relations, and interdependencies.

Theoretically and methodologically, critical realism is well suited for developing research questions tied to the social production of scale. For example, Brenner's "tangled scalar hierarchies" share affinity with the complex operation of contingent mechanisms within critical realism (see figure 10.2), while the search for dispersed horizontal processes is consistent with critical realism's recognition that effects in one locality can share interdependencies with those in another. Researchers within this dialectical tradition therefore employ intensive methods (Sayer 2000), usually based on qualitative data, to trace the complex flows that crisscross and give rise to distinctly social platforms of space (Smith 2000; see also Tickamyer et al. in this volume).

From within this perspective, the missing middle turns out to be more complicated than we might have first thought, for it will always be complex and dynamic, much more like Massey's "power-geometries" (1994; 2004) than simply slipping another layer within Taylor's (1982) original formulation of the global, national, and urban. It would have to be complex because this view of scale admits no easy sorting of social processes to their "appropriate" spatial containers. And it would be dynamic insofar as "social networks, political institutions, economic resources, and territorial rights" are always being reconfigured, creating "new geographies—new landscapes of power and recognition and opportunity" (Howitt 2003:150). Not lastly, at its limit, the relational view of space can make problematic the hierarchy at work in the concept of scale (Martson et al. 2005). As Massey (2004:8) sums it up: "If space really is to be thought relationally . . . then 'global space' is no more than the sum of relations, connections, embodiments, and practices. These things are utterly everyday and grounded at the same time as they may, when linked together, go around the world. Space is not outside of place; it is not abstract, it is not somehow 'up there' or disembodied."

We see two implications of Massey's comments for the "missing middle." First, she implies that this meso-level scale should have a methodological range bounded by the relations and connections that form the practices of social actors, including capital, labor, and the state. These can, of course, be spatially quite extensive, particularly when one thinks of the impact that national-level economic and policy decisions can have on actors' quotidian practices. Yet, second, her comments suggest that it might be most appropriate to think in terms *of* those practices and to follow their relations and connections outward rather than to assume in advance their linkage to wider sets of social relations. The missing middle is thus a valid and worthy object of inquiry insofar as it provides an opportunity to interrogate the links and flows between, and the fixing and breaking apart of, various social and spatial relations.

CONCLUSIONS

We began this chapter by suggesting that geographers and sociologists would benefit from an increased dialogue about social and spatial relations. As this volume makes abundantly clear, sociologists are certainly witnessing their own spatial turn, focusing attention on the complex spatial relationships that constitute social inequality at several scales, including the national, the regional (or subnational), and the urban. Geographers have, for a long time, also been interested in investigating the spatiality of social inequality and often draw from sociology's rich theoretical and empirical research to do so. We argue that two key approaches in geography—a socially-relevant spatial scientific one and a critical realist one—lend themselves well to the research featured in this volume. Spatial scientific approaches provide valuable insights into the generalities of various sociospatial relations, while critical realist approaches point to the importance of studying on-the-ground spatial arrangements and connections.

On balance, the research in this volume can be seen to straddle these two approaches. The socially-relevant spatial science approach comes closer to the interests of some contributors, those particularly concerned with investigating general regional spatial dynamics of inequality through quantitative data analyses. Even here, some elements of a critical realist approach are present, as the authors sketch out various paths of inequality, from the general to the particular, and examine some of the relationships we highlight in figure 10.2. For example, Saenz et al. see discrimination as varying contextually, producing different regions that vary in their welcome of or hostility toward Mexican Americans. They consider how particular regional attributes condition which groups of Mexican Americans are likely to leave their home of origin and migrate to a new place. Oakley and Logan view historical decisions about New York City's zoning policies as filtering down to neighborhoods, creating distinct patterns of service allocation that vary from other cities and from outcomes suggested by general theory. And Cotter et al. recognize that racism results in varying socially constructed environments that reach down to influence family and individual experiences of social inequality.

In other articles, authors are interested in theorizing space in ways that are more relational, closer to the critical realist view. For example, Tickamyer et al. argue for going beyond sociology's past conventional view of ecological units as simple containers and toward a theorization of spaces as constituted through the formation of "regional identity, culture, political economy, and livelihood practices." Leicht and Jenkins and Lobao and Hooks argue for the need to conceptualize the state in a more relational framework that takes into account nesting of political processes and actors in different scales.

As we suggested in the previous section, targeting the missing middle provides a particular opportunity for advancing the study of social inequality for geographers as well as sociologists. By examining meso-level scales we are sensitized to how social and spatial processes operate at levels that mediate and interconnect national- and urban-level processes. At the same time, as we go about studying those processes, new tensions emerge as we try to define how best to understand, study, and theorize that inequality. Thus, while it is safe to say that geographers taking a spatial science position and those taking a critical realist tradition will view these meso-level scalar relations as important in their examinations of social and spatial inequality, they will likely differ in how they theorize those relations. It might therefore be difficult to negotiate between the ontological assumptions that underpin the critical realist and spatial scientific views of those meso-level social *and/or* spatial processes because of their different approaches to those relations.

That said, there are geographers (Del Casino et al. 2000; Jones and Hanham 1995) and other social scientists (Grimes and Rood 1995) writing on behalf of methodological and theoretical commensurability. From this perspective, meso-level scalar analyses directed at the missing middle are less a contradiction of paradigms than a way to bridge the sometimes wide divide between theoretical approaches. Put simply, no single theoretical approach can resolve all the answers to our questions about sociospatial inequality. Thus, it is necessary to think beyond the boundaries of paradigmatic approaches, space and place, generalizability and particularity, and discrete and relational space, and examine social inequality and its inherent spatialities from multiple perspectives simultaneously. Social inequality researchers thus could work productively through multiple paradigmatic frameworks that investigate both general processes and particular practices. For example, Kodras (1997), a geographer, explores the changing "map" of U.S. poverty through both a quantitative study of sociospatial inequalities and a qualitative analysis of how people engage that inequality through real-world experiences.

We therefore see a rich opportunity for geographers and sociologists to continue to dialogue over different views of space. One part of this effort, as Tickamyer et al. in this volume make clear, can be comparative analyses between places complemented by studies that examine the same problems at different scales. As Grimes and Rood (1995) point out, taking multiple theoretical perspectives and applying them to the same case (or cases in a comparative context) may help us to determine where one theory's limits are and another's begins. It is our hope, therefore, that sociologists interested in social inequality continue to expand their vision of spatial relations and consider how they might examine processes that are almost always "messier than our theories of them" (Mann 1986:4, cited in Del Casino et al. 2000:535).

REFERENCES

Berry, Brian. 1964. "Approaches to Regional Analysis: A Synthesis." Pp. 24–34 in *Spatial Analysis*, edited by Brian J. L. Berry and Duane Marble. Englewood Cliffs, NJ: Prentice-Hall.

———. 1973. *Growth Centers in the American Urban System*. Cambridge, MA: Ballinger.

Brenner, Neil. 1998. "Between Fixity and Motion: Accumulation, Territorial Organization, and the Historical Geography of Spatial Scales." *Environment and Planning D: Society and Space* 16:459–481.

———. 2001. "The Limits to Scale? Methodological Reflections on Scalar Structuration." *Progress in Human Geography* 15:525–548.

Brown, Lawrence A., Reginald G. Golledge, and Frank Williamson. 1972. "Behavioural Approaches in Geography: An Overview." *The Australian Geographer* 12:59–79.

Bunge, William. 1962. *Theoretical Geography*. Lund, Sweden: Royal University of Lund, Department of Geography.

Centre for Multilevel Modeling. 2005. *Centre for Multilevel Modeling*. Retrieved May 2005 (http://multilevel.ioe.ac.uk/2005).

Cliff, A., and J. K. Ord. 1981. *Spatial Processes: Models and Applications*. London: Pion.

Conway, Dennis, Adrian Bailey, and Mark Ellis. 2001. "Gendered and Racialized Circulation-Migration: Implications for the Poverty and Work Experience of New York's Puerto Rican Women." Pp.146–163 in *Migration, Transnationalization, and Race in a Changing New York*, edited by H. R. Cordero-Guzmán, R. C. Smith, and R. Grosfoguel. Philadelphia: Temple University Press.

Cox, Kevin R. and Andrew Mair. 1988. "Locality and Community in the Politics of Local Economic Development." *Annals of the Association of American Geographers* 78:307–325.

Del Casino, Vincent J. Jr., Andrew J. Grimes, Stephen P. Hanna, and John Paul Johns III. 2000. "Methodological Frameworks for the Geography of Organizations." *Geoforum* 31:523–538.

Elwood, Sarah and Helga Leitner. 2003. "Community-Based Planning and GIS: Aligning Neighborhood Organizations with State Priorities?" *Journal of Urban Affairs* 25:139–157.

Giddens, Anthony. 1984. *The Constitution of Society: Outline of the Theory of Structuration*. Cambridge: Polity Press.

Glasmeier, Amy. 2006. *An Atlas of Poverty in America: One Nation, Pulling Apart, 1960–2003*. New York: Routledge.

Golledge, Reginald and Robert Stimson. 1997. *Spatial Behavior: A Geographic Perspective*. New York and London: Guilford.

Grimes, Andrew J. and Deborah Rood. 1995. "Beyond Objectivism and Relativism: Descriptive Epistemologies." Pp. 161–178 in *Objectivity and its Other*, edited by Wolfgang Natter, John P. Jones III, and Theodore Schatzki. London: Guilford Press.

Haggett, Peter. 1965. *Locational Analysis in Human Geography*. London: Edward Arnold.

Hart, John F. 1982. "The Highest Form of the Geographer's Art." *Annals of the Association of American Geographers* 72:1–29.

Hartshorne, Richard. 1939. *The Nature of Geography*. Lancaster, PA: Association of American Geographers.

Harvey, David. 1982. *The Limits to Capital*. Chicago: University of Chicago Press.

———. 1989. *The Condition of Postmodernity: An Enquiry into the Origins of Cultural Change*. Oxford: Blackwell.

Herod, Andrew and Melissa Wright. 2002. "Placing Scale: An Introduction." Pp. 1–14 in *Geographies of Power: Placing Scale*, edited by Andrew Herod and Melissa Wright. Oxford: Blackwell.

Howitt, Richard. 2003. "Scale." Pp. 138–157 in *A Companion to Political Geography*, edited by John Agnew, Kathrayne Mitchell, and Gerard Tuathail. Oxford: Blackwell.

James, Preston E. 1952. "Toward a Further Understanding of the Regional Concept." *Annals of the Association of American Geographers* 42:123–135.

Johnston, R. J. 1978. *Multivariate Statistical Analysis in Geography: A Primer on the General Linear Model*. New York: Longman.

Jonas, Andrew. 1994. "The Scale Politics of Spatiality." *Environment and Planning D: Society and Space* 12:257–264.

Jones, John Paul, III. 1987. "Work, Welfare, Poverty Among Black, Female-Headed Families." *Economic Geography* 63:20–34.

Jones, John Paul, III and Emilio Casetti. 1992. *Applications of the Expansion Method*. London: Routledge.

Jones, John Paul, III and Robert Hanham. 1995. "Contigency, Realism, and the Expansion Method." *Geographical Analysis* 27:185–207.

Jones, John Paul III and Janet E. Kodras. 1986. "The Policy Context of the Welfare Debate." *Environment and Planning A* 18:63–72.

———. 1990. "Restructured Regions and Families: The Feminization of Poverty in the U.S." *Annals of the Association of American Geographers* 80:163–183.

Jones, Katherine. 1998. "Scale as Epistemology." *Political Geography* 17:25–28.

Jones, Kelvyn and Craig Duncan. 1996. "People and Places: The Multilevel Model as a General Framework for the Quantitative Analysis of Geographical Data." Pp. 79–104 in *Spatial Analysis: Modelling in a GIS Environment*, edited by Paul A. Longley and Michael Batty. Cambridge: GeoInformation International.

King, Leslie J. 1976. "Alternatives to a Positive Economic Geography." *Annals of the Association of American Geographers* 66:293–308.

Kodras, Janet E. 1986. "Labor Market and Policy Constraints on the Work Disincentive Effect of Welfare." *Annals of the Association of American Geographers* 76:228–246.

———. 1997. "The Changing Map of American Poverty in an Era of Economic Restructuring and Political Realignment." *Economic Geographer* 73:67–93.

Kodras, Janet E. and John Paul Jones III. 1991. "A Contextual Examination of the Feminization of Poverty." *Geoforum* 22:159–172.

Kodras, Janet E., John Paul Jones III, and Karen Falconer. 1994. "Contextualizing Welfare's Work Disincentive: The Case of Female-Headed Families." *Geographical Analysis* 26:285–299.

Lefebvre, Henri. 1991. *The Production of Space*. Translated by D. Nicholas-Smith. Oxford: Blackwell.

Lobao, Linda, Jamie Rulli, and Lawrence Brown. 1999. "Macro-level Theory and Local-Level Inequality: Industrial Structure, Institutional Arrangements, and the Political Economy of Redistribution, 1970 and 1990." *Annals of the Association of American Geographers* 4:571–601.

Longley, Paul A., Michael F. Goodchild, David J. Maguire, and David W. Rhind, eds. 1998. *Geographical Information Systems: Principles, Techniques, Management and Applications*. Cambridge: GeoInformational International.

Mann, Michael D. 1986. *Sources of Social Power*. Cambridge: Cambridge University Press.

Marston, Sallie. 2000. "The Social Construction of Scale." *Progress in Human Geography* 24:219–242.

Marston, Sallie, John Paul Jones III, and Keith Woodward. 2005. "Human Geography Without Scale." *Transactions of the Institute of British Geographers* 30:416–432.

Massey, Doreen. 1984. *Spatial Division of Labour: Social Structures and the Geography of Production*. London: Methuen.

———. 1994. *Space, Place, and Gender*. Minneapolis: University of Minnesota Press.

———. 2004. "Geographies of Responsibility." *Geografiska Annaler* 86:5–18.

McHaffie, Patrick. 1998. "Contingency in the Local Provision of Public Education." *Growth and Change* 29:173–191.

Morrill, Richard, 1969. "Geography and the Transformation of Society." *Antipode* 1:4–10.

Nystuen, John D. 1968. "Identification of Some Fundamental Spatial Concepts." Pp. 35–41 in *Spatial Analysis*, edited by Brian J. L. Berry and Duane Marble. Englewood, NJ: Prentice-Hall.

Peet, Richard. 1977. *Radical Geography: Alternative Viewpoints on Contemporary Social Issues*. Chicago: Maaroufa.

———. 1998. *Modern Geographical Thought*. Oxford: Blackwell Publishers.

Pickles, John. 1995. *Ground Truth: The Social Implications of Geographic Information Systems, Mappings: Society/Theory/Space*. New York: Guilford Press.

Sayer, Andrew. 1984. *Method in Social Science: A Realist Approach*. London: Hutchinson.

———. 1985. "Realism and Geography." Pp. 159–173 in *The Future of Geography*, edited by R. J. Johnston. London: Methuen.

———. 2000. *Realism and Social Science*. London; Thousand Oaks, CA: Sage.

Schaefer, Fred K. 1953. "Exceptionalism in Geography: A Methodological Examination." *Annals of the Association of American Geographers* 43:226–249.

Sheppard, Eric and Robert B. McMaster, eds. 2004. *Scale and Geographic Inquiry*. Oxford: Blackwell.

Simon, Herbert. 1947. *Administrative Behavior: A Study of Decision-Making Processes in Administrative Organization*. New York: MacMillan.

Smith, David M. 1974. "Who Gets What, Where, and How: A Welfare Focus for Human Geography." *Geography* 59:289–297.

Smith, Neil. 1990. *Uneven Development: Nature, Capital, and the Production of Space*. Oxford: Blackwell.

———. 2000. "Scale." Pp. 724–727 in *The Dictionary of Human Geography*, edited by R. J. Johsnston, D. Gregory, G. Pratt, and M. Watts. Oxford: Blackwell.

Soja, Edward. 1989. *Postmodern Geographies: The Reassertion of Space in Critical Social Theory*. London and New York: Verso.

Subramanian. S. V., Craig Duncan, and Kelvyn Jones. 2001. "Multilevel Perspectives on Modeling Census Data." *Environment and Planning A* 33:399–417.

Swyngedouw, Eric. 2004. "Scaled Geographies: Nature, Place, and the Politics of Scale." Pp. 129–153 in *Scale and Geographies Inquiry*, edited by Eric Sheppard and Robert B. McMaster. Oxford: Blackwell.

Taylor, Peter. 1982. "A Materialist Framework for Political Geography." *Transactions Institute of British Geographers* 7:15–34.

Wheeler, Christopher H. 2001. "A Note on the Spatial Correlation Structure of County-Level Growth in the U.S." *Journals of Regional Science* 41:433–449.

Wolpert, J. 1964. "The Decision Process in Spatial Context." *Annals of the Association of American Geographers* 54:537–558.

ELEVEN

Conclusion

An Agenda for Moving a Spatial Sociology Forward

GREGORY HOOKS
LINDA M. LOBAO
ANN R. TICKAMYER

SOCIOLOGISTS STUDY INEQUALITY in a variety of forms and venues. For much of the last century, however, exploration of inequality in the United States proceeded largely without explicit attention to geographic space. But the discipline has entered a new era. A broad movement to spatialize sociology beyond the legacy of past traditions has arisen. New thematic areas for research have emerged while older, familiar ones are being reshaped.

This volume is grounded in sociology's ongoing spatialization project. Its thematic attention to spatial inequality provides a collective vision of a recent generation of work that spans and transcends established research traditions. This work fosters new directions for the sociological imagination, including more holistic understanding of inequality across spatial scales. The term *spatial inequality* describing this body of work has only recently come into more common usage, with this volume the first to our knowledge to make it a sociological centerpiece.

Despite the spatial turn in sociology, even today, well-developed traditions of analyzing inequality are found only at the scale of the city and across nation-states. This stunts the study of stratification in general as well as inequality-related subfields such as political sociology and economic sociology. Further, it has tended to set in stone the way spatial inequality itself is conceptualized and studied, giving rise to a binary sociological view with a large underdeveloped gray area between the two poles. This view obscures commonalities among research traditions. It also crowds out potentially innovative ways of addressing the topic—including bringing in different literatures, spatial scales, and places of study less familiar to sociologists. In noting the tendency toward a binary view of spatial inequality, our purpose is not to diminish the importance of the urban and cross-national inequality traditions. Rather, our point is that sociologists need to devote greater attention to carving out the study of inequality beyond these well-established traditions and to incorporate populations, substantive topics, theoretical debates, and policy and social justice issues at spatial scales omitted from systematic investigation.

This collection features articles by sociologists who seek to make headway against the discipline's spatial impasse. Taken as a whole, the articles emphasize the structural-territorial bases of inequality, extending sociology's inherent concern with stratification processes to geographic space at different scales. Our goal has been to showcase the recent generation of research on spatial inequality, including how it addresses gray areas—issues unresolved or overlooked by past work. In this final chapter, we recapitulate these overlapping themes. We also take stock of the need to advance the study of spatial inequality more broadly throughout the discipline.

SPACES, SPATIAL SCALES, AND PLACES: FILLING IN THE GRAY AREAS WITH A NEW GENERATION OF WORK

The generation of work showcased in this volume can be understood by considering spaces, spatial scales, and places. The contributors have different motivations for examining spatial processes; space, therefore, is not treated as a fixed concept but takes on different meanings depending on theory and research questions. By joining the study of space with the study of inequality, contributors address conceptual gaps in sociological literatures. Some bring in space explicitly to challenge, interrogate, and extend underspatialized literatures on power and inequality, such as found in stratification research, economic sociology, and political sociology. Chapters by Leicht and Jenkins, Cotter et al., and Tickamyer et al. center their work on spatializing such literatures. By contrast, other fields such as demography and rural sociology have long attended to space, but only more recently incorporated a critical analysis of inequality. Chapters by Saenz et al. and McLaughlin et al. seek to move forward the study of inequality within these traditionally spatialized fields. Even within a developed spatial inequality tradition like urban sociology, there are unresolved conceptual issues, as shown in the chapter by Oakley and Logan, which challenges prevailing views about the uneven distribution of services across neighborhoods.

The concept of spatial scales, the territorial resolution at which social processes are studied, illuminates other gaps tackled by the new generation

of work. First, Lobao and Hooks argue there is a missing middle within sociology, the subnational scale. While there has been a great deal of empirical
work at this scale, it is far less visible and routinized compared to research
on the nation-state/global system and the city. A second point is that scales
of social action vary in their importance to inequality processes over time.
While sociologists recognize this point in debates about the declining role
of the nation-state in protecting public well-being in the wake of globalization, there is often little attention to the shifting importance of other scales
of action. For example, in their respective chapters, Leicht and Jenkins,
Lobao and Hooks, and Tickamyer et al. argue the subnational scale is
increasingly significant for understanding inequality processes because
recent changes in state allocate growth and redistribution functions to subnational governments. Finally, contributors recognize, some more explicitly
than others, the need to examine inequality across different scales. While
multilevel quantitative analyses empirically exemplify this approach, there
are broader conceptual issues at hand. Social processes are fluid and to trace
out their operation, one must move between scales. Any one scale provides
a slice in time of inequality processes but, like any slice, truncates the full
picture of these processes.

The new generation of work also calls for us to interrogate how places are
treated in sociology. As discussed in the introductory chapter, discourse about
the concept of place has been shaped largely from the place-in-society
approach that begins with an interest in place character or distinctiveness.
This approach tends to privilege certain places as points of study and units of
analysis, specific cities being a prime example. It sometimes leads to unwar-
ranted generalizations and leaps of faith—that what occurs in one special
place also occurs elsewhere. By contrast, the society-in-place approach—
reflected in most empirical chapters in Part II of this volume—offers an alternative lens from which to view places. It begins with a theoretical question,
then extends it across places, an array of conceptualized territories whose
boundaries may be fixed or fluid. No particular territorial unit is inherently
privileged, but place units must be conceptually scrutinized rather than
treated in an ad hoc manner. Such conceptualization includes drawing out
the content or attributes of places and why they matter to the research question. From the society-in-place approach, the study of spatial inequality can
be thought of as a power-geometry (Massey 1994), where stratification is
examined across a range of places at different scales.

Thus, the new generation of work causes us to rethink how places are to
be studied and the accepted types of territorial units in which to do so. We
argued that place-in-society and society-in-place approaches shed different
but complementary light on inequality processes. Both need to be recognized as offering equally important windows for advancing the study of spatial inequality.

Contributors to this collection also are interested in moving beyond addressing research gaps. They share a broader vision of the study of spatial inequality, in which commonalities across sociological literatures are given greater recognition and development. In this view, questions about power and privilege are framed and empirically examined across and among a variety of spatial scales. The places studied are an array of territorial units. Research is theoretically informed, with capital, labor, the state, and civil society figuring prominently as social forces introduced to analyze spatial inequality. Research designs are comparative. This vision of spatial inequality defies the boundaries of conventional sociological subfields: it bridges and extends spatial traditions and inequality traditions, and it builds from the strengths and commonalities of existing spatial inequality traditions situated at different scales.

In outlining the contours of a new generation of work on spatial inequality, this volume is inherently limited. As discussed in the introductory chapter, we address a broad, ongoing project and cannot capture the full repertoire of substantive topics or approaches to spatial inequality. Relatedly, our interest is inequality across geographic areas within the United States. We have not explored other scales of inequality such as the micro-scale of the household and body, nor featured empirical research on the cross-national scale. The volume reflects the distinct interests and expertise of the scholars brought together by the American Sociological Association/National Science Foundation Fund for the Advancement of the Discipline workshop to advance the study of spatial inequality. While this enabled fruitful dialogue, many other sociologists are involved in carving out the topic of spatial inequality. We have tried to capture their efforts throughout the various chapters in the collection, but in a burgeoning field much more remains to be addressed.

Finally, the volume itself needs to be contextualized within the status of current work on spatial inequality in sociology, an incomplete and evolving project. Del Casino and Jones take stock of sociology's spatialization project—and the chapters from this book—from the vantage of geography. They consider how the research approaches featured here overlap with the manner in which space is studied in their discipline. Geography's dominant spatial science approach takes a variable-based view with an interest in charting spatial patterns and contextual variability. This approach gave rise to quantitative methodologies such as GIS and spatial analytical regression, now widely used to study spatial relationships. Here space tends to be treated as external to social processes and there are fixed scales from which these processes are customarily studied. This approach yields a broad view of the various determinants of inequality across scales. In contrast, critical realism views spatial and social processes as dialectically constituted and argues they must be theorized jointly. Scale itself is seen as socially produced and there-

CONCLUSION   257

fore not inherently fixed. Research tends to be more qualitative. This approach challenges researchers to come to terms with the manner in which space is integral to social relations, including race, gender, class, and other dimensions of inequality.

Del Casino and Jones see contributors to this volume as spanning these two metatheoretical camps and individual articles sharing some elements of each. Some contributors fall closer to geography's spatial science approach because their interest lies in identifying and attempting to explain specific measures of social inequality through variable-based analyses. A spatial science approach once was associated with acceptance of the status quo. The articles in this volume are in step with a more recent trend where the spatial science approach is deployed to address structural inequities and social justice concerns. Other contributors are closer to the second camp, critical realism, which views spatial and social processes as intertwined at every scale and molding inequality in a variety of ways.

Although Del Casino and Jones do not pose the spatial science approach and critical realism as mutually exclusive, there are tensions between them. Axes of tension include the manner by which we conceptualize the link between social and spatial aspects of human life, views of geographic scales, and research strategies to tap the complexities of spatial-social relationships, including both the general and place-specific ways in which these relationships work out. These tensions pose challenges to all social scientists undertaking the study of spatial inequality. They require sociologists to rethink customary ways of studying the topic and to more self-consciously examine the role of space in the creation and reproduction of inequality. We hope this volume will spur greater collective activity in those directions.

SPATIAL INEQUALITY: CREATING A
COMMON AGENDA FOR FUTURE WORK

How can we further advance the sociological study of spatial inequality across geographic areas? In the section above and throughout this volume, contributors have discussed the continuing need to address gray areas of sociological research. These include: spatializing underspatialized inequality traditions; advancing the critical study of inequality within conventional spatially oriented traditions; ironing out conceptual gaps that persist in different traditions; developing the body of research at the subnational scale; and recognizing alternative ways of conceptualizing places and employing territorial units.

We close this book by outlining a broader project for sociology, one that we hope will advance and integrate the study of spatial inequality more holistically across the discipline. To that end, we set out an ambitious agenda for future work.

First, sociologists need to expand the substantive scope of the study of spatial inequality. Most research on the topic, including the studies in this book, centers on how inequality based on class, race, gender, or other dimensions of well-being is distributed across space. A related question is how territories themselves become stratified, such as occurs in the creation of chronically poor or prosperous regions. To address this question requires attention to how distinct social forces create uneven development, how they shape a gestalt of place attributes, and how they set in motion potential path-dependency in subsequent development. In sociology, this second question is explored in studies of urban and cross-national development, and directed toward select regions such as Appalachia and the south. However, it is a much broader research question that extends across other regions and spatial scales. Uneven development today is visible in prosperous bicoastal states juxtaposed with an increasingly depopulated and often impoverished rural heartland. It is seen within regions such as the intermountain west, where new pockets of economic growth bring housing and commuting hardships to residents across neighboring communities. Chapters in this volume by Leicht and Jenkins, Lobao and Hooks, Oakley and Logan, Saenz et al., and Tickamyer et al. echo this need to give greater attention to the process of uneven development.

Second, we need to develop a more systematic conceptual template, grounded in sociological thinking that can be used to study both distribution of inequality and the social forces creating uneven development at different scales. We are by no means advocating one-size-fits-all theory. Our point here is that sociology's comparative disciplinary strengths in studying stratification should be harnessed to develop more general understanding about the operation of stratification processes across scales. The chapter by Lobao and Hooks begins to get at this issue. They note there is little collective effort in sociology to theorize inequality at the subnational scale. They argue for giving primary attention to economic structure and institutional arrangements as social forces that create and maintain inequality. This view is grounded in sociology's stratification heritage and also builds upon insights from economic and political sociology about the role of the market and state in reproducing inequality. Lobao and Hooks see the operation of economic structure and institutional arrangements as contingent upon place-specific attributes including past history, which results in present patterns of place stratification. While the focus here is subnational, one might expand on this logic by systematically studying how key social forces from sociology's inequality heritage operate across and are nested in different scales, from local to global. Certainly such systematic efforts are ongoing *within* literatures. For example, the literature on urban poverty denotes key attributes that stratify neighborhoods and create unequal life chances for residents (Pebley and Sastry 2004). The task is to extend these efforts and draw connections across literatures and spatial scales.

A collective effort toward better theoretical understanding of how social forces from sociology's stratification heritage operate at different scales would accomplish several things. It would bridge research traditions in sociology. It would create a more systematic knowledge base, where repeated use of similar concepts would yield insights into inequality at different scales. It would broaden knowledge about a range of social forces implicated in uneven development. Most important, such efforts would foster a distinct overarching sociological approach to spatial inequality. Efforts to theorize how inequality is reproduced across spatial scales is ongoing in human geography and economics. For example, in geography, the infusion of critical approaches from the 1970s onward resulted in collective theoretical efforts to apply these approaches across scales, resulting in literatures on the geography of poverty (Smith 1982), Massey's explication of power-geometries (1994), and recent work on the geography of power (Herod and Wright 2002). In economics, Krugman (1991) reformulated neoclassical theory to include space, resulting in an outpouring of work that extends neoclassical principles at different scales. Sociology has yet to put forth such holistic efforts in understanding inequality across scales.

Third, we should give increased attention to spatial flows and processes, moving beyond the sui generis nature of territories. Recent calls for a "relational sociology" (Emirbayer 1997; Tilly 1995; Urry 2000) emphasize the importance of shifting attention to flows—or to state this in terms of an admonition, to avoid overemphasizing the nodes, the inert structures, and the frozen moments in social life. From its inception, sociology has been fascinated with typologies classifying nodes of social life in taxonomic fashion, but that risk losing sight of dynamic processes molding the social world. To the extent that space is incorporated into sociological analysis, it is often tacked on as a single categorical concept—such as urban or rural location—or viewed from the vantage of a fixed territorial unit. The result is that researchers miss the dynamic exchanges occurring within and between different units at various spatial scales. As Del Casino and Jones argue, for that reason also—to better understand how urban and national processes are connected—social scientists need to give greater attention to their point of intersection, the subnational scale.

By adding a focus on flows and processes, we can better address the continuity between social processes in cities, the countryside, regions, nation-states, and the world. People across territories are increasingly linked through technology, employment, and daily life (Urry 2000). The demarcation between the urban and countryside is becoming blurred (Champion and Hugo 2004). And local, regional, national, and global structures and processes are increasingly intertwined (Castells 1996). These changes argue for a shift in focus. For the study of inequality, it is important to avoid fixing the study of inequality in any single place or scale and instead to move the focus toward the connections among them. Social processes internal to a place and the connections between this place and other places (at similar or different scales) influence the degree of poverty or prosperity experienced by residents. Capital-labor-state struggles over resources also move across scales, affecting the fortunes of populations (Castells 1996). For example, the conservative right has pushed for a limited national state with its resources channeled subnationally, through localities and states. This, however, creates the potential for place-based social movements that press for resource claims from all levels of government and for progressive subnational governments to challenge the national state. Conflict over the allocation of state resources continually moves up and down places across spatial scales, particularly given the federalist nature of American government.

Fourth, we need greater attention to human agency and how social actors strategically use and create spaces and places. Numerous historical examples demonstrate the strategic use of space and place to achieve political ends, ranging from the deliberate location of new settlements to selection of battlefields. In his examination of power, Clegg (1989) points out that social action is channeled—sometimes constrained and sometimes amplified—by the terrain on which it occurs. He illustrated this point by reviewing the Battle of Thermopylae (5th century BCE) where three hundred Spartan soldiers held tens of thousands of Persian soldiers at bay, a feat made possible by a narrow mountain pass that prevented all but a small portion of the Persian force to advance. As the Greeks did at Thermopylae, social actors (whether individuals or collectives) purposefully choose *where* to pursue objectives. Logan and Molotch (1987) advance such a view when they propose a "shopper model" to examine the choices of large corporations in selecting where to locate facilities. Hooks (1994) and Markusen et al. (1991) also adopt this view when examining decisions of military planners regarding the locations of bases and defense production facilities. These decisions are strategic in the sense that agents of large, powerful organizations scan the terrain to identify places affording advantages in pursuing organizational goals. The manner in which they treat land and people is often at odds with the needs and attachment of local residents. Strategic decisions by powerful external actors such as the military can degrade the environment and endanger residents (Hooks and Smith 2004). Similarly, location decisions of corporations and the state profoundly influence the welfare of residents and communities. In turn, decisions of powerful social actors may generate significant opposition movements grounded in the strategic protection of places.

Fifth, sociologists need to build a stronger methodological-empirical foundation for studying inequality across geographic space. Across the social sciences, researchers are increasingly aware of the need to develop methodologies applicable to analyzing a variety of spatial data and to address other empirically-related concerns. An example is the recent effort by the Center for Spatially integrated Social Sciences (CSISS) (Goodchild and Janelle 2004), which seeks to move forward spatial thinking and analyses across disciplines. Within sociology, much research on spatial inequality in the United States is quantitative, based on large samples using secondary data. Qualitative, comparative case study designs and collection of primary data are particularly needed to explain relationships and address topical issues bypassed by quantitative work.

In addition, we need to recognize that geographic data present common challenges which are conceptual in nature and never easily sorted out. The urban poverty literature (Pebley and Sastry 2004) has been particularly attentive to some of these issues, but they crosscut literatures and geographic scales. One is the modifiable areal unit problem (Sweeney and Freser 2004), where results may vary under different levels of areal aggregation or boundary change. Irwin's chapter in this book, for example, illustrates how inequality relationships may shift by different levels of spatial aggregation. Another issue is potential endogeneity in regional processes, where cause-effect are difficult to disentangle (Moffit 2005). For example, is a region chronically poor because disadvantaged populations have chosen to move there? Or does a long history of uneven development and/or current regional characteristics undermine the life chances of those who reside there? The chapter by Cotter et al. speaks to such questions. A third issue is spatial autocorrelation, examined in Irwin's chapter. Finally, determining appropriate units and scales for particular research questions and the feasibility of collecting sociologically relevant data for those units/scales continues to present challenges. Sociologists studying spatial inequality at different scales and from the vantage of different literatures need to engage in a more holistic dialogue about these common issues.

Sixth, to build a more comprehensive sociology of spatial inequality, we should continue to learn from other traditions and disciplines both within sociology and beyond. As discussed above and elsewhere in this volume, we have argued for better linkages between sociology's spatial traditions and inequality traditions, and for greater integration of knowledge among existing literatures on spatial inequality, those that tap the urban, subnational, and cross-national scales.

Within sociology, the comparative-historical literature grapples with many of the same issues noted here but with regard to time rather than space. The temporal context of social action is marked by discontinuities in time. For social action, uniform slicing of time by clocks and calendars is arbitrary (Urry 2000). Instead, time is demarcated by events that define social relationships and processes at the micro- and macro-levels. Sewell (1996) eschews the quest for sociological laws applicable over all historical periods. Instead he calls for a careful consideration of the events that demarcate historical periods and to the social structures molding action at any given time.

Just as events punctuate history, so places demarcate geography. The decision as to which research questions can be pursued given the territorial units at hand requires conscious consideration. Just as the received temporal units (hours, days, and years) may or may not capture the rhythm of social life, so the study of spatial inequality requires ongoing concern with the selection of appropriate territorial units, with their conceptualization, and with the spatial boundaries of social processes. As Ragin (1992) forcefully argues, what constitutes a case in social science requires interrogation—and this self-conscious casing applies to spatial analyses as well.

In a similar vein, spatial approaches need to pay heed to other developments in the study of inequalities, most notably the current effort to analyze and understand intersectionalities—the ways that different domains of inequality overlap and intersect to create patterns of oppression and privilege for individuals and groups. Race, ethnicity, class, gender, sexuality, and age have all been offered as primary loci of inequality, and how they influence life chances requires analysis of the "matrix of domination" created by their intersections (Collins 2000). Spatial inequality needs to be added to this matrix to the benefit of both approaches both to create a more complex and nuanced understanding of stratification and inequality via the inclusion of spatial factors, and to advance understanding of spatial inequality by explicitly taking account of the connections with other dominant dimensions of power and privilege.

Linkages with geography need to continue to be cultivated. Sociology has been enlivened over the past two decades by the steady infusion of conceptual frameworks and methodologies developed by geographers. Indeed, as we noted, this infusion of knowledge has in part contributed to the new generation of studies featured in this volume. We have drawn from geographers' work on spatial scales and places to situate the contours of the new generation of sociological research on spatial inequality, while many of the contributors employ geographic methods and frameworks. The previous chapter by Del Casino and Jones builds further bridges between the two disciplines, outlining metatheoretical traditions on the study of space which overlap with approaches taken by sociologists. Del Casino and Jones also point to the challenges facing those studying spatial inequality irrespective of discipline, challenges which require continual, self-conscious reflection about the manner in which space is intertwined with inequality processes. Geographers and sociologists have much to learn from each others' disciplinary strengths. We must continue to blend the geographical and sociological imaginations to move research on spatial inequality forward.

In the last analysis, however, sociology needs to bring its distinct voice and perspective to the study of spatial inequalities. Thus our final prescription requires learning from sister disciplines but at the same time moving beyond and not being trapped by their visions. In putting forth this agenda, we are arguing for the development of a deeper and more comprehensive sociological approach to the study of spatial inequality. We see this approach as grounded in sociology's stratification heritage, where questions about power and privilege are framed and empirically examined across a variety of spatial scales. This approach views social processes as being fluid across places at any single scale and across spatial scales themselves. It bridges spatial and inequality traditions, and well-developed approaches to spatial inequality, as seen in urban and cross-national sociology, with those that are less developed. It entails an awareness of and respect for different research traditions, places of study, and scales of social action, but the vision is ours. The studies in this volume provide examples of this endeavor and illustrations of the prospects for a vigorous new sociology of spatial inequality that addresses the original question of this volume: *Who gets what—where?*

REFERENCES

Castells, Manuel. 1996. "The Reconstruction of Social Meaning in the Space of Flows." Pp. 493–498 in *The City Reader*, edited by Richard T. LeGates and Frederic Stout. London: Routledge.

Champion, Tony and Graeme Hugo, eds. 2004. *New Forms of Urbanization: Beyond the Urban-Rural Dichotomy*. Aldershot, England: Ashgate.

Collins, Patricia Hill. 2000. *Black Feminist Thought: Knowledge, Consciousness, and The Politics of Empowerment*. 2nd ed. New York: Routledge.

Emirbayer, Mustafa. 1997. "Manifesto for a Relational Sociology." *American Journal of Sociology* 103:281–317.

Goodchild, Michael F.and Donald G. Janelle, eds. 2004. *Spatially Integrated Social Science*. New York: Oxford University Press.

Herod, Andrew and Melissa W. Wright, eds. 2002. *Geographies of Power: Placing Scale*. Malden, MA: Blackwell.

Krugman, Paul. *Geography and Trade*. Cambridge, MA: MIT Press.

Lobao, Linda and Gregory Hooks. 2003. "Public Employment, Welfare Transfers, and Economic Well-Being Across Local Populations: Does Lean and Mean Government Benefit the Masses." *Social Forces* 82:519–556.

Massey, Doreen. 1994. *Space, Place, and Gender*. Minneapolis: The University of Minnesota Press.

Moffitt, Robert. 2005. "Remarks on the Analysis of Causal Relationships in Population Research." *Demography* 42:91–108.

Pebley, Anne R. and Narayan Sastry. 2004. "Neighborhoods, Poverty, and Children's Well-Being." Pp.119–145 in *Social Inequality*, edited by Katherine M. Neckerman. New York: Russell Sage Foundation.

Ragin, Charles C. 1992. "'Casing' and the Process of Social Inquiry." Pp. 217–226 in *What Is a Case? Exploring the Foundations of Social Inquiry*, edited by Charles C. Ragin and Howard S. Becker. New York: Cambridge University Press.

Sewell, William H. 1996. "Historical Events as Transformations of Structures: Inventing Revolution at the Bastille." *Theory and Society* 25:841–881.

Smith, David M. 1982. *Where the Grass Is Greener: Living in an Unequal World.* Baltimore: Johns Hopkins University Press.

Sweeney, Stuart H. and Edward J. Feser. 2004. "Business Location and Spatial Externalities." Pp. 239–262 in *Spatially Integrated Social Science*, edited by Michael F. Goodchild and Donald G. Janelle. New York: Oxford University Press.

Tilly, Charles. 1995. "To Explain Political Processes." *American Journal of Sociology* 100:1594–1610.

Urry, John. 2000. *Sociology Beyond Societies.* New York: Routledge.

About the Editors and Contributors

EDITORS

LINDA M. LOBAO is Professor of Rural Sociology, Sociology, and Geography, at The Ohio State University. Her work focuses on state and market processes in creating inequality across geographic space. Publications include a book monograph, *Locality and Inequality*, a coauthored volume, *Beyond the Amber Waves of Grain*, and numerous articles. Currently, she is engaged in a long-term study of decentralized government and its uneven subnational effects.

GREGORY HOOKS is Professor and Chair of the Department of Sociology at Washington State University. His research focuses on the role of the state, particularly the defense industry and prisons, in producing regional inequality. He is also examining environmental (in)justice issues, with a focus on Native American exposure to toxins created by the military. He has served as a Senior Justice Soros Fellow, and his recent articles have appeared in *Social Forces* and *American Sociological Review*.

ANN R. TICKAMYER is Professor and Chair of the Department of Sociology and Anthropology at Ohio University. Her research focuses on poverty, gender, and development. She is coeditor of a recent volume, *Communities of Work*, a former editor of *Rural Sociology*, and the author of numerous articles in journals and edited volumes. Recently, she has been engaged in a longitudinal study of welfare reform in Appalachia.

CONTRIBUTORS

DAVID A. COTTER is Associate Professor of Sociology at Union College in Schenectady, New York. His research interests include work-related gender inequality and poverty across labor markets. His articles on these topics have been published in the *American Sociological Review*, *Rural Sociology*, and other journals.

CYNTHIA M. CREADY is Assistant Professor of Sociology at the University of North Texas. She has published in the areas of race/ethnic differentiation and inequality, family, and long-term care of the elderly.

VINCENT J. DEL CASINO JR. is Associate Professor of Geography and Liberal Studies at California State University, Long Beach. He has published research on a number of areas of interest to sociologists, including health geography, organizational studies, representational analysis, and geographic methodologies.

DEBRA A. HENDERSON is Associate Professor of Sociology at Ohio University. She specializes in inequalities and family. She and her coauthors have been collaborating on a longitudinal study of devolution and welfare reform in the Appalachian region of Ohio.

JOAN M. HERMSEN is Associate Professor of Sociology at the University of Missouri-Columbia. Her research explores gender inequality and economic hardship across labor markets as well as the impact of interpersonal violence on women's economic well-being.

MICHAEL D. IRWIN is Associate Professor of Sociology at Duquesne University. His research focuses on spatial analytic methods and the role of civic society in creating inequalities across regions. His articles on regional processes are published in *American Sociological Review*, *Social Forces*, and elsewhere.

J. CRAIG JENKINS is Professor and Chair of Sociology and Professor of Political Science at The Ohio State University. In addition to other projects, he is examining the role of state government in economic development, with articles on this topic published in the *American Journal of Sociology*, *Social Forces*, *Economic Development Quarterly*, and elsewhere.

JOHN PAUL JONES III is Professor and Head of the Department of Geography at the University of Arizona. Jones is a former editor of the *Annals of the Association of American Geographers*, the discipline's flagship journal. His work is concentrated in social theory, geographic thought, and social science methodology.

KEVIN T. LEICHT is Professor of Sociology at the University of Iowa and Co-Director of the Iowa Center for Inequality Studies. With Jenkins, he is examining state governments' role in regional economic development. Leicht is a former editor of *The Sociological Quarterly*.

JOHN R. LOGAN is Professor of Sociology and Director of Spatial Structures in the Social Sciences at Brown University. He has published numerous articles on inequality in the city and urban change and coauthored the now classic volume, *Urban Fortunes: The Political Economy of Place.*

DIANE K. MCLAUGHLIN is Associate Professor of Rural Sociology and Demography at The Pennsylvania State University. She is examining the effects of poverty and inequality on mortality and also the factors influencing changes in income inequality in counties across the United States.

MARIA CRISTINA MORALES is Assistant Professor of Sociology at the University of Nevada Las Vegas. Her areas of interests are social inequality, with a focus on race/ethnicity, gender, and immigration/citizenship, and social demography, with a focus on labor and immigration.

ATSUKO NONOYAMA is a researcher engaged in evaluating HIV/AIDS prevention programs implemented in California counties. Her past work has focused on the impact of HIV/AIDS on food security in African countries and on childhood obesity.

DEIDRE A. OAKLEY is Assistant Professor of Sociology at Northern Illinois University. Her recent articles include "The American Welfare State Decoded: Uncovering the Neglected History of Public-Private Partnerships" published in *City and Community.* She is working on a project funded by the National Poverty Center at the University of Michigan that addresses the effectiveness of the Federal Empowerment Zone and Enterprise Community initiative.

ROGELIO SAENZ is Professor of Sociology at Texas A&M University. His research is concerned with race/ethnic inequalities across U.S. regions. He is the author of *Latinos and the Changing Face of America,* recently published by the Russell Sage Foundation and the Population Reference Bureau.

P. JOHNELLE SMITH is a graduate research assistant in rural sociology and demography at The Pennsylvania State University. Her research interests are health and mortality and the relationships among stratification, residence, and health.

C. SHANNON STOKES is Professor of Rural Sociology and Demography at The Pennsylvania State University where he teaches courses in research methods and demography. His research focuses on health in the U.S. population and development in Asia and Africa.

BARRY L. TADLOCK is Assistant Professor of Political Science at Ohio University. His research focuses on American government and politics, with publications in the areas of identity politics and the impacts of welfare reform in Appalachian Ohio. He is co-editor of *Gays and Lesbians in the Democratic Process: Public Policy, Public Opinion, and Political Representation.*

REEVE VANNEMAN is Professor of Sociology at the University of Maryland. He served as Program Director for the Sociology Program at the National Science Foundation. His research investigates variations in gender inequality across metropolitan areas in the United States and across districts in India.

JULIE ANNE WHITE is Associate Professor of Political Science at Ohio University specializing in political theory, feminist ethics, and public policy. She is the author of *Democracy, Justice and the Welfare State: Reconstructing Public Care.* Along with her coauthors she has been studying the impacts of welfare reform in Appalachian Ohio.

Index